Better Homes and Gardens®

PLAYSETS

IDEAS AND PLANS FOR PLAY STRUCTURES

Meredith® Books
Des Moines, Iowa

Better Homes and Gardens® Playsets
Editor: Larry Johnston
Copy Chief: Terri Fredrickson
Publishing Operations Manager: Karen Schirm
Senior Editor, Asset and Information Manager: Phillip Morgan
Edit and Design Production Coordinator: Mary Lee Gavin
Editorial and Design Assistant: Renee E. McAtee
Book Production Managers: Pam Kvitne, Marjorie J. Schenkelberg, Rick von Holdt, Mark Weaver
Contributing Copy Editor: Michael Maine
Contributing Proofreaders: Julie Cahalan, Sue Fetters, David Krause
Indexer: Donald Glassman
Contributing Editorial Assistant: Janet Anderson

Additional Editorial Contributions from Abramowitz Creative Studios
Publishing Director/Designer: Tim Abramowitz
Writer: Jeff Day, Heartwood Books
Graphic Designers: Kelly Bailey, Joel Wires
Photo Research: Amber Jones
Photography: donna h chiarelli studio
Assistant: Tom Wolf
Illustration: Art Rep Services, Inc.
Director: Chip Nadeau
Illustrator: Dave Brandon
Thanks to:
Jack Bowser
4419 Wee Laddie
Houston, TX 77084

Meredith® Books
Executive Director, Editorial: Gregory H. Kayko
Executive Director, Design: Matt Strelecki
Managing Editor: Amy Tincher-Durik
Executive Editor/Group Manager: Benjamin W. Allen
Senior Associate Design Director: Ken Carlson
Marketing Product Manager: Brent Wiersma

Publisher and Editor in Chief: James D. Blume
Editorial Director: Linda Raglan Cunningham
Executive Director, New Business Development: Todd M. Davis
Executive Director, Sales: Ken Zagor
Director, Operations: George A. Susral
Director, Production: Douglas M. Johnston
Director, Marketing: Amy Nichols
Business Director: Jim Leonard

Vice President and General Manager: Douglas J. Guendel

Meredith Publishing Group
President: Jack Griffin
Executive Vice President: Bob Mate

Meredith Corporation
Chairman and Chief Executive Officer: William T. Kerr
President and Chief Operating Officer: Stephen M. Lacy

In Memoriam: E. T. Meredith III (1933-2003)

Library of Congress Control Number: 2005929350
ISBN: 0-696-22555-7

All of us at Meredith® Books are dedicated to providing you with the information and ideas you need to enhance your home and garden. We welcome your comments and suggestions. Write to us at:
Meredith Books
Home Improvement Books Department
1716 Locust St.
Des Moines, IA 50309-3023

Note to the Readers: Due to differing conditions, tools, and individual skills, Meredith Corporation assumes no responsibility for any damages, injuries suffered, or losses incurred as a result of following the information published in this book. Before beginning any project, review the instructions carefully, and if any doubts or questions remain, consult local experts or authorities. Because codes and regulations vary greatly, you always should check with authorities to ensure that your project complies with all applicable local codes and regulations. Always read and observe all of the safety precautions provided by manufacturers of any tools, equipment, or supplies, and follow all accepted safety procedures.

TABLE OF CONTENTS

CHAPTER HIGHLIGHTS

- Groundcovers and Edging
- Accessories
- Ladders, Bridges, and Steps
- Swings
- Climbing Walls
- Playhouses
- Playing with a Theme

GREAT PLACES TO PLAY

Playing is a child's business

Children are naturally energetic and inquisitive. Playing is one of the ways they learn and exercise their imaginations. Active outdoor play also helps youngsters stay healthy while they develop strength and coordination. And playing with other children is an essential part of developing social skills. So an outdoor playset could be considered an important part of a child's world, not just a frill. If, as is often said, play is the business of children, then a playset is a child's office.

This book shows playsets of all types, from basic swings to forts and playhouses suited for any backyard. Manufacturers offer a variety of styles of playsets, some that you assemble yourself and some that are built by professionals. By browsing through manufacturers' catalogs, you're sure to find a style that has just the accessories your kids want.

You'll also find plans and instructions in this book that show you how to build your own playset. Here, too, you can let your childrens'–and your own–imagination run wild. Select a basic structure, then add readily available features and accessories–such as a slide or climbing wall–to create the best backyard playset ever.

Groundcovers and Edging

▶ Grass under a playset soon gets trampled down and scuffed away, making the ground a muddy mess whenever it gets wet. Mulch and resilient groundcovers make a nicer play area.

▼ Edging helps contain the groundcover under a playset. This commercial plastic edging installs easily with spikes and allows you to create your own shape. Wooden landscape timbers also work well.

Falling is practically guaranteed when children are playing. Dirt and grass are a hard surface to land on, and a fall from a high place onto turf can cause injuries.

Loose-fill material under a playset creates a resilient surface that makes the play area safer and more fun. Loose-fill surfaces also drain better, so rain and irrigation won't make the area unusable. You can choose from several materials:

■ Wood chips or bark mulch are inexpensive and readily available. You'll need to add more periodically as it decomposes.

■ Sand and gravel can pack down, making a hard surface. Sand is easily tracked out of the play area, and a big sand area may become a popular rest stop for neighborhood animals.

■ Rubber mulch is a low-maintenance material that doesn't pack down and remains resilient. It is more expensive, but it is probably the best choice overall.

Loose-fill material should be placed only over bare ground, not concrete or paving. The fill material should be at least 6 inches deep (see chart on page 29). It's easiest to place the fill material after the playset has been built.

Surround the filled area with wood or commercial edging. Rake sand, gravel, or mulch surfaces periodically to keep them loose.

▲ Resilient mulch ensures a soft landing at the foot of the slides. And should someone fall, a mulch surface is more forgiving than the cold, hard ground.

▼ The raised edging helps keep the groundcover from being kicked out into the grass.

ACCESSORIES

▲ Mount a steering wheel like this one on a railing or post and see what it becomes. It could be a tall ship's helm one day, a space shuttle control the next.

The basic playset is only a starting point. Adding accessories broadens the range of possible activities and increases the opportunities for imaginative play. By adding accessories to a basic structure, you can change things over time, too, so the playset can grow with your children or accommodate more kids.

Almost anything you see in a school or park playground can be added to your backyard playset, although you may want a scaled-down version in some cases. An Internet search on "playground equipment," "playset accessories," and similar terms will point you toward a number of sources for imaginative playset parts. (See page 191 for some sources.)

Let the children decide

When you're shopping for accessories and add-ons for a playset, it's easy to take an adult approach and look for function and value and other adult attributes as if you are buying a new appliance. But a playset should be fun and exciting, so take your inner child–and your real one–when you go shopping.

See what attracts your child's attention. Look for things that are colorful and have motion, and try to imagine how many ways a child could have fun with something.

Then, turn the shopping over to your outer adult. Make sure the parts are sturdy and don't have sharp ends or edges.

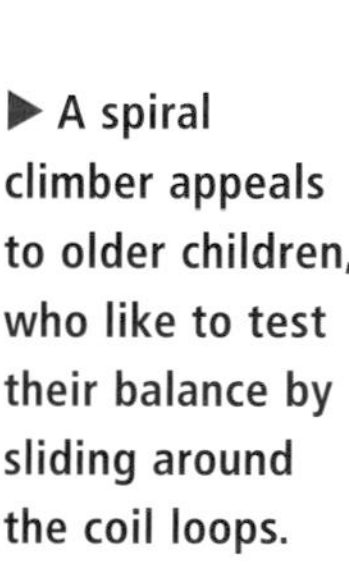

▶ A spiral climber appeals to older children, who like to test their balance by sliding around the coil loops.

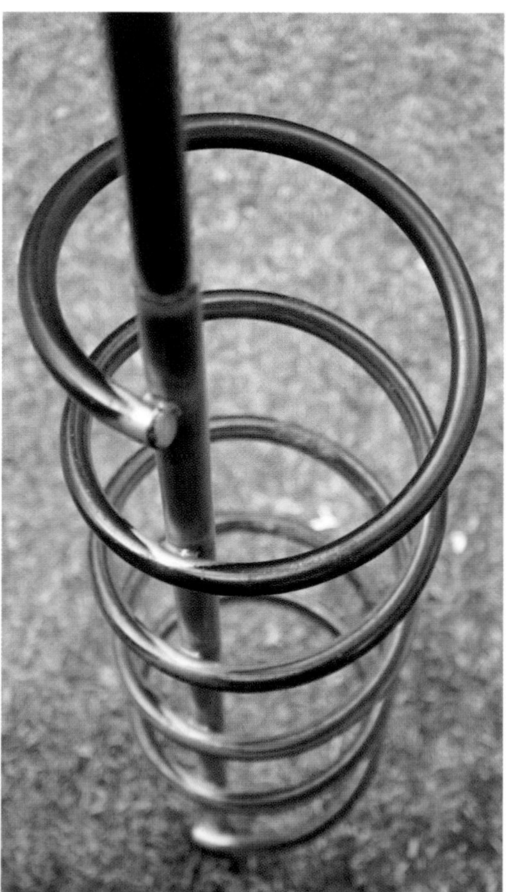

▲ Active kids can swing from end to end on a row of rings. A pair of rings is great for swinging and pull-ups.

◀ A giant tic-tac-toe board gives children a break from the physical work of play.

◀ Mushroom-style climbers are placed at different heights for varied ages and abilities.

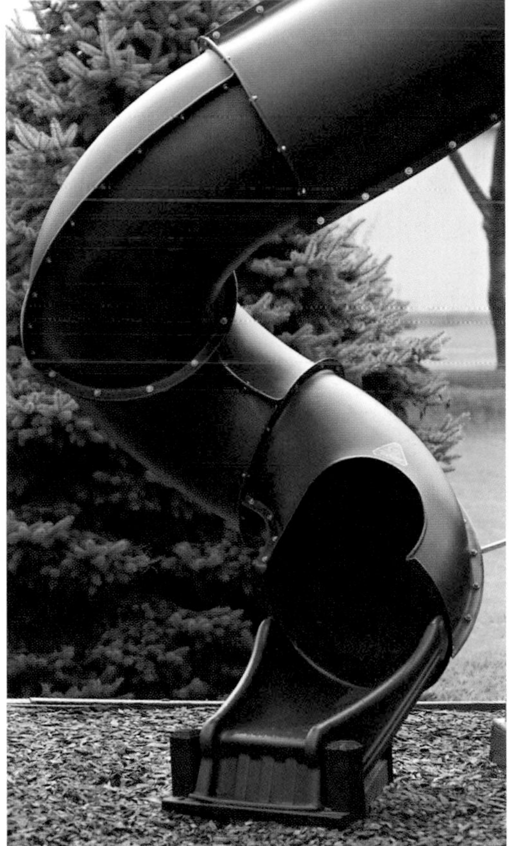

◀ A tubular slide with turns gives a thrill ride. A slide is a great addition to any playset.

◀ A child must to be able to jump high enough to hang from this handle so put it on a low beam first and move it higher as the child grows (and becomes a better jumper).

Ladders, Bridges, and Steps

Climbing and being up high are big parts of the fun offered by any playset. Youngsters love the thrill of exploring high places, and walking across a wobbly rope bridge or climbing a ladder to a platform on a playset gives them a chance to do it safely.

Several of the projects in this book (Chapter 3) incorporate raised platforms, ladders, and stairs. You can build one or more separate platforms, using the basic instructions for post structures, and link them with a series of bridges. Ramps can replace stairs for access too.

Bridges and steps should always have handrails for safety. On a bridge, the handrails should include guardrails to keep children from falling off below the handrail. Chains can be stretched between posts for guardrails. Ladders that lead to platforms need handrails or grab handles above the top step.

A ladder should always be securely attached to the structure at the top so it won't fall over backward with someone climbing it. Check ladders and bridges periodically for loose rungs and secure mountings.

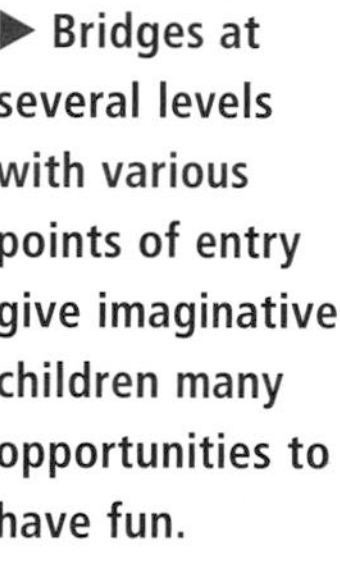

▶ Bridges at several levels with various points of entry give imaginative children many opportunities to have fun.

▶ A rope ladder is exciting to climb and just looks cool on a playset. Nylon rope is better than natural-fiber rope. It's easier on the hands and less likely to rot and break.

■ Planks bolted to chains make an adventurous swaying bridge. Be sure to put handrails on a bridge like this. The old-style monkey bars below still have great appeal.

▼ Spiral stairs could be in a castle or a haunted house. Either way, they are fun for kids of all ages. You could build them of wood or use ready-to-assemble steel ones like these.

◀ Chains with rungs make a ladder that is sturdy and a blast to climb. A ladder like this adds to the fun of the slide.

SWINGS

A swing is a playset staple. A playset at its most basic, in fact, is usually a frame with two swings. When you plan any play structure, you should include a swing or two.

You should avoid the traditional backyard swing–an old car tire hanging from a tree limb on a manila rope. An auto tire is heavy enough to cause injury if it hits a child, and a natural-fiber rope out in the weather is liable to rot and break. The rope can abrade and break where it's tied around the branch or tire too. Another traditional type of swing to stay away from is the knotted rope hanging from a tree limb. This Tarzan-style swing is responsible for many injuries. Tying a rope–or anything–around a tree branch is bad for the tree too. It can damage thin bark or girdle the branch, killing it.

The best swing sets have a sturdy frame with soft seats hanging from chains. (Seats made of wood, metal, or other heavy, solid materials are a hazard.) The chains should be attached to pivoting hangers at the top.

▲ **A porch swing is a great addition for a playhouse. Make a child-size swing wide enough for two so friends can swing and visit.**

▼ **A soft canvas swing is a fine place to sit and read or relax, but it just wouldn't be suitable for high swinging.**

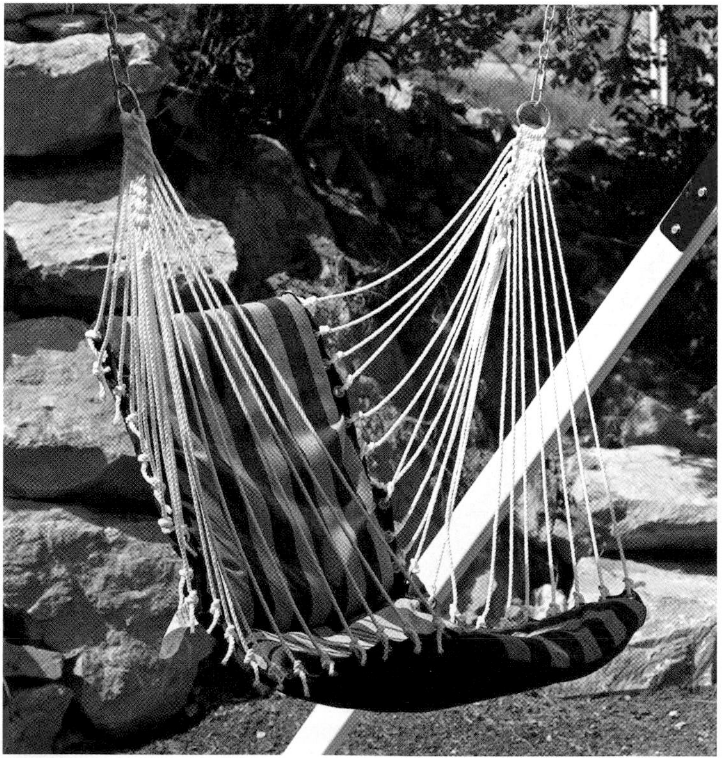

▲ Ready-made tire swings use a special tire rather than an old car tire. A tire swing should be on a beam separate from other swings.

▼ A bucket swing is best for toddlers under age 3. You can replace the bucket with another type of seat as your child gets older.

A swing should be 30 inches from any supporting structure on the side. Place swings 24 inches apart and at least 6 feet from buildings or other obstructions. Attach the chains to the pivots and swing seat with snap links or other closed fittings; clothing might snag on open S-hooks, posing a hazard.

▲ A belt swing, trapeze, and glider ensure plenty of opportunities for fun on this swing set.

Climbing Walls

Climbing walls—artificial rocks that mountaineers and rock climbers practice their skills on—are becoming more popular for backyard play.

You can add a smaller, simpler climbing wall to any playset. You could build a separate one as a freestanding feature or against a garage or house wall. The structure is basic—a surface of decking or 2× boards over some stringers. The wall can be vertical or on a slant, depending on the age and skill of the child climber. The wall should be firmly attached to a solid structure at the top so it won't fall over on the climber.

Grips for climbing are available in a number of styles from several sources. Some are random shapes, while others resemble animals or fish.

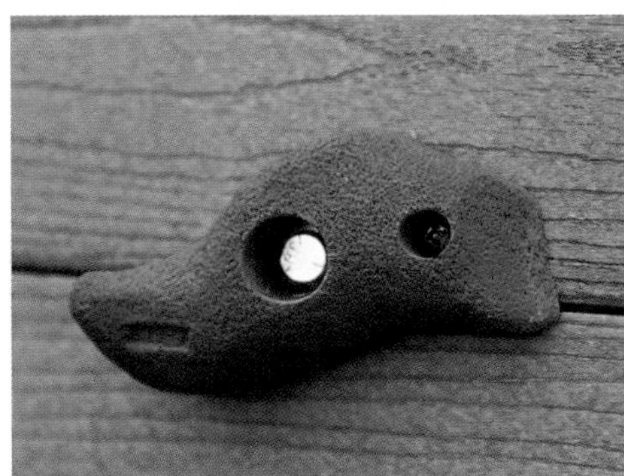

▲ Screw-on grips make any vertical or near-vertical surface a climbing wall.

▶ A few grips placed on a flat wall give children lots of ways to scale the surface, be it a medieval castle keep or an outlaw's desert lair.

◀ The boards at the edges of this climbing surface offer additional footholds for a young climber.

▼ Send a youngster who is driving you up the wall in the house outside to climb a wall. This wall is faced with stone veneer for a realistic look. Gaps and stone ledges give a climber places to step and grip.

The grips attach to the surface with screws or bolts. As your child grows, you can remove the grips and move them to a larger wall. An Internet search on "climbing wall," "climbing wall grips," or "climbing wall holds" will direct you to several sources for ready-made grips.

You could make your own climbing grips from short lengths of 2×2 or 2×4 lumber. Cut the wood to shape and form the edges with a rasp or belt sander. Make a slight bevel on the top edge and place the short side of the bevel against the wall to provide a better fingerhold. Attach the grips securely with lag screws or carriage bolts–your child's weight at times will be hanging from the fasteners for only one grip.

A rope attached at the top of a climbing wall provides another way to scale the wall. Secure it with a snap link to make it removable.

Playhouses

Playing house is at its best in a child-scale house. A playhouse is a perfect project to build for and with your kids. (Plans for two playhouses start on pages 92 and 128.)

A playhouse is really little more than a garden shed with decorative details added. So the easiest way to build a playhouse is to start with a ready-made garden shed or a precut kit, available at many lumberyards and home centers and through mail-order dealers.

▼ A rustic log cabin with a porch and swing is a retreat any child would love.

▲ A full-size door awaits the day when this playhouse becomes home to the lawn mower and other outdoor equipment. In the meantime, larger guests can enter through it to visit the playhouse.

Starting from the basic structure, you can make the playhouse look like your real house or turn it into a fantasy vision. It depends on the kind of details you add. This is where you and your children can work together on the project. The kids will love dreaming up details, and you can let them help with things like painting and attaching pieces.

One detail you should always consider for a playhouse is a porch. A porch with room for a couple of child-size chairs and a table will make a place children will treasure for years to come.

Your children will inevitably outgrow a playhouse. A well-built structure can continue to serve as a garden or storage shed. In time, though, grandchildren may show up, eager to stake their own claim on the space their mom or dad remembers so fondly.

◀ **It's the details that make a playhouse a playhome. A window box and shutters lend this playhouse a country look.**

▼ **Without anything to give scale, this playhouse looks almost like a real house.**

Playing with a Theme

Imagination makes a playset into anything a child wants it to be. But there are times when a little design help can take that imagination even further.

The pirate ship on these pages is based on a fortress-style playset with raised platforms. But in this case, the platforms have become boat decks. A mast with trapeze bars, a wooden ship's helm, a telescope on the rail, a gangplank for entry, and other clever details turn an ordinary playset into the feared barque of the dreaded Cap'n Kid.

You could build a playset as a pirate ship too. Or it could be an airplane, a submarine, a castle, a spaceport, an Antarctic weather station, or whatever your child wants it to be.

▼ Cap'n Kid, whose headwear leaves no doubt what kind of ship he runs, sails to an island. Buried treasure awaits at a spot marked X.

▼ A pirate ship in the backyard provides swings, slides, places to climb, and more. But it also lets an imaginative young pirate safely prowl the seven seas.

■ Peering through the telescope, Cap'n Kid searches for signs of lunch. A nearby house appears to have a refrigerator he can raid.

For a theme playset, start with a basic structure, such as the Kid's Retreat on page 78. The facade on that structure could be painted to fit almost any theme. A spaceship? Paint the pointed facade to look like a rocket. Or you could extend the facade past the rafters and give it a crenellated top to look like a castle. With just minor design changes, you can make it look like it belongs in a dusty Old West town.

Accessories and other features shown in this chapter will help you further the theme you create. A climbing wall would be a natural part of a castle. A steering wheel right below the window in the facade makes an airplane cockpit, a submarine, a space shuttle, or a hundred other fantasy places.

Other projects in this book can be customized to follow a theme. Or you can just leave it to your child's imagination.

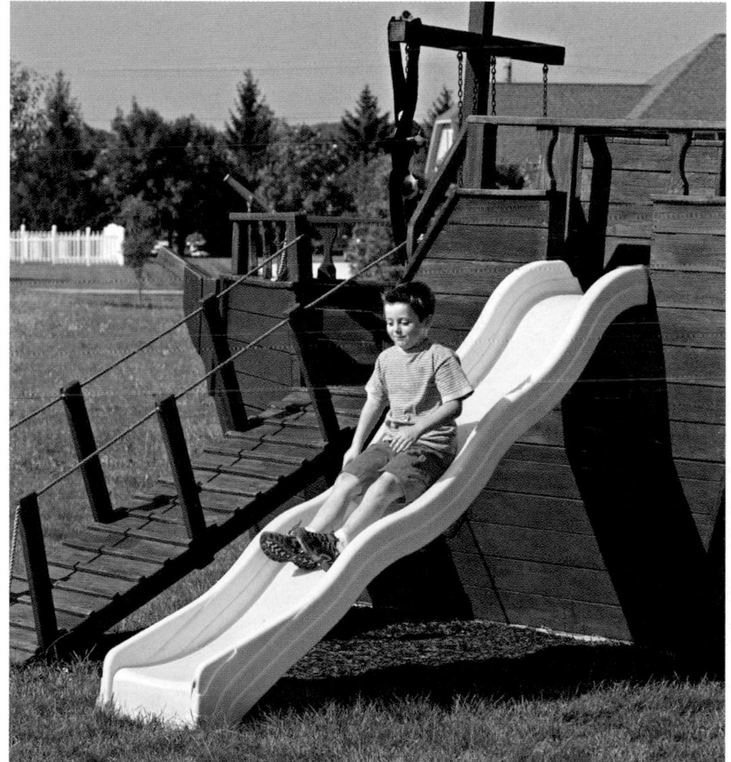

▲ At the end of a long morning of pirating, going down the slide is certainly better than walking the plank.

CHAPTER HIGHLIGHTS

- Assessing Your Needs
- Buying Components for Your Structure
- Choosing a Site
- Playing Safe
- Building with Kids

PLANNING

Memories are made of this

Swings, slides, forts, playhouses, and similar outdoor playthings are the stuff of childhood memories. These memories take on an extra dimension when the play item is homebuilt. By building the project yourself, you are in control of the quality, features, and safety of your child's play structure. You can also save some money; your only cash costs are the materials and any tools you buy or rent. If you include your child in the planning and building, you have a winning proposition all around.

Building the projects in this book requires a basic understanding of woodworking and the skills to use several portable power tools, including a drill and a circular saw. Larger tools, such as the tablesaw, will be helpful for the more complex projects. The larger play structures also require more planning. You will need to consider the nature of your children who will be using the equipment and their ages. Also consider safety concerns and available space.

The first step in getting started, and the purpose of the next few pages, is to help you think about, plan, and decide what you're going to build.

ASSESSING YOUR NEEDS

Play structures come in many sizes and shapes for all kinds of activities. Some features, such as ladders and swings, promote motor skills and coordination. Others, such as sandboxes and playhouses, foster creative and imaginative play. You may choose to build one type of play structure or combine several for a backyard play zone that will attract the entire neighborhood.

Children under the age of 5 are usually happy with basic play structures: a swing set, a small slide, a teeter-totter. They often do not feel comfortable playing on large playsets with multiple climbing levels, so begin with a small project; sandboxes and wading pools are ideal.

Slightly older kids, ages 5–10, want more complex play structures. Tented or roofed platforms and huts built on top of climbing towers provide great spaces for creative play. Climbing ropes, cargo nets, bridges, and firefighter poles are appropriate for this age group as well.

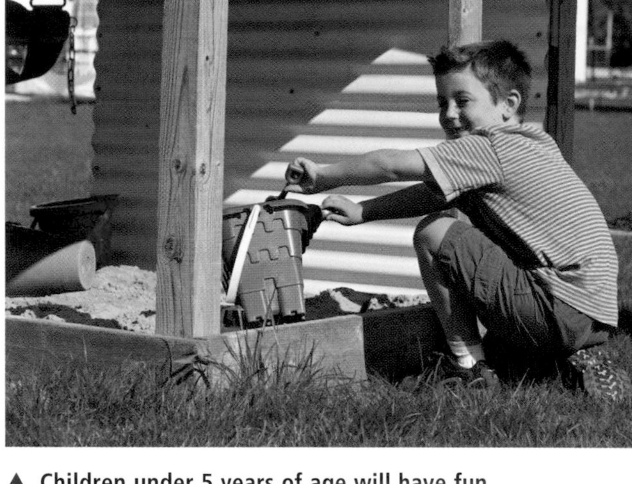

▲ Children under 5 years of age will have fun playing in a sandbox, but the appeal of digging and playing with toy construction equipment makes a sandbox good for older kids too.

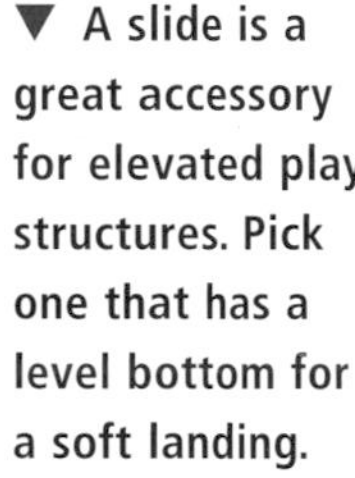

▼ A slide is a great accessory for elevated play structures. Pick one that has a level bottom for a soft landing.

Swings are favorites for kids of all ages. Soft strap-type seats or lightweight rigid seats have replaced the wooden and metal seats you may have grown up with. But swings will take kids anywhere their imaginations will go, so don't stop with the basics. Kids will enjoy options such as disks, tire swings, buoy-ball swings, trapeze-and-ring combos, and gliders. Tire swings come both as single-axis swings, which travel back and forth like regular swings, or as universal swings that can be propelled in any direction. (For safety, each universal swing must be mounted on a separate swing set with no other swings.)

◀ A picnic table, like this one cleverly built into the supports of an elevated playset, provides a place to play games, work on craft projects, or eat a playtime lunch outdoors.

In addition to swings, slides are extremely popular. Gone are the days when they were made of metal and prone to overheating during hot weather. The new slides are molded of strong plastics and come in a variety of shapes. For the very young, there are extra-wide slides. For older kids, the slides can be fast or slow, with or without waves, and enclosed or open. Enclosed tubes are often spiral shape for added excitement. Today's slides allow for soft landings by leveling off for a couple of feet at the end of the slide.

Size and number of children

Kids tend to use play structures with their friends, so build your structure with enough features to accommodate your child and several friends as well. The more children you expect to use this play structure, the more features you will want to add so that every child can find something to do.

If there's an elevated platform in your design, make it big enough to hold several children, and be sure it has a sturdy safety rail. A ground-level picnic table is also a smart addition to any play zone for use in warm weather. In a child's imagination it becomes a boat, a plane, a mountain, or the moon. It's a great place for the neighborhood kids to eat lunch (instead of in the kitchen) and provides a place to play games or do messy art and crafts projects.

Allow enough space around play areas such as platforms, swings, slides, and sandboxes. If you pack features too close together, they will be hard to use and may be dangerous. For more on spacing, see page 26.

Buying Components for Your Structure

Two of the most important components for any playset are swings and slides. You'll find several types of swings to choose from. Some of the most popular ones include sling seats, flat plastic seats, or tire swings. (See pages 12–13.)

The sling seat that looks like a wide belt is most common, but older children sometimes complain that this kind is too tight around the hips. A flat plastic seat solves that problem and still meets safety standards.

Bucket seats are a good option for toddlers and young children because the design gives them a backrest and is difficult to fall out of. Choose a full-bucket seat, not a half-bucket seat, for children under age 3.

■ **A full bucket swing (above) is best for a toddler. Attach the swing with chains and clips so you can change to a half bucket, sling, or flat seat as a child grows. Accessories such as the pivoting telescope (left) add opportunities for imagination and fun to a playset.**

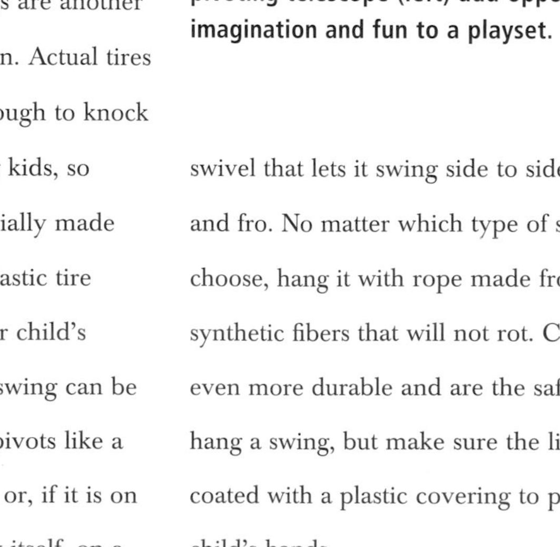

Tire swings are another popular option. Actual tires are heavy enough to knock over even big kids, so choose a specially made lightweight plastic tire swing for your child's safety. A tire swing can be mounted on pivots like a regular swing or, if it is on a swing set by itself, on a swivel that lets it swing side to side as well as to and fro. No matter which type of swing you choose, hang it with rope made from strong synthetic fibers that will not rot. Chains are even more durable and are the safest way to hang a swing, but make sure the links are coated with a plastic covering to protect your child's hands.

There are also many kinds of slides. Aside from the traditional flatbed slide, you can buy slides with waves or bumps. Slides that spiral are another way to add excitement to the sliding experience. Tube slides are a good way to add extra safety. You can add a slide to almost any playset with an elevated platform.

A popular feature you can add to almost any play structure is a climbing wall (pages 14–15). The easiest way to add a climbing wall to your play structure is to buy a preassembled climbing wall or a kit of parts and install them according to the manufacturer's directions. Climbing walls are not recommended for kids under age 6.

You can customize a playset to match your child's interests and preferences with a variety of accessories. Steering wheels, play telephones, periscopes, and telescopes are available from many of the suppliers listed on page 191. Also see pages 8–9 for accessories.

▲ A climbing wall is fun and also helps a child build strength and develop coordination.

▶ Mounted so it turns freely, this wheel can be a big-rig steering wheel, a power-plant control valve, or whatever else the moment's play demands.

Choosing a Site

A playset should be in a location that is well shaded. Otherwise you will have to contend with the sun, sunburn, and heat. If natural shade from a building or tree is not available, consider shading play areas such as a sandbox or wading pool with a large umbrella made of a fabric that blocks UV light.

Place your backyard play zone so that you can see it from the house, patio, or deck, so you can keep an eye on what's going on. This is especially important if your children are young. Make sure the site is free of obstructions such as clotheslines, stones, buildings, fences, exposed roots, or tree trunks for at least 6 feet in all directions. Keep play structures that are more than 30 inches tall at least 9 feet apart. Add a fence to separate play structures from the street.

Swings, slides, and seesaws should be placed so they (and kids playing on them) won't collide with children on the ground. A child should be able to go from one element of the play area to another without crossing in front of swings. Provide enough space to keep areas where younger children play separate from areas for older children.

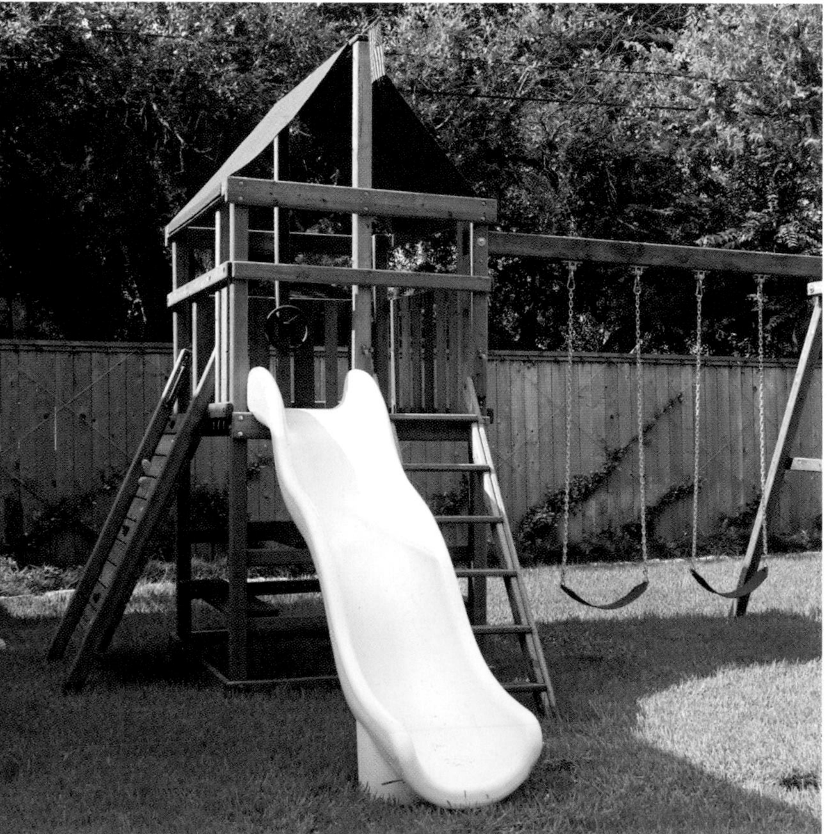

■ **The slide on the play structure below is too close to the evergreen. The plant could scratch children playing on the slide and could be damaged. The slide at left has no obstructions and ends where there is room to land.**

◀ Mulch makes a safe surface for play, but the stone wall is close enough that children could fall on or against it. A child on the swing could hit the wall too. The slide ends at the foot of the ladder, making collisions likely.

On the level

Make sure the site is flat and level. On a slope, an elevated play structure could be unstable. Uneven ground will cause falls.

To check for level, tape a level to a straight 2×4. Move the board sideways over the ground to check for high spots. You may be able to level minor high spots with a rake. More likely, you will have to dig down high spots and fill in low spots with a shovel. Once the ground is relatively flat, put the level and 2×4 on the ground and lift an end until the bubble centers in the vial. The distance between the bottom of the 2×4 and the ground is the amount the ground is out of level. Move soil from the high end of the area to the low end. Keep removing soil from the high end and spreading it out at the low end until you get a level reading. If the ground is quite uneven, you may have to bring in truckloads of soil to level the area. If you do, rent a power tamper to pack the soil down once you've leveled it.

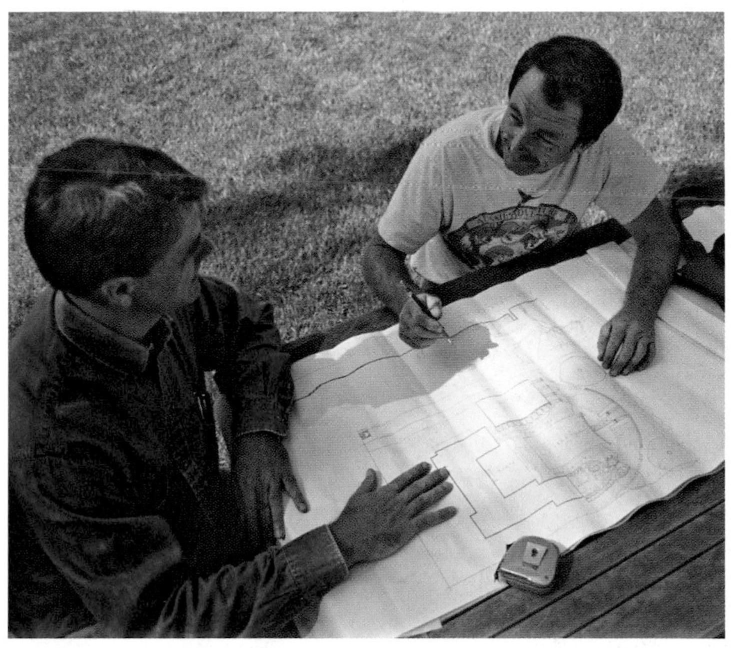

▲ Start with a drawing of your yard to determine the best location for a playset. Consider distances to landscape features, buildings, and hard areas such as driveways or sidewalks.

Playing Safe

Safety covers three broad categories: preventing falls, providing soft landings, and keeping kids from getting stuck, scraped, cut, or bruised.

Preventing falls is the most important. Most playground injuries are caused by falls. The height of a play structure depends on the age of the children using it. The Consumer Product Safety Commission recommends structures for preschoolers be no more than 5 feet tall. Playsets for school-age children should be no more than 7 feet tall. A child's head should never be more than 12 feet above the ground when the child stands on the structure.

If your play structure is more than 30 inches tall, a guardrail should surround the play surface, except at entrances and exits. The top surface of the guardrail should be at least 29 inches above the platform; the lower edge should be no more than 23 inches above the platform. For older children, the top should be at least 38 inches and the bottom should be no more than 28 inches above the platform.

That type of guardrail is acceptable on a structure 30–48 inches tall, but a barrier that extends from the surface to the top guardrail height is preferable. Structures more than 48 inches tall must have a barrier. The barrier can be solid or made of slats spaced no more than 3 inches apart.

Providing soft landings

No matter how safe you play it, kids jump and fall. Make sure there is a soft landing zone for them around your play structure. Nothing provides complete protection, but wood chips, sand, shredded tires, or even gravel all provide a soft enough landing as long as they are installed over dirt.

Wood chip surfaces have a low initial cost, but they decompose and will need to be replenished. Rain, humidity, and freezing

Maintaining Wood Play Structures

Check play structures regularly to make sure there are no problems. Check all nuts and bolts at the beginning of the play season and twice monthly for the rest of the season.

Remove plastic swing seats and take them indoors when the temperature drops to the point specified by the manufacturer.

Oil all metallic moving parts monthly during the play season.

Check all coverings for bolts and sharp edges at the beginning of the season and twice monthly for the rest of the season. Make sure they are tight and properly attached. Replace as necessary.

Check swing seats, ropes, cables, and chains monthly during the play season. Replace as directed by the manufacturer.

Stain or paint regularly as directed by the manufacturer of the finish you're using.

▲ **Shredded rubber mulch in colors makes a cheerful and bright play area. The resilience of the material makes the area safe too.**

weather make the surface harder, lessening its effectiveness. Sand and gravel are also relatively inexpensive and will not decompose. Both are abrasive, however, and like wood chips, they are affected by rain, freezing weather, and humidity.

Shredded tires–often sold as rubber mulch–will not deteriorate, have the best cushioning features, and are less likely to compact. But rubber mulch is more expensive. Untreated, it may stain clothing.

Tires have steel belts in them, so make sure you get rubber mulch that's guaranteed to be wire free.

Lay 4×4s or a similar barrier around the play area to keep the surface material in place.

Recommendations for the size of the soft surface vary with use:

■ The soft surface around climbing equipment should extend beyond the structure for 6 feet in every direction.

■ The ground around slides should be covered with a soft material 6 feet in every direction. The area in front of the slide should be covered for a distance equal to the height of the slide plus 4 feet.

■ The ground around swing sets should be covered 6 feet on each side and twice the height of the swing set in front and back.

LANDING ZONE THICKNESS

HEIGHT OF STRUCTURE	**5'**	**6'**	**7'**	**8'**	**9'**	**10'**	**11'**
SURFACE MATERIAL							
WOOD CHIPS	6"	6"	6"	9"	9"	9"	12"
DOUBLE-SHREDDED BARK MULCH	6"	6"	9"	9"	9"	9"	12"
FINE SAND	9"	12"	12"	12"	12"		
COARSE SAND	9"	12"					
FINE GRAVEL	6"	6"	9"	12"	12"	12"	
MEDIUM GRAVEL	9"	12"					
SHREDDED TIRES	6"	6"	6"	6"	6"	6"	6"

SOURCE: CONSUMER PRODUCT SAFETY COMMISSION

Cuts, bruises, and getting stuck

Here's where common sense prevails. Round over all wooden edges to prevent slivers and cuts. Nuts and bolts should be recessed, or extend by no more than the diameter of the bolt, to prevent scrapes, cuts, and catching children's clothing. Use lock washers to keep hardware from working loose.

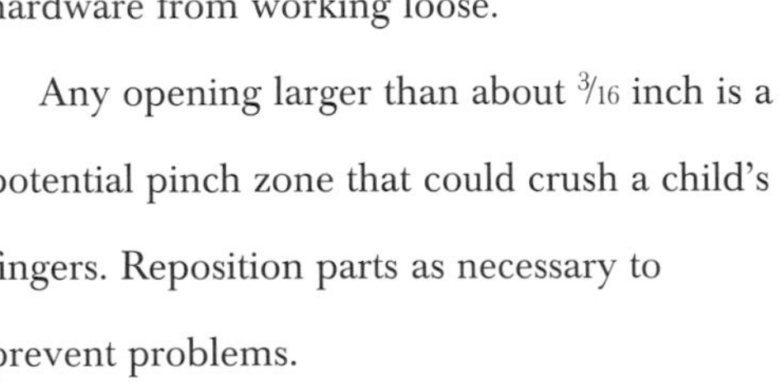

Any opening larger than about 3/16 inch is a potential pinch zone that could crush a child's fingers. Reposition parts as necessary to prevent problems.

Balusters in railings should be no more than 3 inches apart so that kids can't slip their heads between them and get stuck.

▲ **A sturdy handle solidly attached makes a safe handhold for a child. Rounded edges on the railing prevent cuts and splinters.**

▼ **Hang swings from strong swivels. A snap link makes it easy to adjust the chain for swing height and allows you to remove swings for the winter.**

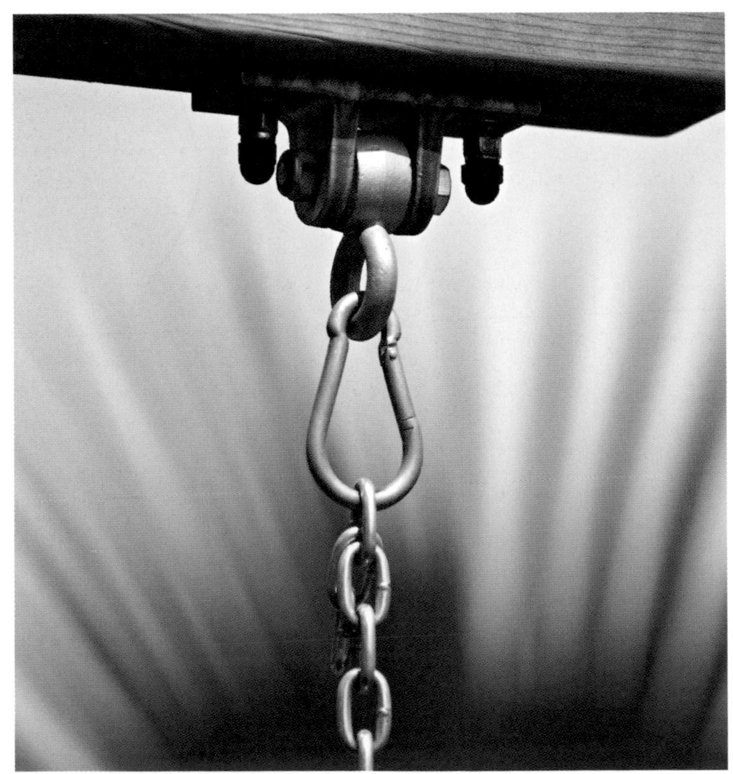

Fasten ropes, rope ladders, and cargo nets at both ends so that they can't form a loop that could strangle a child.

Swings should be rubber or canvas–not wood or metal. The hooks that attach them to the chains should be closed so clothes can't get caught on them. Snap links are even better to use. Hang the swing at least 8 inches above the ground; higher for older, taller kids.

CHAPTER 2

Building with Kids

Children love to get involved in building a playset. The easiest way to involve your child is with the planning. Show your child the plans in this book. Discuss which ones they'd prefer. Where there are choices as to which features to add, such as with a swing set, go to the websites listed on page 191 and look over the choices together.

You can also have your children help choose where in the yard they would like to place the play structure. Give them paper and pencils and show them how to sketch the project. You can have an older child draw the plan to scale on graph paper and show it in relationship to existing structures, trees, and garden beds. For a younger child, this might be an exercise in imagination, such as drawing a playhouse and imagining the doors and windows.

Once you've settled on the site, get out the shovels and have the kids help level things out. They probably won't be interested in getting everything perfectly flat or level, but you can always have them dig a hole somewhere off to the side. Use the soil to fill in the low spots. If the hole amounts to anything by the time they're done–and given the way children take to shovels, it usually will–fill it back in so no one steps into it and gets hurt.

Have the kids help you pick out the lumber and assist in measuring the wood and marking it for cutting. Even the youngest can help by holding one end of a tape measure in place. When it comes to actual cutting and drilling, however, it's best to keep children under age 12 on the sidelines. Don't let the kids use a circular or tablesaw under any circumstances. Older kids may be able to help with easy cutting tasks involving a jigsaw, but keep them under your constant supervision. Equip them with safety equipment–goggles, gloves, and hearing protectors around power tools–and set an example by wearing it yourself. Carefully set up for each task and follow safe tool use and woodworking practices.

Finishing offers some opportunities to involve children. If you're working with cedar or redwood, wrap sandpaper on a sanding block and let the young ones get busy rounding over corners and smoothing out surfaces. (Wear a dust mask for any sanding.) Older kids can handle palm sanders. (Leave the sanding of pressure-treated lumber to adults.)

Painting or staining is also relatively safe, as long as you're using latex paints or stains. Have the kids don rubber gloves and old clothes. Getting paint out of a child's hair is sure to cause unhappiness, so a painter's hat is a good idea. And eye protection is a must. Be sure to follow the manufacturer's safety precautions on the product label.

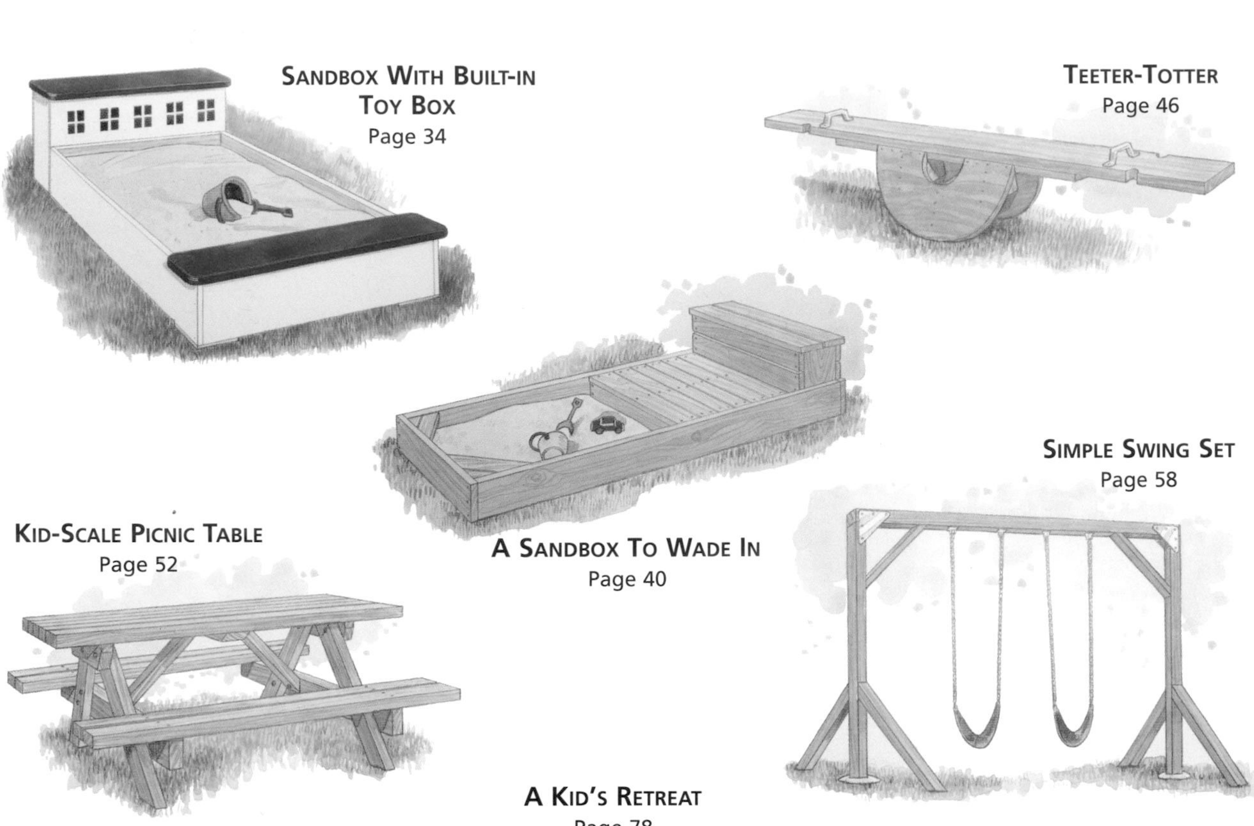

Sandbox With Built-in Toy Box
Page 34

Teeter-Totter
Page 46

A Sandbox To Wade In
Page 40

Kid-Scale Picnic Table
Page 52

Simple Swing Set
Page 58

A Kid's Retreat
Page 78

Swing Under Cover
Page 64

High Rise Playhouse
Page 92

Fort Frolic
Page 108

Cottage Playhouse
Page 128

PROJECTS

Plans and instructions in this chapter show you how to build 10 different playsets, shown opposite. From simple sandboxes to complex multiactivity play centers, these projects are sturdy enough to stand up to the rambunctious use active children will give them.

Before you begin a project, read through the instructions a couple of times and study the drawings so you will be familiar with the structure. Check with your local building department before you begin, too, to find out whether the structure you plan to build will require a building permit.

If you want more information about materials, construction techniques, or tools, refer to chapters 4 and 5. You'll find the answers to many basic construction questions there, along with information that will help you buy materials and pick the right tools for the job.

Special hardware, swing seats, and accessories that will make your playset look like it was professionally built are available at many home centers, lumberyards, and toy stores. If you can't find what you want locally, check the sources listed on page 191 or search on the Internet for playset parts.

SANDBOX WITH BUILT-IN TOY BOX

Having a sandbox in the backyard is the next best thing to building sand castles on the beach. Playing in the sand is one childhood diversion that never seems to lose its appeal, generation after generation. Kids like to dig in the dirt, no matter what their parents say, and dirt doesn't come any cleaner than bagged sandbox sand. This sandbox has an attached toy box to store shovels, buckets, and toy tractors between playtimes. You can make the toy box look like a garage by painting lines or black rectangles on it to simulate windows and doors, if you wish.

The sandbox is easy to construct–it's just a bottomless box made from 2×12s. For a simpler sandbox, replace the toy box with another seat.

The toy box is built from one and one-half 4×8-foot sheets of $\frac{3}{4}$-inch exterior plywood. A full sheet of plywood is awkward to transport and handle, so have the dealer cut the sheet into two pieces. Cut it off-center so you'll have a $49\frac{1}{2}$-inch-long piece for the lid **(E)**. Some home centers and lumberyards will cut all the pieces to size at little cost, which is even handier.

Another way to make this project a little easier is to prime and paint the components of

Sandbox exploded view

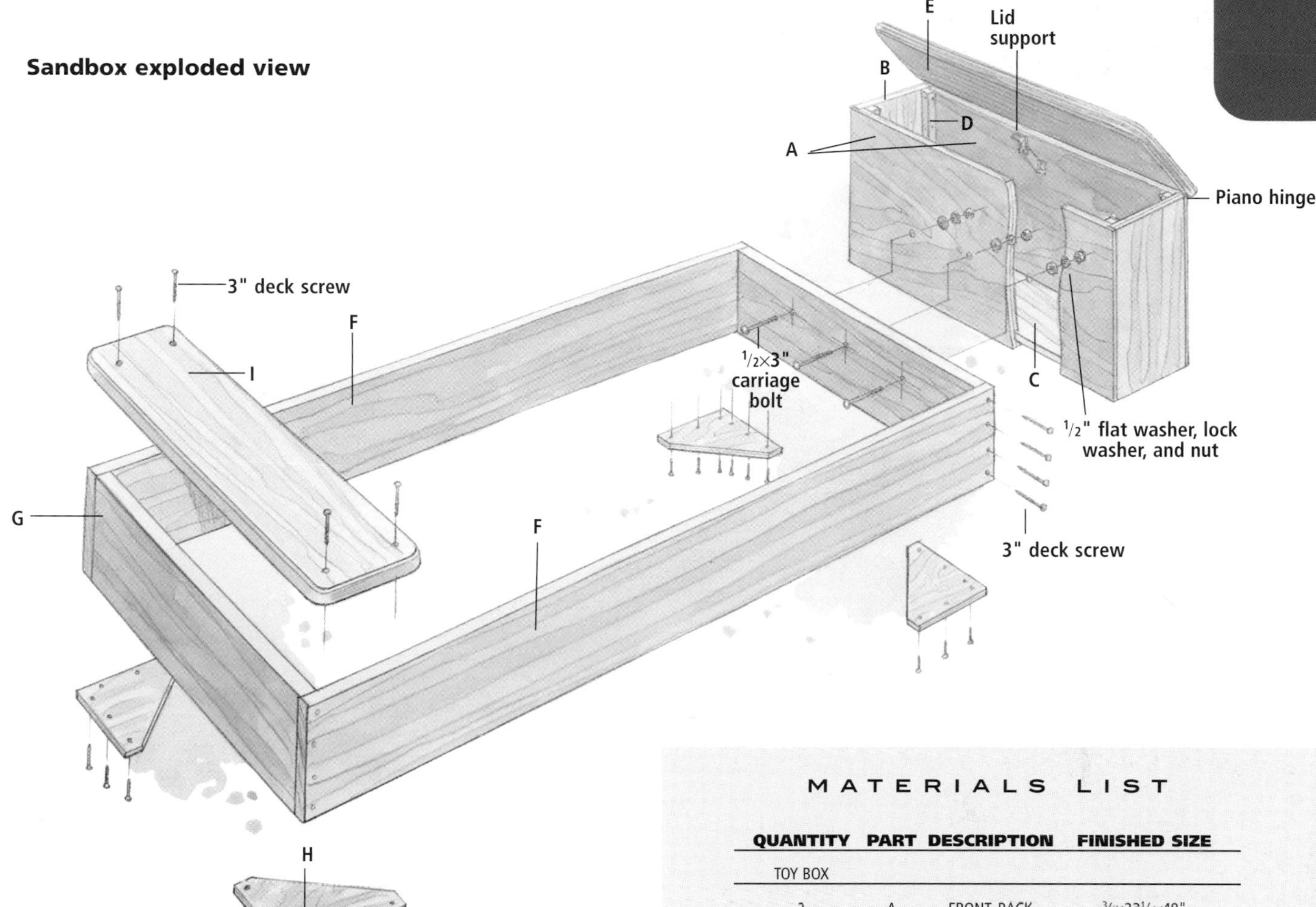

the box before assembly. If you do this, mask off the areas where you will apply glue so the assembled joints will be strong.

Both the toy box and the sandbox are assembled with galvanized deck screws and construction adhesive. Carriage bolts attach the two. The toy box calls for a long piano (continuous) hinge and a lid support. If you can't find them in local stores, you can buy them through a woodworking supply catalog or an Internet site.

MATERIALS LIST

QUANTITY	PART	DESCRIPTION	FINISHED SIZE
TOY BOX			
2	A	FRONT, BACK	¾×23¼×48"
2	B	ENDS	¾×23¼×14½"
1	C	BOTTOM	¾×14×47"
4	D	CLEATS	¾×1×21¾"
1	E	LID	¾×16½×49½"
SANDBOX			
2	F	SIDES	1½×11¼×96"
2	G	ENDS	1½×11¼×45"
4	H	GUSSETS	¾×12×12"
1	I	SEAT	1½×11¼×51"

GALVANIZED DECK SCREWS: 1⅝" AND 3"

CONSTRUCTION ADHESIVE OR POLYURETHANE GLUE

EXTERIOR PRIMER

EXTERIOR ENAMEL

PAINTER'S MASKING TAPE

1½×47" BRASS PIANO HINGE

FLATHEAD BRASS WOOD SCREWS, #6×½"

TOY BOX LID SUPPORT

ROUND-HEAD BRASS WOOD SCREWS, #8×½"

½×3" CARRIAGE BOLTS, FLAT WASHERS, LOCK WASHERS, AND NUTS

BAGGED SANDBOX OR PLAYGROUND SAND

SANDBOX WITH BUILT-IN TOY BOX (CONTINUED)

Cut and assemble the toy box parts

1 Cut plywood for the front and back (**A**), ends (**B**), and bottom (**C**) of the toy box to the sizes shown in the materials list.

2 Rout a 3/4-inch-wide groove 1/4 inch deep and 3/4 inch from the bottom of the front and back panels and a dado of the same dimensions on the end panels, as shown right. (A dado and a groove look the same; a dado runs across the grain and a groove runs with the grain.) With a router or tablesaw, cut a 3/4-inch-wide rabbet 1/2 inch deep along the inside vertical edges of the front and back panels, as shown right.

3 Cut four corner cleats (**D**) 3/4×1×21 3/4 inches. You can cut these parts from scraps of 1× lumber (3/4 inch thick) or 5/4 (five-quarter) wood decking (1 inch thick). Drill and countersink screw holes through the cleats with a combination countersink bit.

4 Assemble the box, applying construction adhesive or polyurethane glue along the mating surfaces of the front, back, ends, and bottom. Drive 1 5/8-inch screws through the holes in the cleats. Make sure the box is square by measuring the diagonals, as shown below. If the diagonals are the same, the box is square. If not, push gently on the longer diagonal to square the box.

Routing

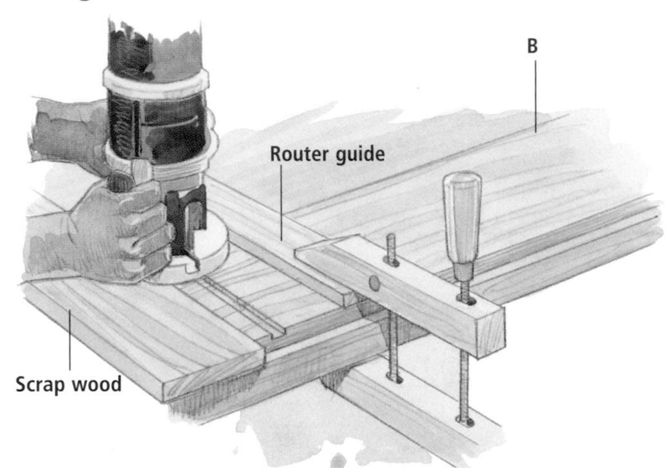

Toy box exploded view

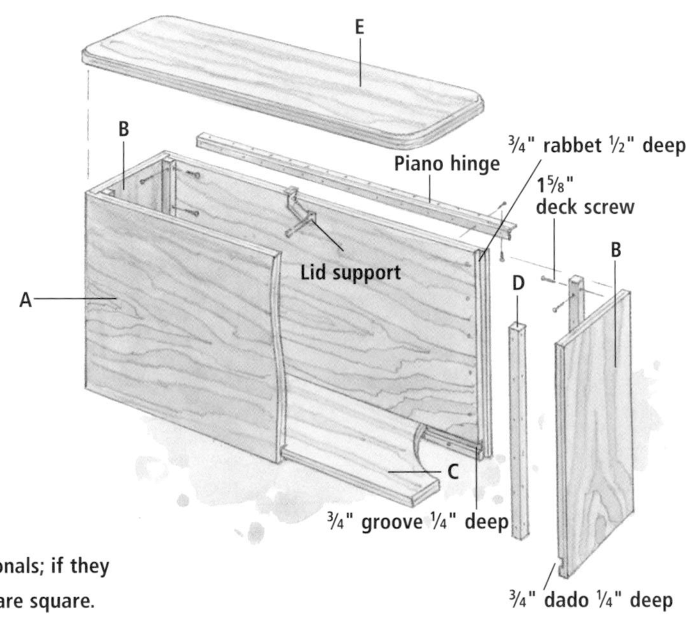

Checking for square

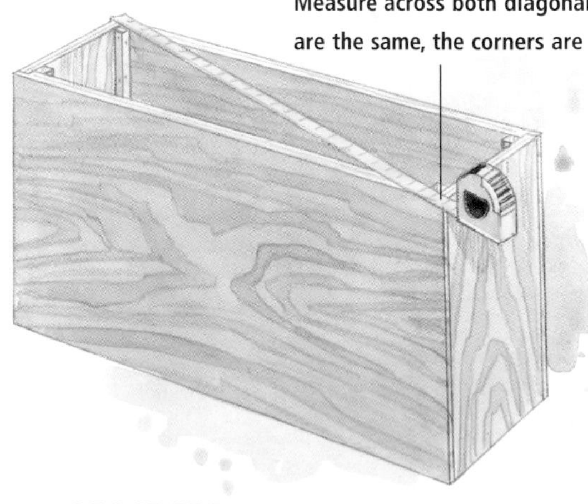

Measure across both diagonals; if they are the same, the corners are square.

5 Cut the lid (**E**) from plywood. Use a compass to draw a 1 1/2-inch radius at each corner. Cut and sand the corners to shape. Rout all around the top and bottom edges of the lid with a 3/16-inch roundover bit.

6 Cut the piano hinge to 47 inches long. Cut it with a hacksaw, and file or grind the sharp corners at both ends. Set it aside for now.

Cut and assemble the sandbox parts

1 Cut 2×12 boards to the lengths shown in the materials list for the sides **(F)** and ends **(G)**.

2 Drill pilot holes for screws at both ends of the sides as indicated in the Exploded View illustration on page 35. Apply construction adhesive or polyurethane glue to the mating surfaces and assemble the parts on a level surface. Drive 3-inch screws at each corner, making sure the box is square.

Gusset

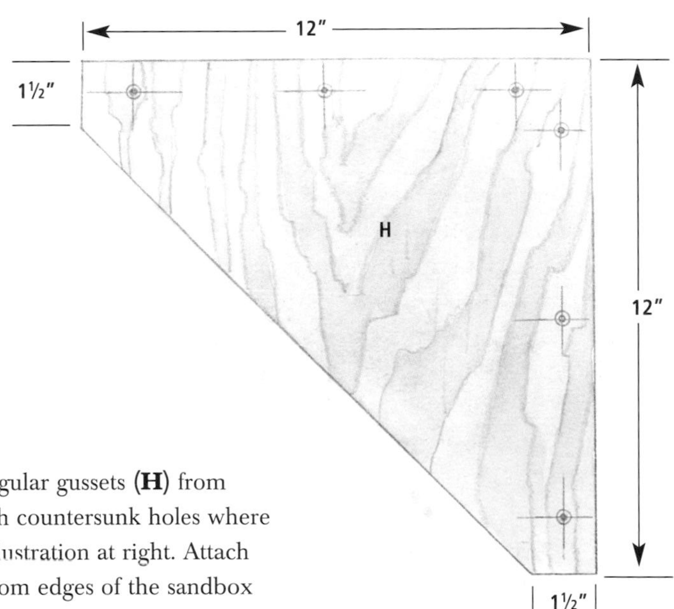

3 Cut the four triangular gussets **(H)** from plywood. Drill 5/32-inch countersunk holes where shown in the gusset illustration at right. Attach the gussets to the bottom edges of the sandbox with adhesive and 1⅝-inch screws.

4 Cut the seat **(I)** to length from 2×12 stock. Draw a 1½-inch radius at each corner. Cut and sand the corners to shape. Rout all around both the top and bottom edges of the seat with a 3/16-inch roundover bit.

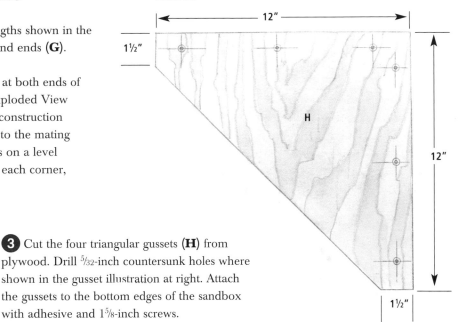

Section view

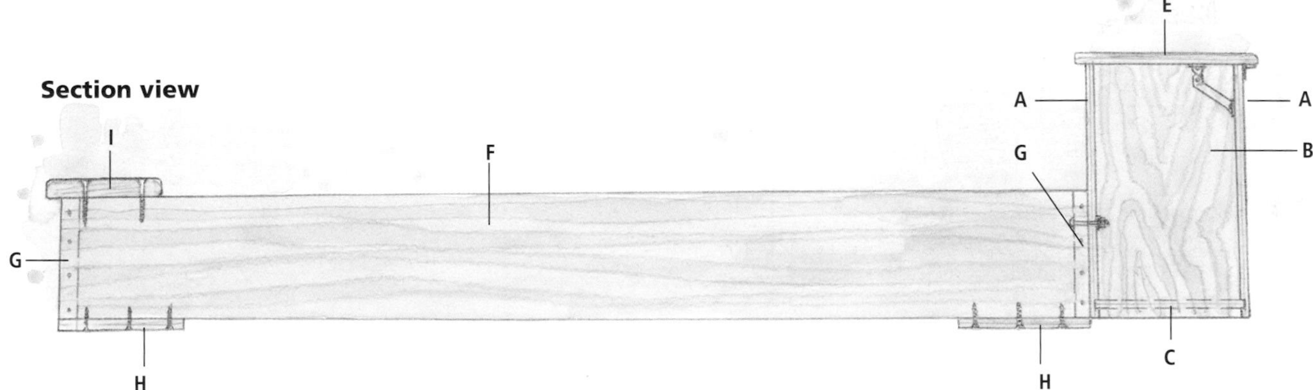

5 Drill pilot holes for the seat and attach it to the box with adhesive and 3-inch screws.

Sandbox with Built-In Toy Box (continued)

Painting the windows

Attaching the toy box

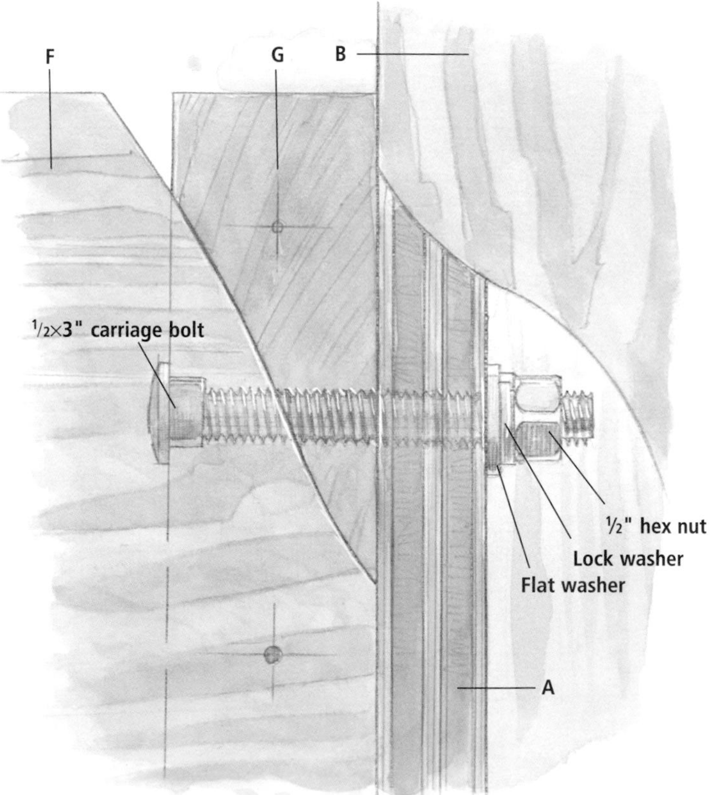

Final assembly

1 Sand all the pieces, rounding and smoothing the edges that children will come in contact with when the sandbox is completed. Wear a dust mask while sanding.

2 Apply a coat of exterior primer to all surfaces, including the inside of the toy box. Follow with two coats of exterior enamel.

3 When the paint is thoroughly dry, lay out windows and doors on the toy box in pencil, if you wish. Outline the windowpanes and door with painter's masking tape. Use a small brush to apply black exterior enamel, as shown left. Remove the tape within an hour or so to prevent it from leaving a residue or lifting the underlying paint.

4 On a flat surface, position the toy box flush against the end of the sandbox opposite the seat. Center the toy box on the end of the sandbox. On the inside face of the sandbox end, locate three ½-inch holes for the carriage bolts that will hold the two box assemblies together, as indicated in the illustration on page 35. Using either ballast or a helper to keep the assemblies together, drill ½-inch holes from the sandbox through the front of the toy box. Insert the bolts, with the head of each bolt on the sandbox side. Inside the box, place a flat washer, then a lock washer, then a nut, as shown at left. (The toy box can be detached readily if you want to store it inside over the winter months.) You can push a plastic cap over the end of the bolt inside the toy box, if you wish.

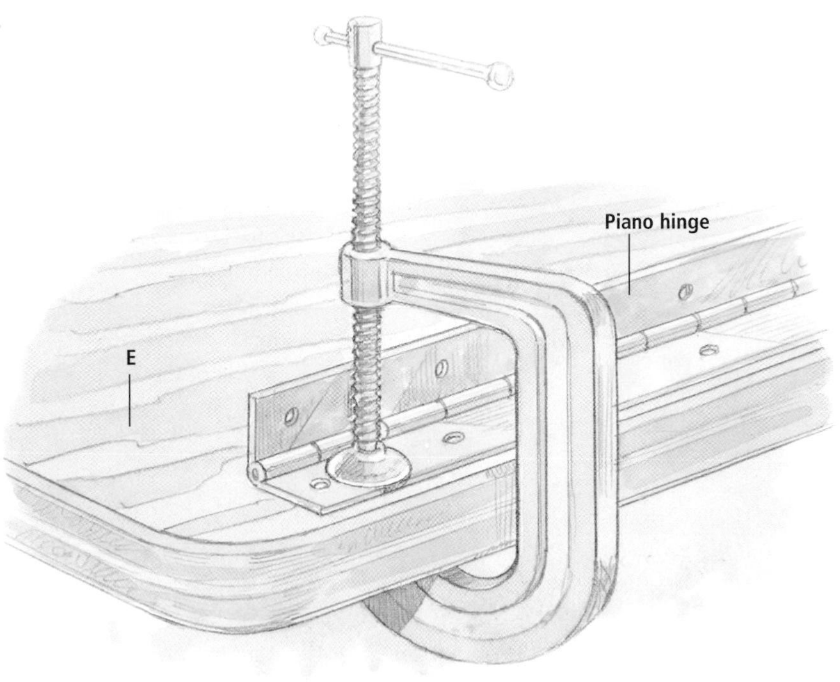

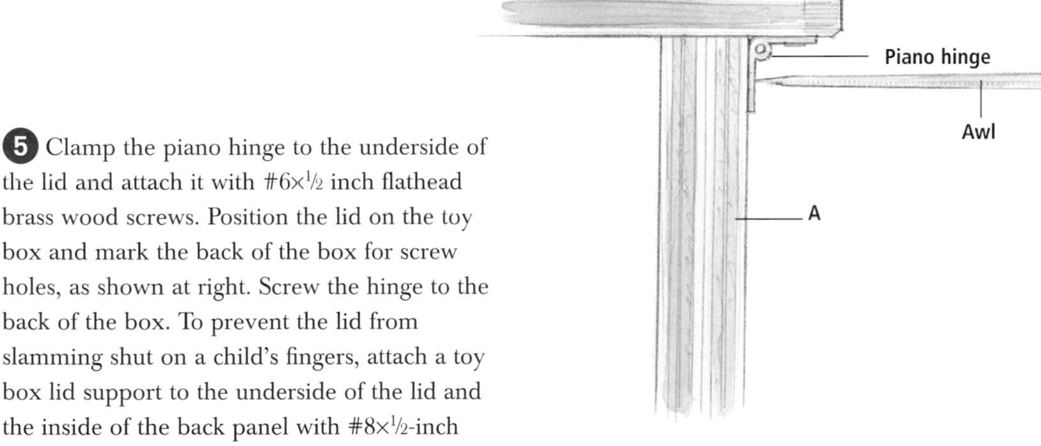

5 Clamp the piano hinge to the underside of the lid and attach it with #6×½ inch flathead brass wood screws. Position the lid on the toy box and mark the back of the box for screw holes, as shown at right. Screw the hinge to the back of the box. To prevent the lid from slamming shut on a child's fingers, attach a toy box lid support to the underside of the lid and the inside of the back panel with #8×½-inch brass roundhead wood screws.

6 When placing the sandbox in the yard, consider sun and shade and whether it will be visible from a window of the house. Make sure it is on level ground. Fill with bagged playground or sandbox sand. To keep out cats and prevent rain from making the sand soggy, place a lid of ¾-inch plywood over the box when it isn't in use.

A Sandbox to Wade In

This compact plaything can be a wading pool or a sandbox. With a tarp as a liner, it holds just enough water to cool off in. Or you can fill the box with sand. An elevated deck adds even more play area, and the hinged lid of the bench makes a handy storage area for playtime paraphernalia. Because this project is so straightforward, you might want to build a pair and place them side by side, one for building sandcastles and the other for splashing.

The sandbox frame is made from 2×10s and has a plywood bottom under the open end to support the tarp when you make a wading pool. The deck, bench, and corner seats are made from 5⁄4 (five-quarter) decking that is 1 inch thick with rounded edges.

You should make a cover of 3⁄4-inch plywood too. It will help keep the sand cleaner or prevent kids from taking an unintended dip.

Sandbox exploded view

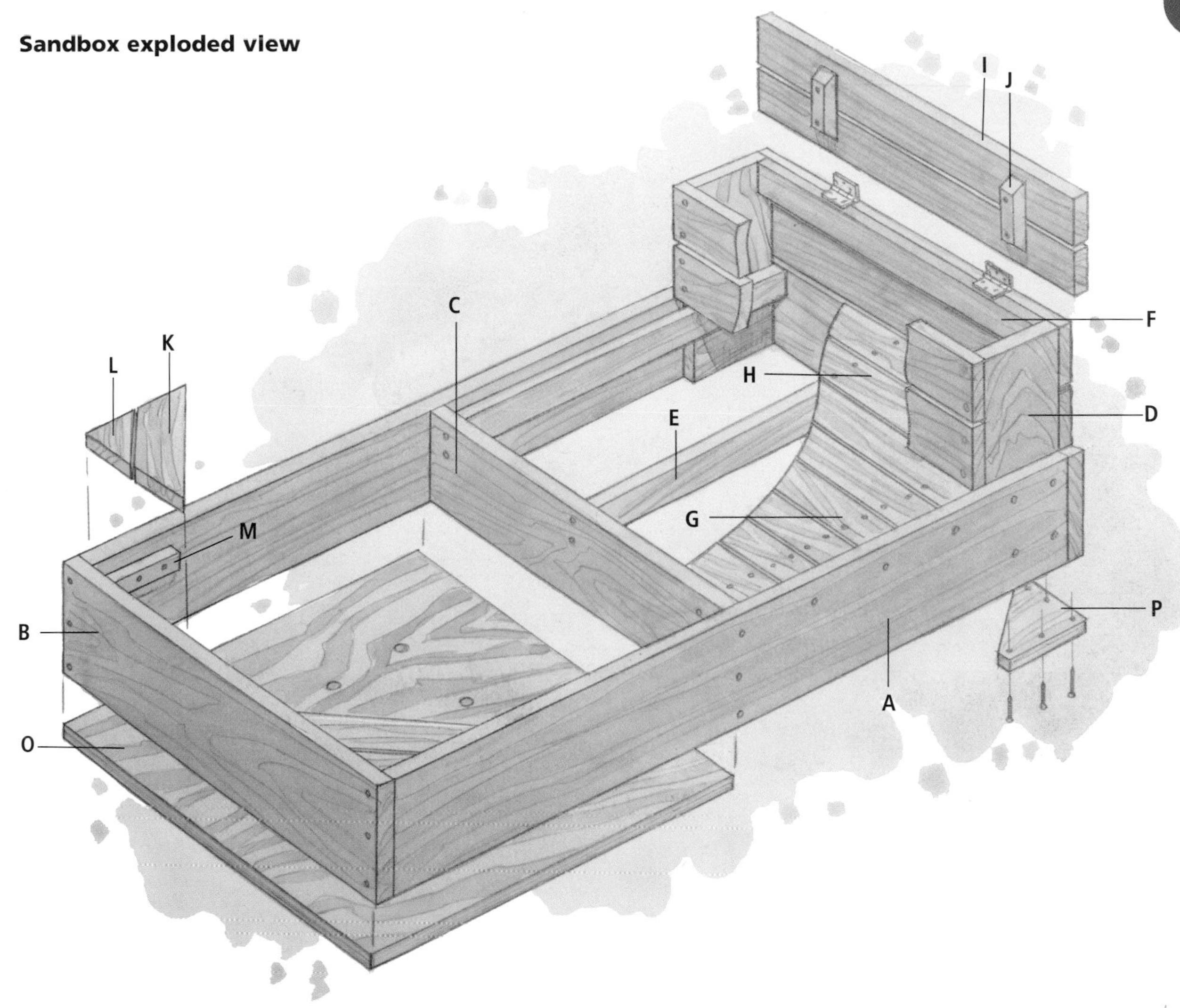

MATERIALS LIST

QUANTITY	PART	DESCRIPTION	FINISHED SIZE
2	A	FRAME SIDE	1½×9¼×90½"
2	B	FRAME END	1½×9¼×48"
1	C	FRAME CROSSPIECE	1½×9¼×45"
2	D	BENCH ENDS	1½×9¼×21"
3	E	JOISTS	1½×3½×44"
1	F	BENCH SUPPORT	1½×3½×42"
10	G	DECKING, BENCH SIDES	5/4×5½×45"
2	H	BENCH FLOOR	5/4×5½×42"
2	I	LID	5/4×5½×47"
2	J	BENCH CLEAT	1½×1½×7½"
2	K	LONG SEAT PIECE	5/4×5½×21¾"
2	L	SHORT SEAT PIECE	5/4×5½×10¾"
2	M	LONG CLEAT	2×1½×13½"
2	N	SHORT CLEAT	2×1½×12"
1	O	SANDBOX BOTTOM	¾×48×48"
2	P	FEET	¾×12×12"
2	Q	RIM SUPPORT	CUT TO FIT
1	R	RIM SUPPORT	CUT TO FIT
1	S	RIM SUPPORT	CUT TO FIT

#8×2½" DECK SCREWS

CONSTRUCTION ADHESIVE

TWO 3" HINGES WITH SCREWS

EXTERIOR PAINT OR WATER-REPELLENT SEALER

7×7' SQUARE OF HEAVY-PLASTIC TARP (FOR POOL LINING)

BAGGED SANDBOX OR PLAYGROUND SAND (FOR SANDBOX)

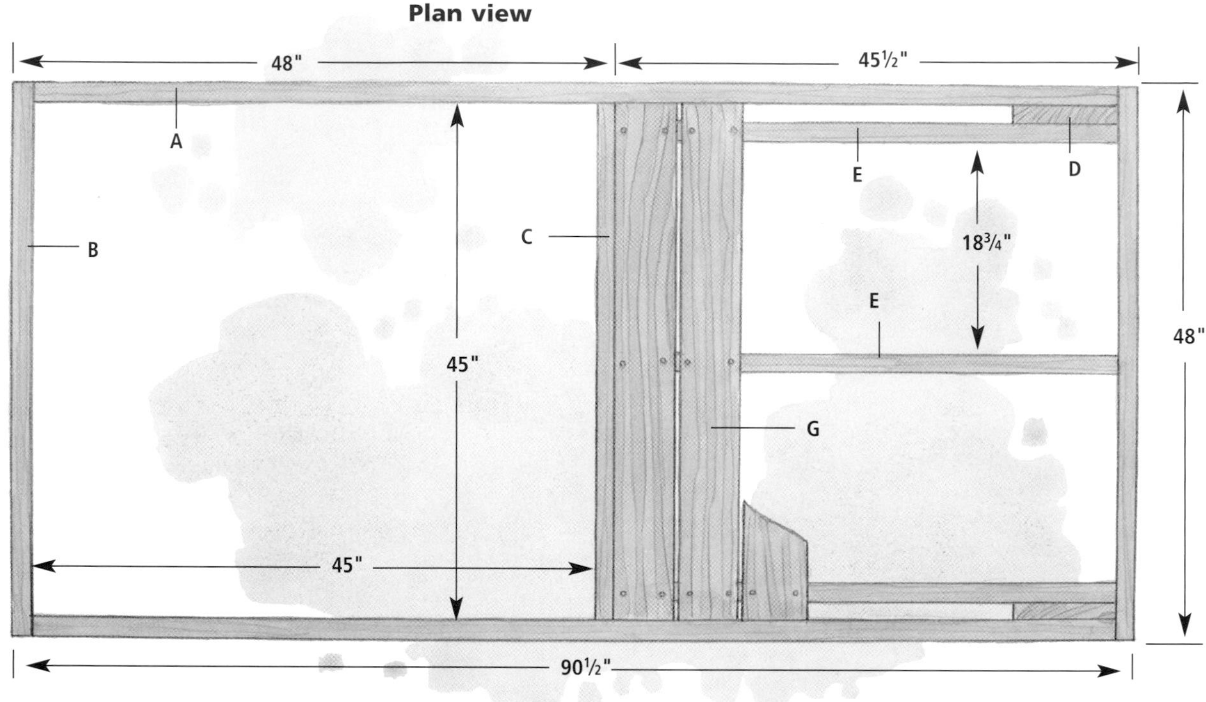

Cut the pieces to size

1 It will be easiest to finish the parts before assembly. Apply exterior primer and exterior enamel or a water-repellent sealer to both sides and all edges of the parts. Mask off areas where you will apply glue.

2 Cut the 2×10 frame sides (**A**), ends (**B**), and crosspiece (**C**) to the lengths shown in the materials list.

3 Cut the bench ends (**D**) to size.

4 Cut the three 2×4 joists (**E**) that run under the deck, and the bench support (**F**).

5 Cut a pair of cleats (**J**) for the bench lid from 2×2 stock. Also cut long cleats (**M**) and short cleats (**N**) for both seats. For the pool, cut two rim supports for the sides (**Q**), one for the center (**R**), and one for the end (**S**).

6 Cut ten pieces of 5/4×6 decking 45 inches long for the deck (**G**) and bench front and back. Also cut two pieces 47 inches long for the bench lid (**I**), two pieces 42 inches long for the bench floor (**H**), two long seat pieces (**K**), and two short seat pieces (**L**).

7 The plywood bottom **(O)** is half of a sheet of ¾-inch exterior plywood. You can buy a half sheet at most home centers and lumberyards.

8 Cut two legs **(P)** from plywood. Refer to the Gusset drawing on page 37 for dimensions.

Bottom installation

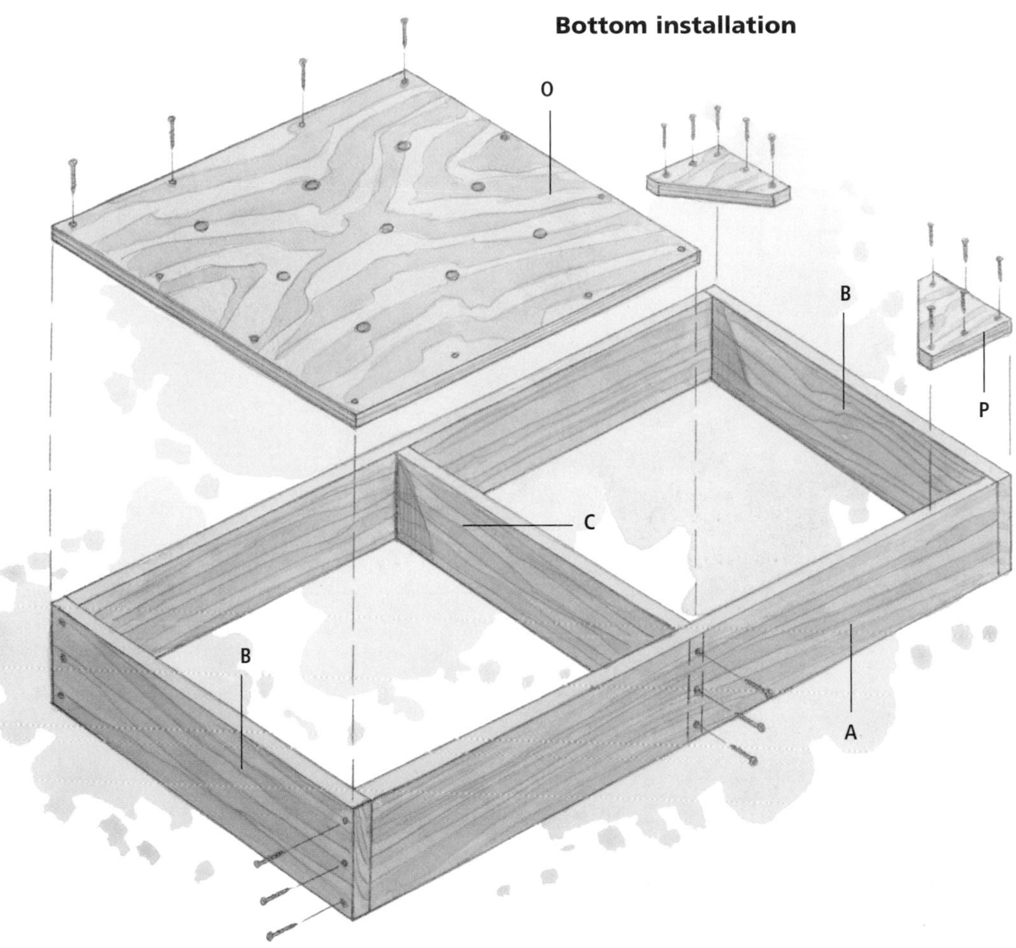

Assemble the frame

1 Build the frame with construction adhesive or polyurethane glue along the mating surfaces and #8×2½-inch deck screws driven through pilot holes. (Deck screws are galvanized, made of stainless steel, or coated to prevent rust.) Working on a flat surface, put one of the frame sides **(A)** in place next to one of the ends **(B)**. Use a framing square to make sure they form a square corner, then hold them together as you drill 7/64-inch diameter pilot holes through the end **(B)** and into the side **(A)**. Apply adhesive on one of the mating surfaces, and then drive screws through the pilot holes. Repeat on the remaining corners.

2 Attach the frame crosspiece **(C)** between the ends. See the drawings above and opposite. Carefully turn the assembly upside down and attach the plywood bottom **(O)** to the edges of the frame at the end opposite where the bench will be. Cut and install the legs **(P)** at the end where the bench will be.

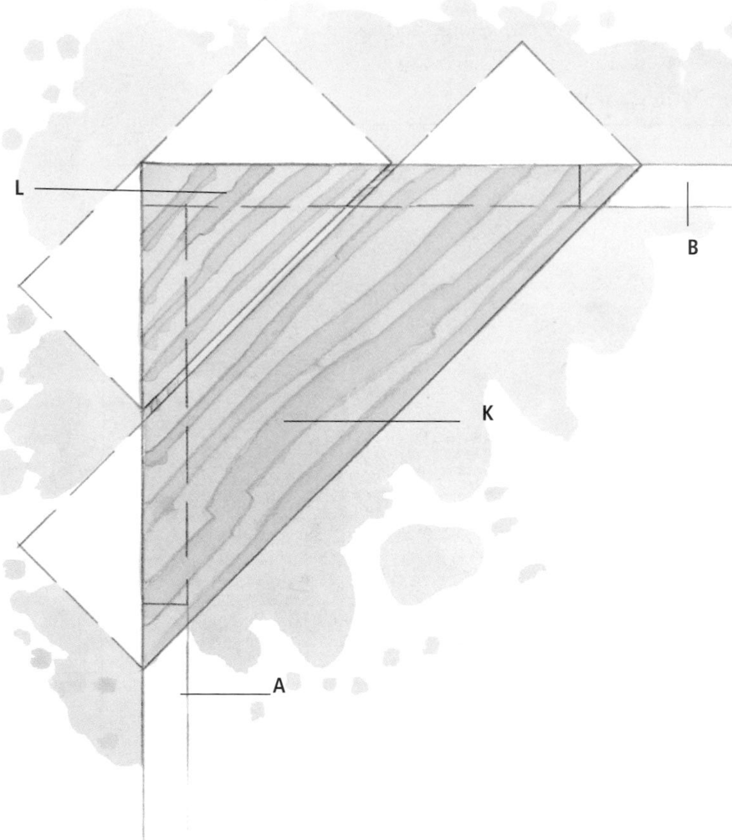

3 With the frame right side up, drill pilot holes to attach the bench ends **(D)** to the inside face of the frame sides, driving screws from the outside. Screw in the three joists **(E)**, placing them 1 inch below the top edge of the frame sides, end, and crosspiece. Drill pilot holes first, driving screws at the ends of each joist and through the outer joists into the bench ends.

4 Lay out the six decking pieces **(G)**, allowing an even spacing, as shown in the Plan View drawing on page 42. Decking width sometimes varies–if six boards are too wide to fit in the opening, notch the last piece to fit around the bench ends. Drill pilot holes through the decking and into the joists, and attach the decking to the joists with screws.

5 Attach the two 42-inch pieces of decking **(H)** to make the floor of the bench between the bench ends **(D)**. If necessary, rip the end piece to fit.

6 Attach two 45-inch decking pieces to the front edge of the bench ends **(D)**, and two to the back edge to form the bench front and back. Leave gaps between the two pieces if necessary to bring the front and back flush with the top of the bench ends.

7 Position the bench support **(F)** between the ends and flush with the top of the bench; attach it by driving screws from the outside face of the bench back. Make the lid **(I)** from two 47-inch pieces of decking. Lay them side by side, spacing them to make the lid the same width as the outside distance from the front of the bench to the back.

8 Position one brace **(J)** 6 inches in from each end on the underside of the lid, drill pilot holes, and attach them with screws. Position a 3-inch hinge 8 inches from each end and mount with the screws in the package.

Pool liner

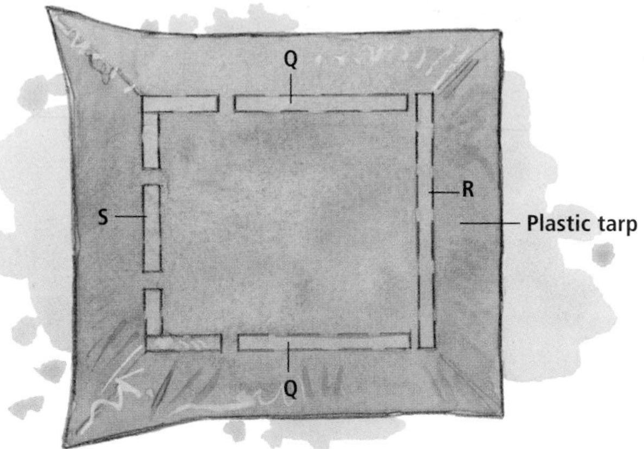

9 Attach the seats. As shown in the illustration opposite, lay out and cut 45-degree miters at the ends of the two pieces of decking **(K and L)** that form the seats. Attach one long cleat **(M)** and one short cleat **(N)** to inside corners of the sandbox frame, keeping them 1 inch below the top edge of the pool. Drill pilot holes and drive screws from inside the frame. Attach the seat pieces to the cleats with screws.

Liner installation

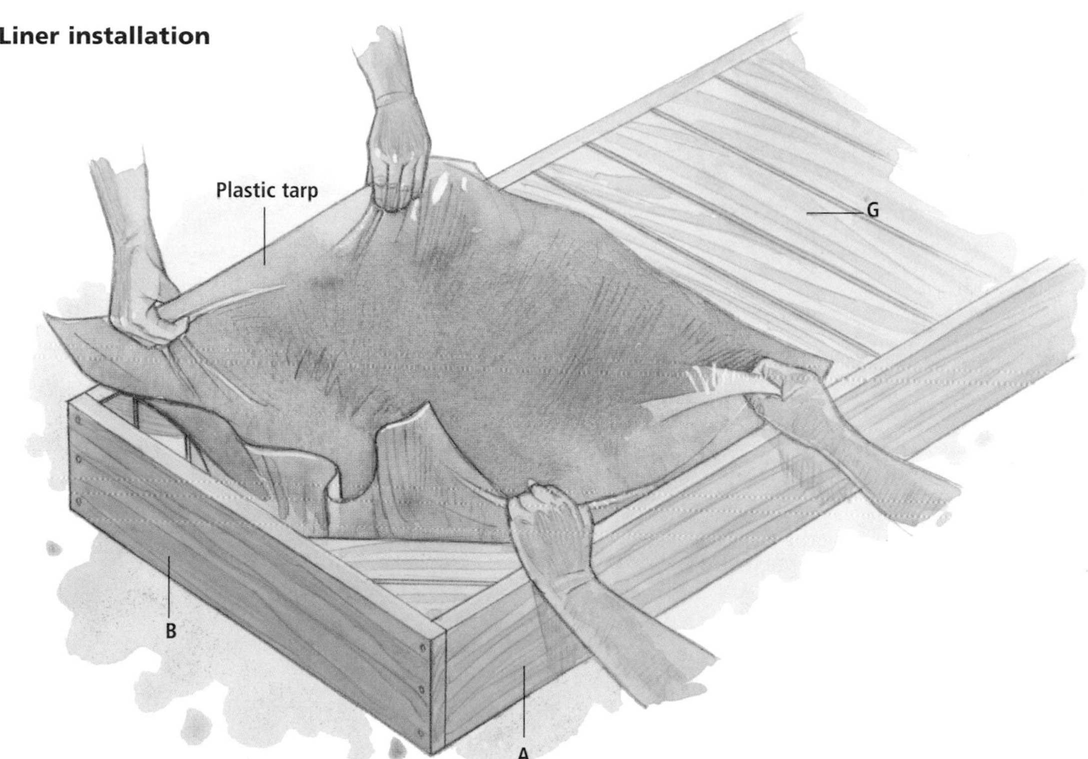

10 Line the pool end of the frame with the tarp, allowing 12 inches on all sides beyond the bottom dimension of 45×45 inches, with extra-long ears at the corners that will be under the seats. See the drawing top. With the structure positioned in the yard, arrange the tarp as shown in the Liner Installation drawing above. Secure the tarp with the four rim supports **(Q, R,** and **S)** around the perimeter of the pool. Note that the supports don't extend under the seats because of the cleats; the excess material at these corners helps to keep the pool watertight. Place the supports over the tarp and flush with the top edges of the frame, then secure them by drilling pilot holes and driving screws into the sides **(A)**, end **(B)**, and center **(C)**. To convert the pool to a sandbox or replace the lining, back out these screws to remove the supports.

TEETER-TOTTER

Teeter-totters are guaranteed to make kids giggle, especially the young ones. Building this one is likely to make Mom or Dad a hero.

The skill required to build this teeter-totter is somewhere between that required for a sandbox and that required for a swing set. This one requires use of a jigsaw when making the rockers and seat as well as bevel-cutting. You could probably cut the bevel angles on top of the rockers and the support board with a portable circular saw, using a straight board as a saw guide, but it will be easier to cut them accurately on a tablesaw.

This teeter-totter is designed for kids 8 years old or younger. Older children would probably find it a bit tame: At the highest your tyke will be only about 32 inches off the ground. As a result, this teeter-totter isn't built for the stress older kids will put on it.

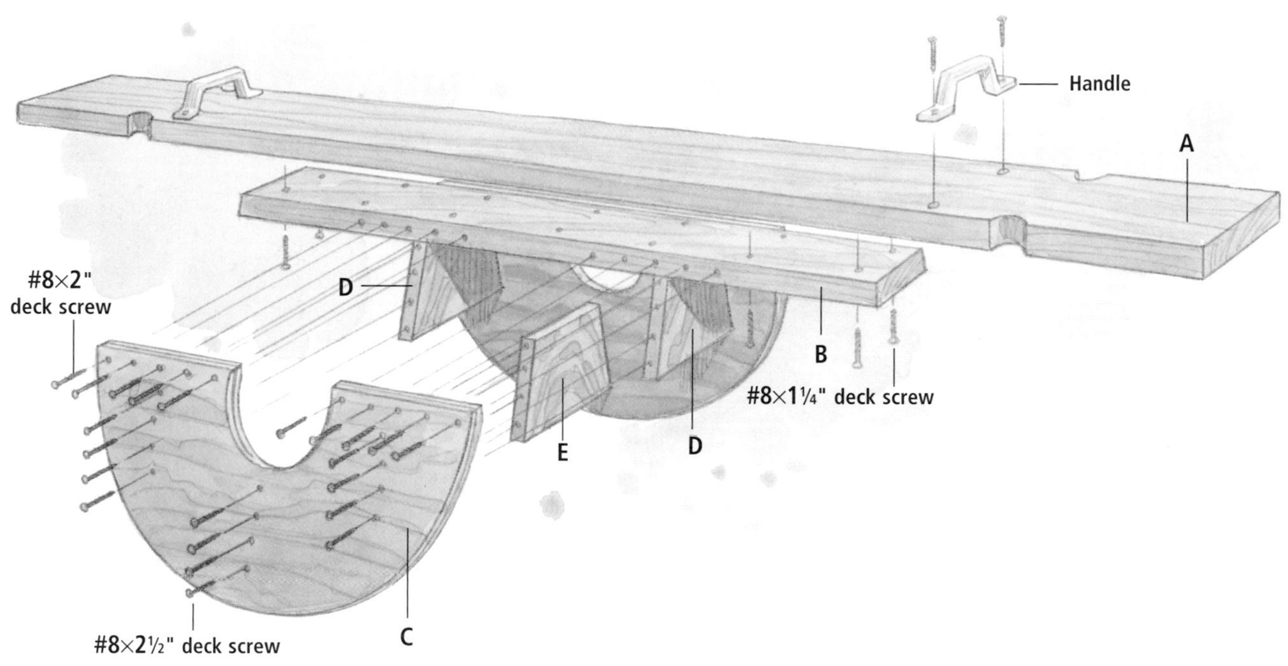

MATERIALS LIST

QUANTITY	PART	DESCRIPTION	FINISHED SIZE
1	A	SEAT	¾×7½×108"
1	B	SUPPORT BOARD	¾×5×60"
2	C	ROCKERS	¾×15×30"
2	D	SPACER	¾×9¾×8½"
1	E	SPACER	¾×11⅛×8½"
		#8×1¼" DECK SCREWS	
		#8×2" DECK SCREWS	
		#8×2½" DECK SCREWS	

TEETER-TOTTER (CONTINUED)

Rocker layout

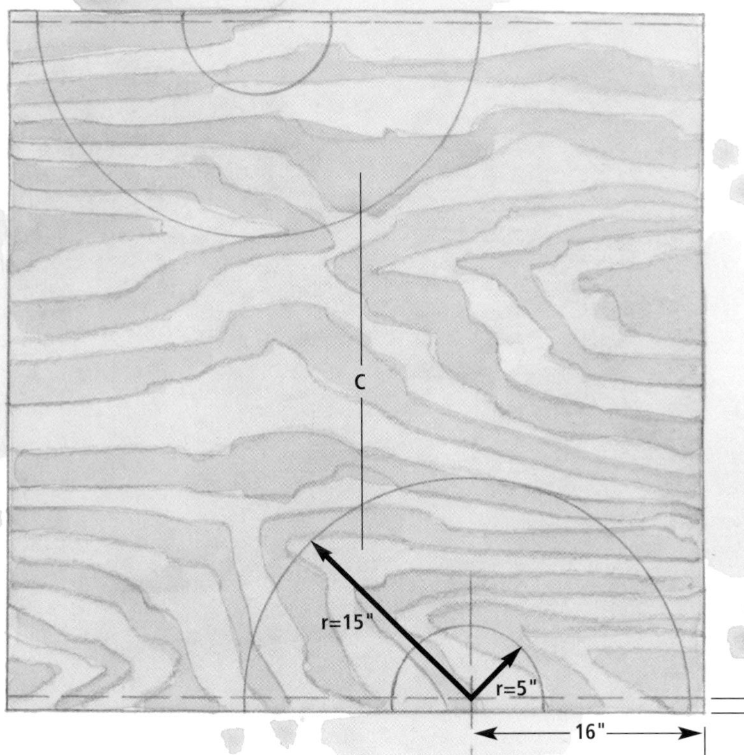

1 You can make both rockers **(C)** from a half sheet of A-C plywood. To lay out the rockers, draw a line 1 inch from each of two opposite edges, as shown at left. Drive a nail into one of the lines 16 inches from one of the edges, and tie a 20-inch string to it. Wrap the string around a pencil until the distance from the nail to the pencil point is 15 inches. Draw an arc, then wrap the string around the pencil until the distance is 5 inches and draw a second arc. Repeat to lay out the second rocker.

Spacer layout

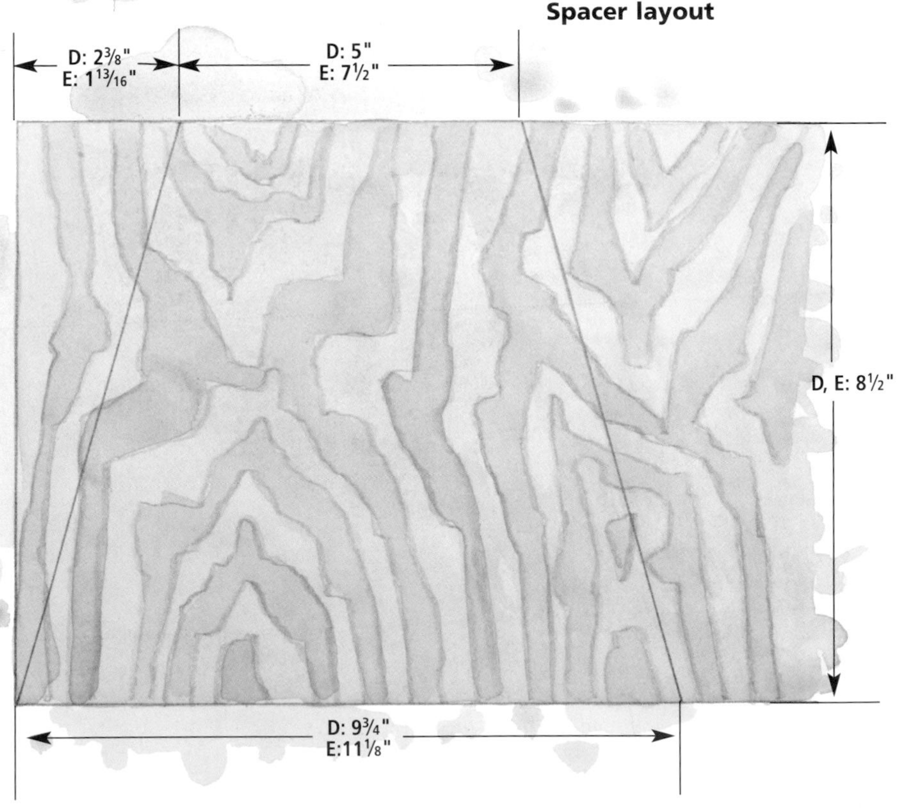

2 Saw a 15-degree bevel for the top of each rocker, following the lines 1 inch from the edges. (The bevel splays the rockers to help keep the teeter-totter stable from side to side.) Then cut the arcs with a jigsaw. Sand the edges smooth. Round over all curved edges with a ¼-inch roundover bit in a router.

3 Cut blanks for the spacers (**D, E**) from 1×12 lumber. Cut two pieces 9¾ inches wide × 8½ inches long for parts **D** and one piece 11⅛×8½ inches for part **E**. Lay out the parts as shown in the Spacer Layout drawing opposite, and cut along the lines with a circular saw. The spacers will slope at the same 15-degree angle at which the rockers splay.

4 Screw the rockers to the spacers with four 2½-inch screws per joint driven through each rocker. Place spacer **E** at the middle of the rockers below the cutout arc and a spacer **D** 9½ inches from each side of **E**. Leave ¾ inch between the spacers **D** and the top of the rockers so that you can put the support board in later.

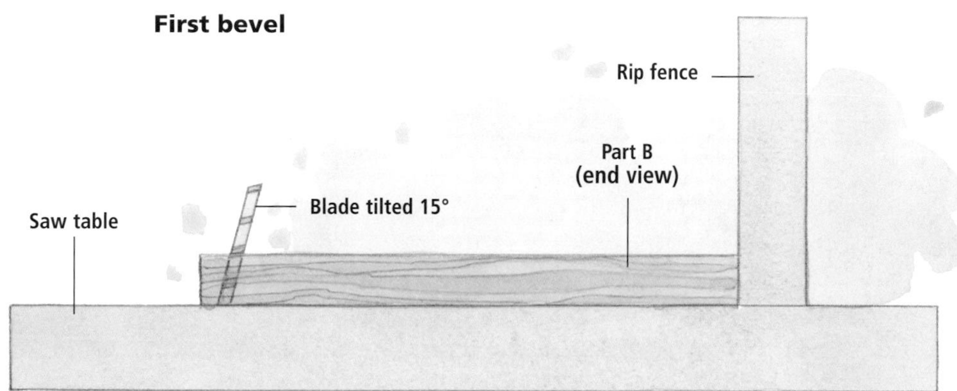

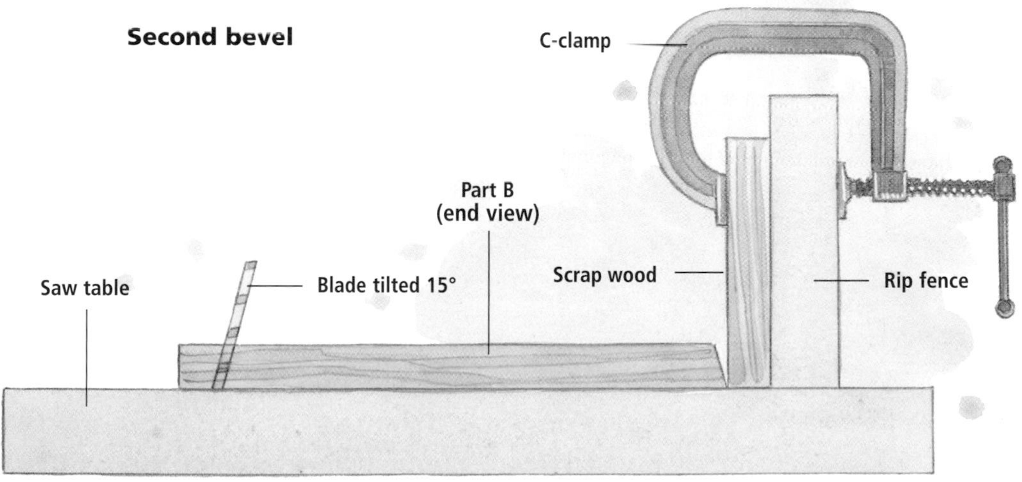

Make the seat

1 Start with a straight 1×8 that has good edges and no loose knots to make the seat (**A**). A board with splintery edges will leave slivers in anyone using the teeter-totter. Cut the board to 9 feet long.

2 The support board (**B**) strengthens the seat and is beveled along the edges to fit between the rockers. First cut a 15-degree bevel on one edge of a 1×6 board 5 feet long, as shown in the First Bevel illustration above.

3 Once you have cut the first beveled edge, put the assembled rockers upside down on a workbench. Place the beveled edge of part B against the appropriate rocker. Trace along the other rocker to mark the position for the bevel on the other edge of the support board. Clamp a piece of scrap wood onto the rip fence to keep the point of the bevel from slipping under the fence. Cut the second bevel as shown in the Second Bevel illustration on page 49. Hold the board firmly against the fence.

Support board

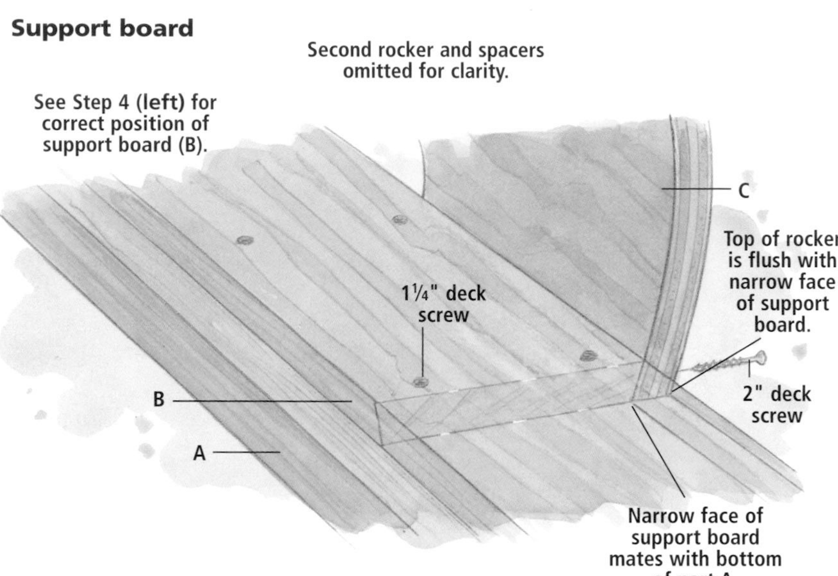
Second rocker and spacers omitted for clarity.
See Step 4 (left) for correct position of support board (B).
C
Top of rocker is flush with narrow face of support board.
1¼" deck screw
2" deck screw
B
A
Narrow face of support board mates with bottom of part A.

4 With the rockers still upside down on the bench, slip the support board between them and center it so that equal lengths extend beyond each end of the rockers. (If the board won't slide easily, loosen the screws on one of the rockers, slide the board in, and then retighten.) Apply glue, and drive 2-inch screws through each rocker into the support board. Space the screws about 2 inches apart.

Seat notches

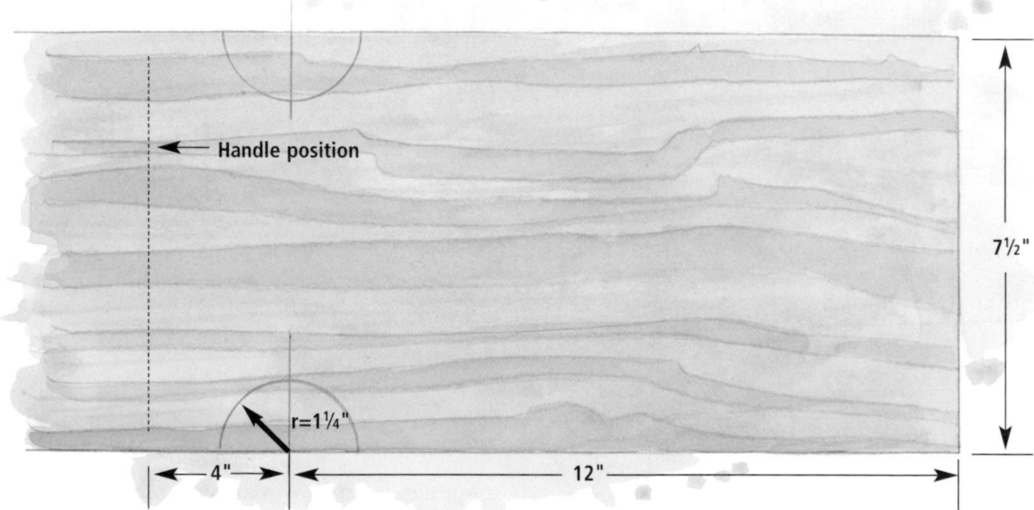
Handle position
r=1¼"
4"
12"
7½"

5 Lay out two notches at each end of the seat, as shown above. Draw a circle with a 1¼-inch radius on a piece of paper. Fold the paper in half, and put the fold on the edge of the board. Trace the notches onto the board using carbon paper, and cut out the notches with a jigsaw.

6 Round over all the exposed seat edges with a ¼-inch round-over bit chucked in a router. You can sand or plane the round-overs if you don't have a router. Then sand until the board is smooth and completely free of splinters with a palm-grip sander.

Assembly

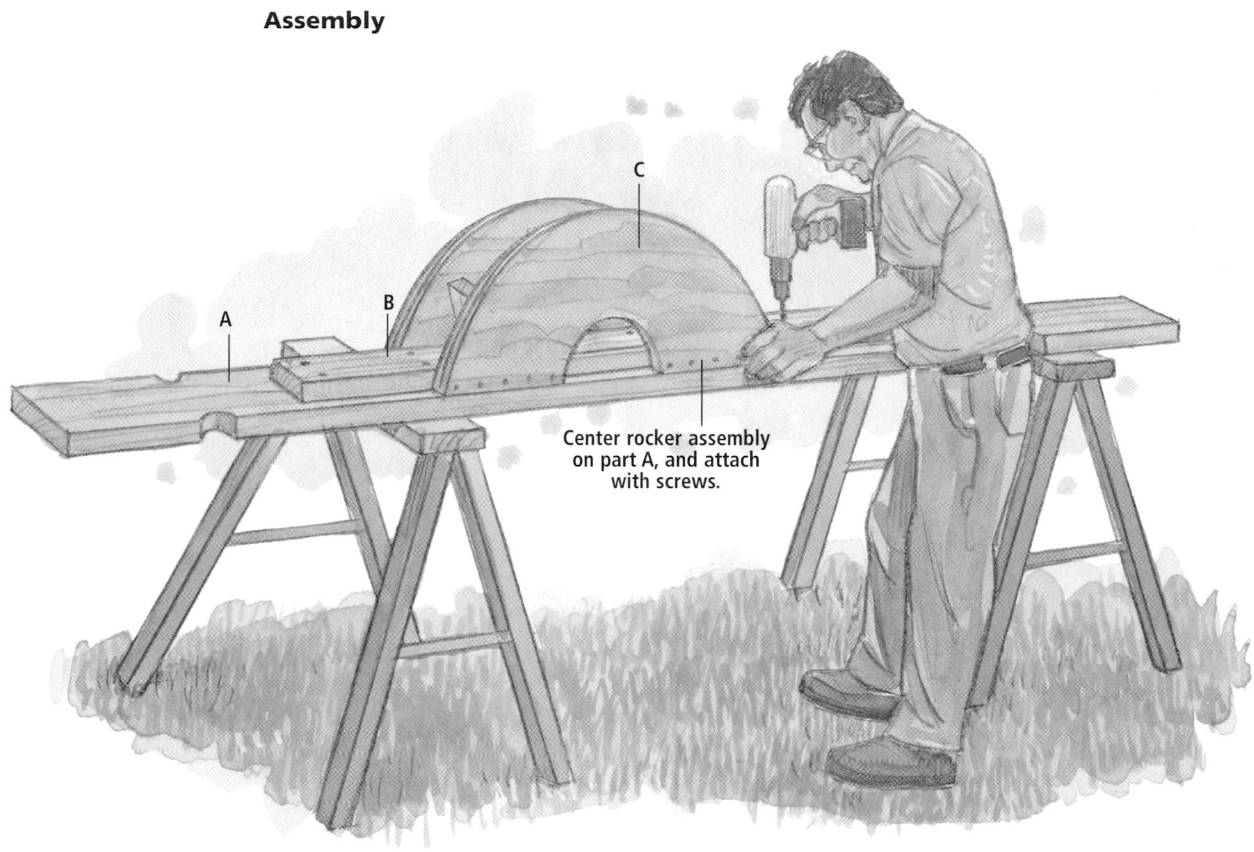
C
B
A
Center rocker assembly on part A, and attach with screws.

Final assembly

1 Slide the support board and rockers along the seat, and center them along the length of the board. Mark the location, remove the assembly, and apply glue to the area where the rockers and support board attach to the seat.

2 Screw the support board to the seat with 1¼-inch deck screws. Put in two rows of screws, spacing the rows about 2½ inches apart and the screws in each row about 8 inches apart.

3 Prime and paint all exposed surfaces. Use a light color if you live in a hot, sunny climate. Surfaces painted in dark colors can get hot and uncomfortable to tender skin. Painting is a great time to involve the kids in the project. Just be sure they're wearing old clothes!

4 Attach the handles to the board, positioning them as shown in the Seat Notches drawing opposite. Follow the manufacturer's instructions for mounting the handles.

KID-SCALE PICNIC TABLE

Every meal will be a picnic for the younger members of the family at this downsized table. The table is also a great place to do the messier sorts of arts and crafts projects on pleasant days. The entire project is built from 8-foot 2×4s with minimal cutting, and assembly is a snap.

Once the kids grow too big for the little table, you can use it as a two-tiered plant stand at the edge of the patio or deck.

Picnic table exploded view

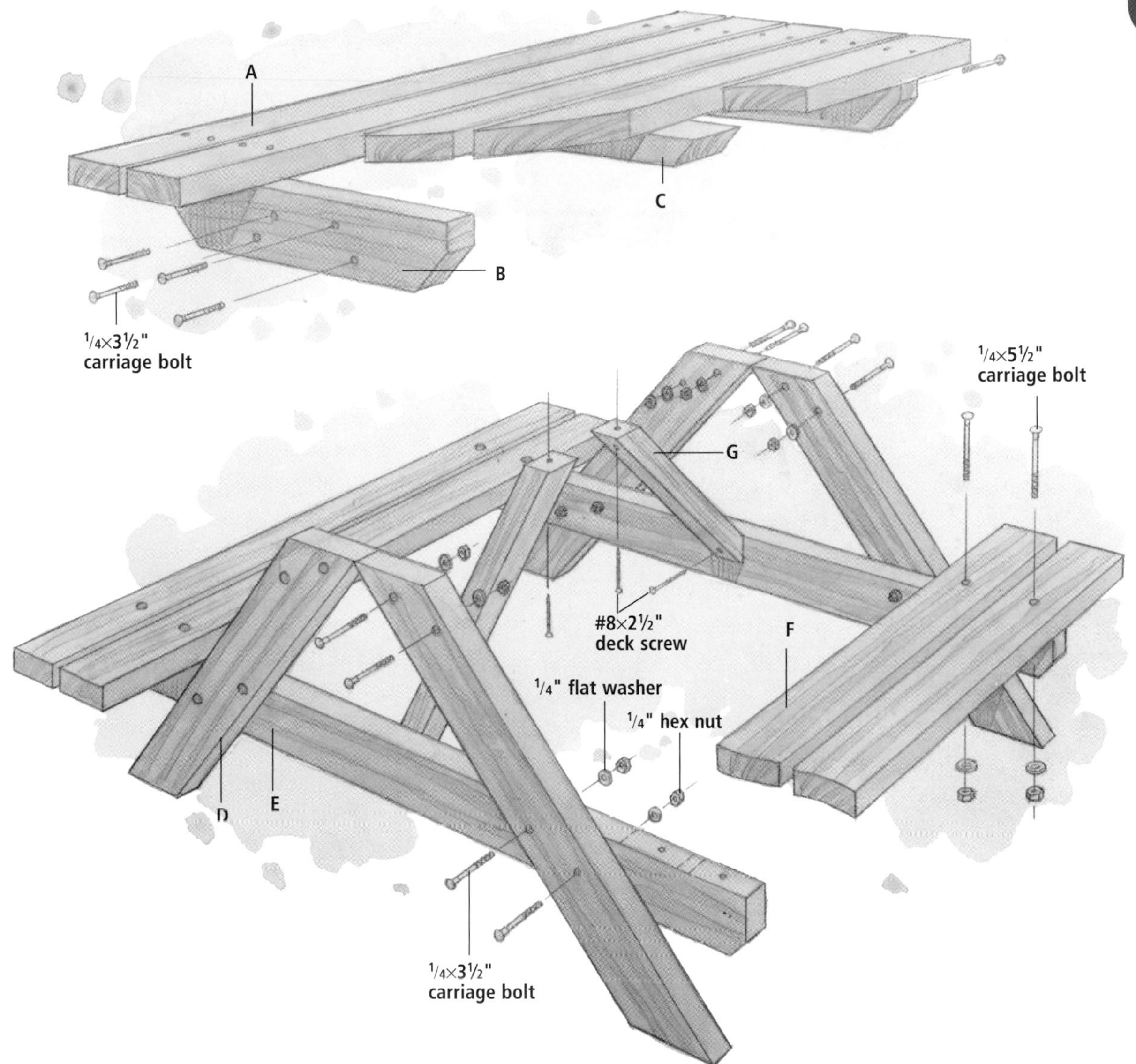

MATERIALS LIST

QUANTITY	PART	DESCRIPTION	FINISHED SIZE
5	A	TABLETOP PIECES	1½×3½×48"
2	B	END SUPPORTS	1½×3½×18"
1	C	CENTER SUPPORT	½×3½×18"
4	D	LEGS	1½×3½×29"
2	E	SEAT SUPPORTS	1½×3½×44"
4	F	SEAT BOARDS	1½×3½×48"
2	G	BRACES	1⅝×1⅝×18"
	#8×2½" GALVANIZED DECK SCREWS		
16	¼×3½" CARRIAGE BOLTS, FLAT WASHERS, NUTS		
8	¼×5½" CARRIAGE BOLTS, FLAT WASHERS, NUTS		

Cut and assemble the tabletop parts

1 Cut the tabletop pieces **(A)** and the three supports **(B, C)** to length. Use a combination square to mark 45-degree angles at the ends of the supports as shown right, then cut these bevels.

Tabletop bottom view

#8×2½" deck screw

B

1½"

A

C

#8×2½" deck screw

2 Rip a 5/8-inch-wide strip from a piece of scrap wood. Cut the strip into eight 2-inch lengths for use as spacers in positioning the tabletop pieces and seat boards.

3 Select the better face of each tabletop piece **(A)** and place the pieces next to each other good-side down on a flat surface. Insert the 5/8-inch spacers to establish consistent spacing between the pieces. Align the ends of the tabletop pieces using a straightedge. Clamp the assembly together as shown right. Measure from end to end and draw a line across the center of the table. Position the center support **(C)** so it straddles the line and screw it to the underside of the tabletop with #8×2½-inch galvanized deck screws.

Tabletop assembly

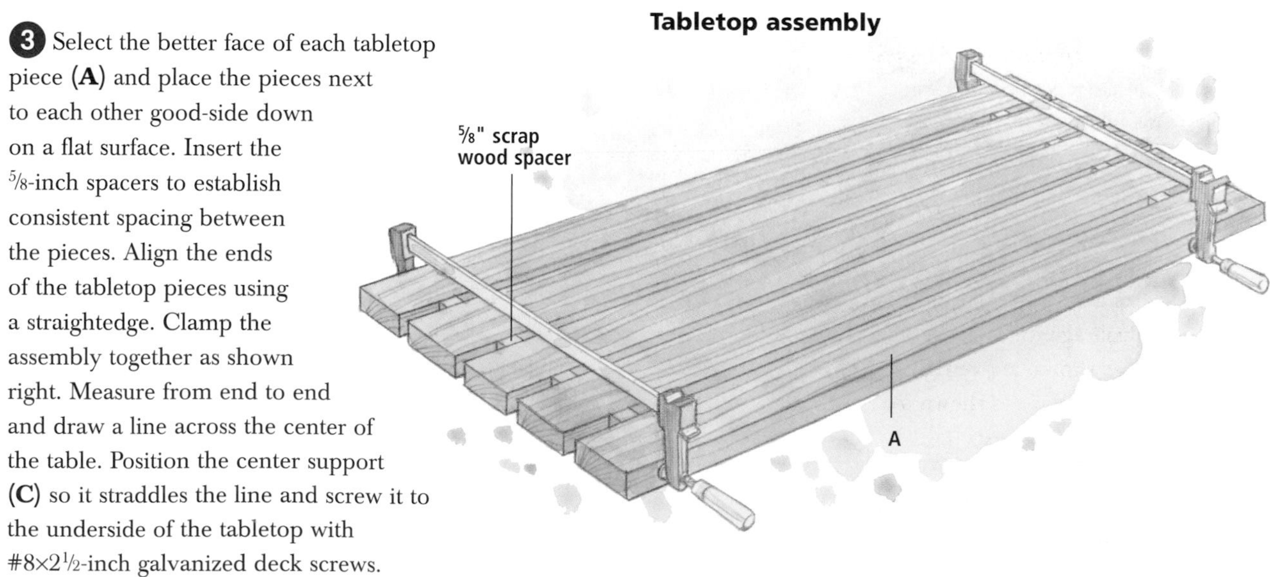

Tabletop screw

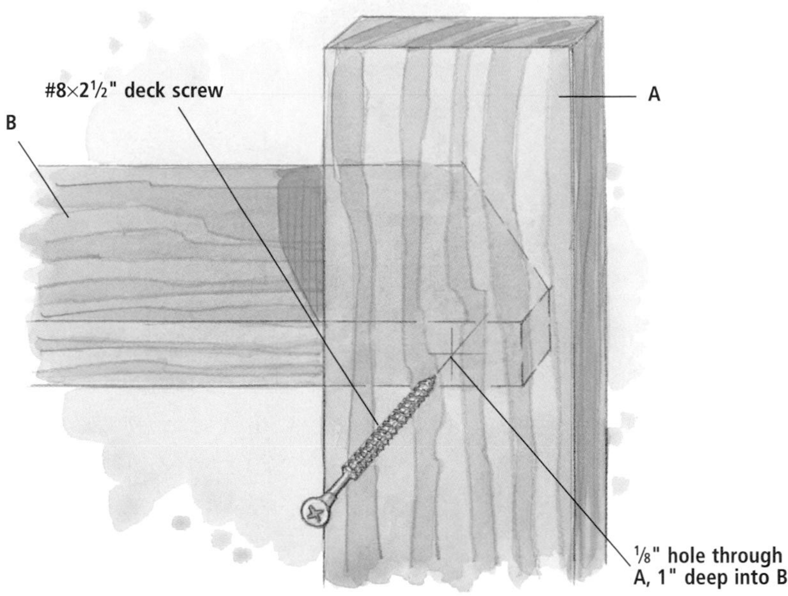

4 With the clamps still in place, carefully turn the tabletop right side up. Position the two end supports **(B)** under the table, 4½ inches from each end. Clamp the supports in place. Drill two ⅛-inch-diameter pilot holes through the top **(A)** and 1 inch into the support **(B)** for each screw, as shown left. Drilling pilot holes prevents splitting the wood when you drive screws into the narrow edge of the supports **(B)**. Screw the top to the supports with #8×2½-inch galvanized deck screws, as shown in the End Section View illustration (page 56).

Making the seat support

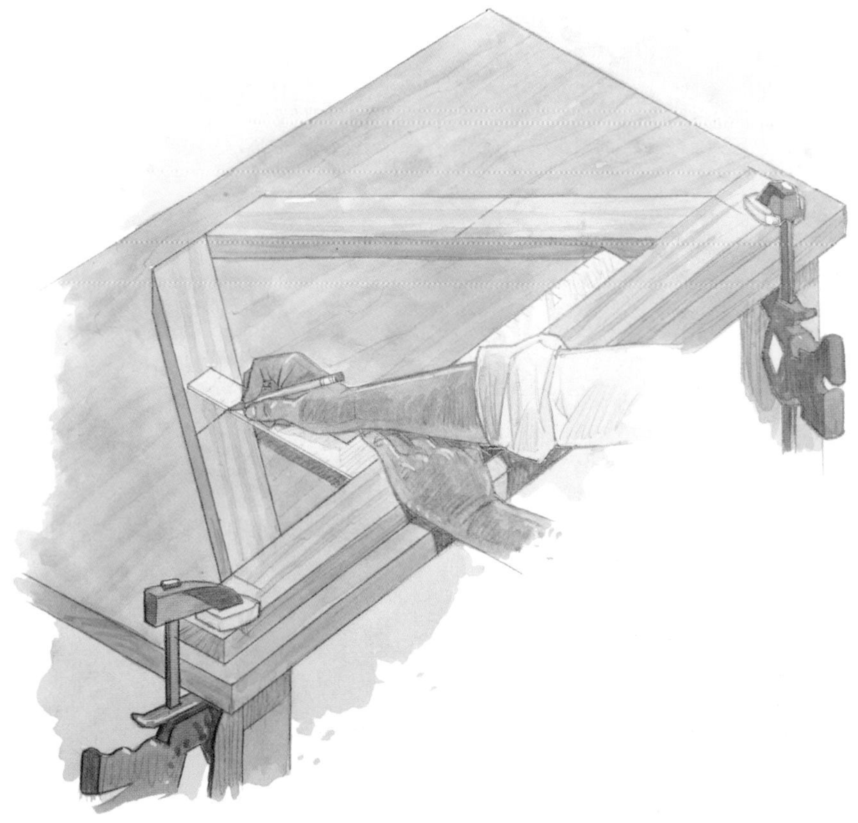

Attach the leg assemblies

1 Both ends of the legs **(D)** are cut at an angle (mitered). Cut one end at a 40-degree angle. At the other end, make a parallel cut at the same angle as shown in the End Section View drawing (page 56) to make a finished overall length of 29 inches.

2 Cut the seat supports **(E)** and seat boards **(F)** to lengths shown on the materials list. Cut off the bottom corners of the seat supports at a 45-degree angle.

3 For each leg assembly, arrange a pair of legs on a flat surface with their lower ends flush against a straightedge, as shown above right. Use the framing square as shown to measure up 9 inches on each leg. (Measure vertically, not along the leg itself.) Make a mark at 9 inches to lay out the top edge of the seat support. Center the seat support on the legs.

5 Drill two pairs of ¼-inch holes in each leg. Stagger the holes in each pair as shown below to help keep the wood from splitting. Attach the legs with ¼×3½-inch carriage bolts, flat washers, and nuts as shown in the Picnic Table Exploded View drawing on page 53.

End section view

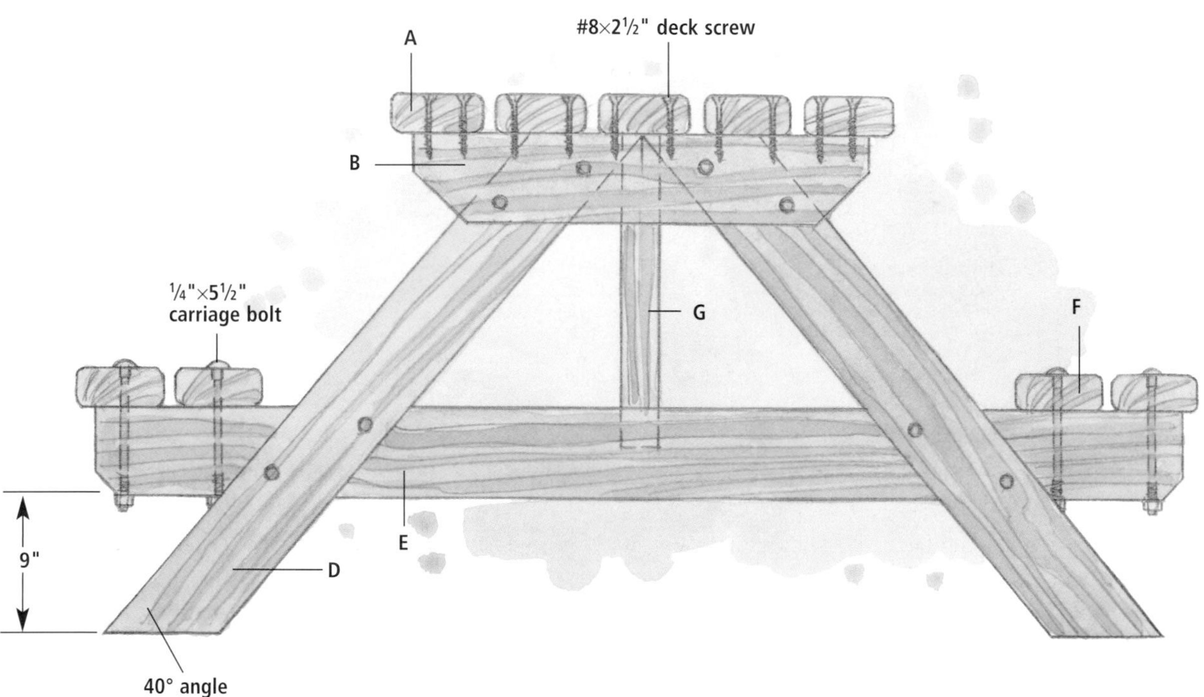

Complete the table

1 The leg assemblies attach to the inside of the tabletop supports (**B**). With the tabletop upside down on a flat surface, clamp the legs in place. Drill ¼-inch holes through the supports and the legs. Fasten the legs to the supports with ¼×3½-inch carriage bolts, flat washers, and nuts.

2 Turn the table right side up. Position the seat boards better side up so that the edge of the outside board overhangs the seat support by ⅝ inch. Center the boards along the length of the table so that the ends of the boards extend equal distances beyond the legs. Clamp the seat boards to the seat supports, again using the spacer blocks to maintain spacing between them. Drill ¼-inch holes through the seat boards and supports and attach the boards with ¼×5½-inch carriage bolts, flat washers, and nuts.

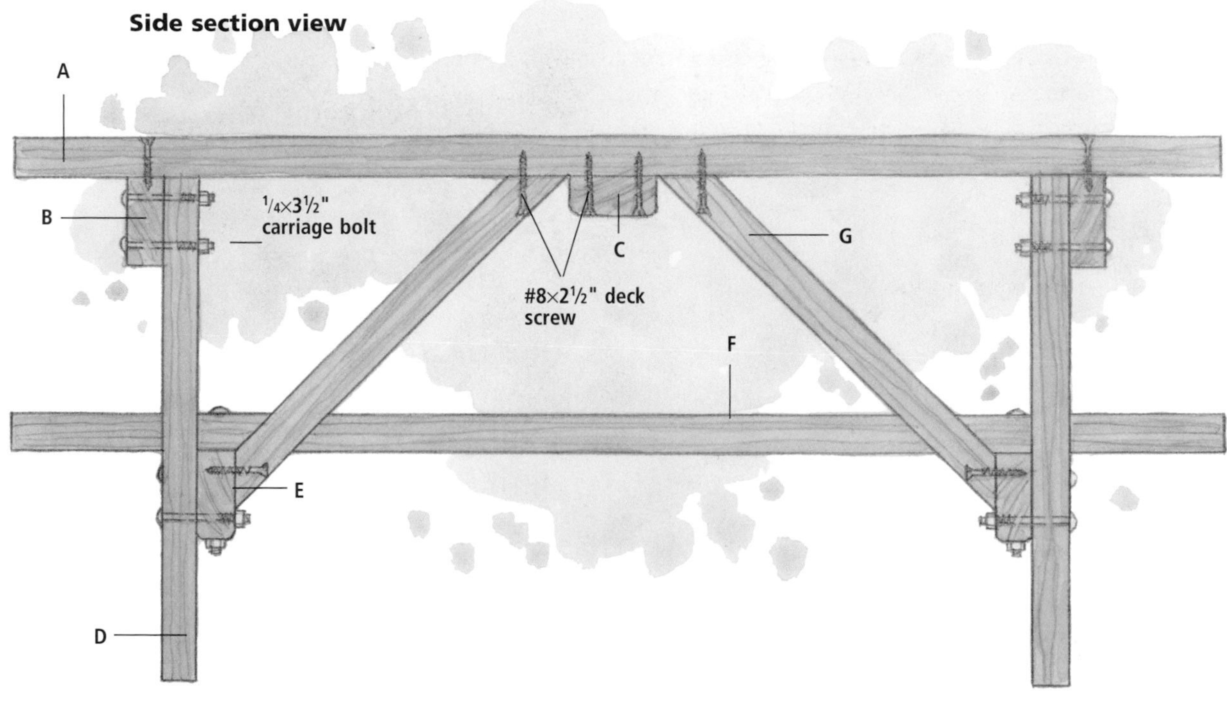

❸ The diagonal braces (**G**) will help keep the table from racking. Begin by crosscutting a 2×4 to 20 inches long and ripping it in half to make two pieces. Mark the ends of both braces for 45-degree miter cuts to arrive at a finished length of 18 inches. (Note that the two cuts are not parallel, but are at right angles to each other.) Position each brace between one side of the center support and the adjacent seat support, as shown above; check the table for square. Drill 1/8-inch pilot holes through the brace and 1 inch into both the underside of the tabletop and the support. Attach the braces with #8×2 1/2-inch galvanized deck screws.

❹ Round over sharp corners and edges with sandpaper. Paint the table or apply a clear finish to protect the table from the weather.

Simple Swing Set

Swings are at the heart of most backyard play areas–even older kids like them. This swing is basic but safe and sturdy. Posts anchored in concrete and stout bracing keep this swing set stable.

The three sets of braces have different functions: The lower braces help keep the posts from swaying; the upper braces reduce the unsupported span of the beam; and the metal braces reinforce the post-to-beam joints.

The concrete poured around the underground section of the posts is necessary because the crossbeam is hung on posts rather than A-frames. Generally the concrete anchor should be three times the width of the post and one-third its overall length, as it is here.

And because kids often jump from swings, make sure they have a soft landing. Spread soft surfacing materials under the swing. See pages 6–7 for more about surfacing materials.

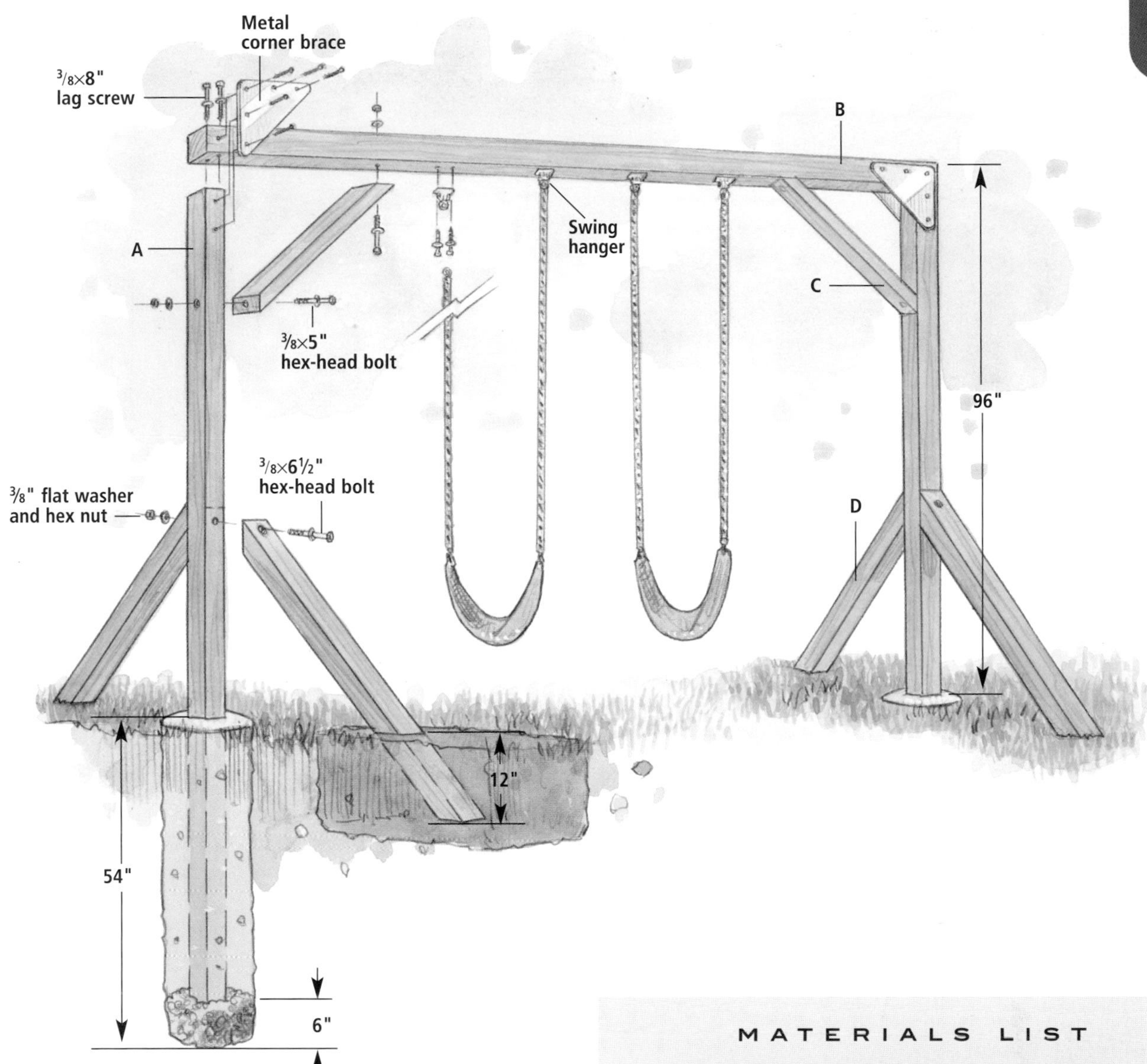

MATERIALS LIST

QUANTITY	PART	DESCRIPTION	FINISHED SIZE
2	A	POSTS	$3^1/_2$×$3^1/_2$×144"
1	B	CROSSBEAM	$3^1/_2$×$3^1/_2$×144"
2	C	TOP BRACES	$3^1/_2$×$3^1/_2$×36"
4	D	BOTTOM BRACES	$3^1/_2$×$3^1/_2$×62"
5	8-FOOT 1×3" FOR TEMPORARY BRACES		
	2" DRYWALL OR DECKING SCREWS		
2	SWINGS		
2	SWING HANGER PAIRS		
4	TRIANGULAR STEEL BRACES		
4	3/8×8" LAG SCREWS AND WASHERS		
4	3/8×5" HEX-HEAD BOLTS, NUTS, AND WASHERS FOR TOP SUPPORTS		
2	3/8×6 1/2" HEX-HEAD BOLTS, NUTS, AND WASHERS FOR BOTTOM SUPPORTS		
	SOFT PLAYGROUND SURFACING MATERIAL, SUCH AS WOOD CHIPS, SHREDDED RUBBER, OR SAND		
12	60-POUND BAGS OF READY-MIXED CONCRETE		

Assemble the frame

1 Lay out the two 4×4 posts (**A**) and the crossbeam (**B**) on a flat surface, such as a driveway or lawn. If the surface where you're working isn't flat, slide a sheet of plywood underneath the joint. Cut 45-degree miters for the top braces (**C**), cutting them to length at the same time.

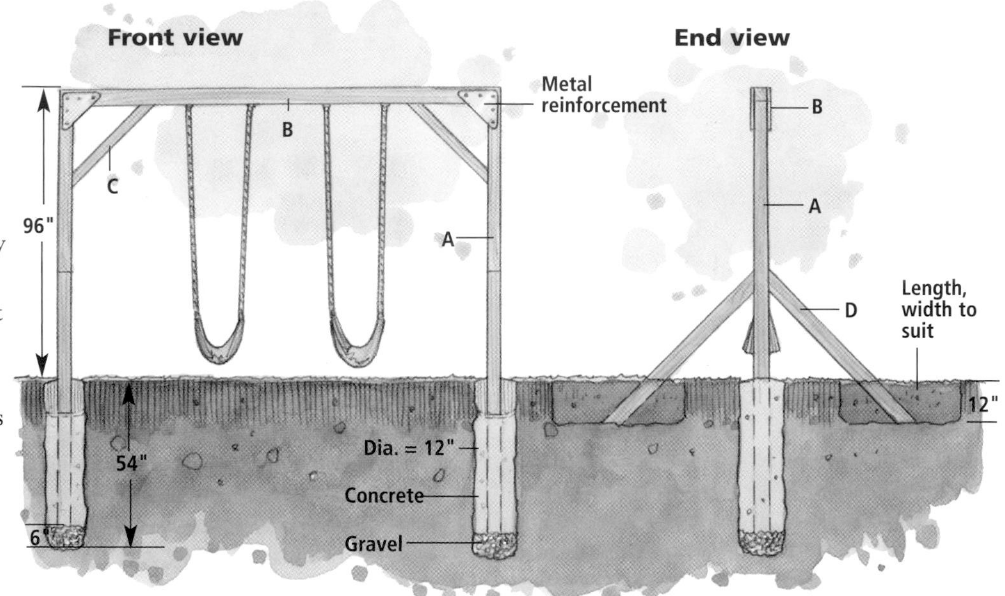

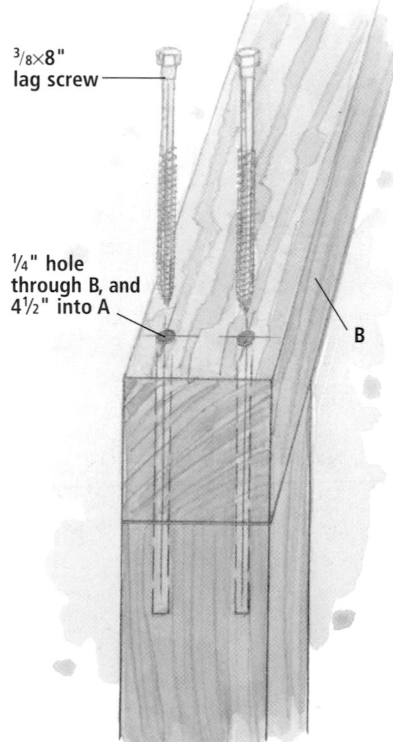

2 Bore two 1/4-inch-diameter holes at each end of the crossbeam for the lag screws that attach the crossbeam to the post. To keep the holes straight, put a square to the side of the drill and keep the bit parallel with the square. For best results, have a helper watch the drill from another side, as shown in the Boring Straight Holes drawing below. Once you've drilled the holes, place the beam on top of the posts and use the holes in the beam as guides to drill holes 4 1/2 inches deep into the posts.

Joint reinforcement

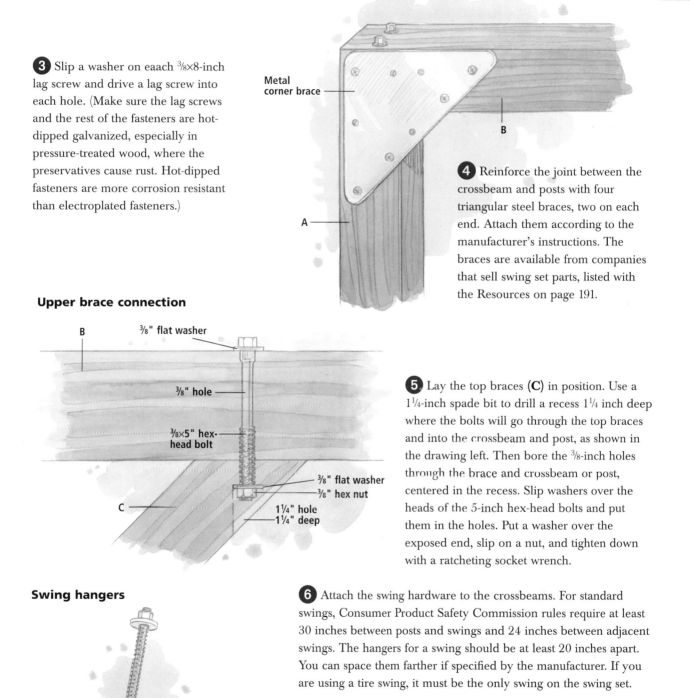

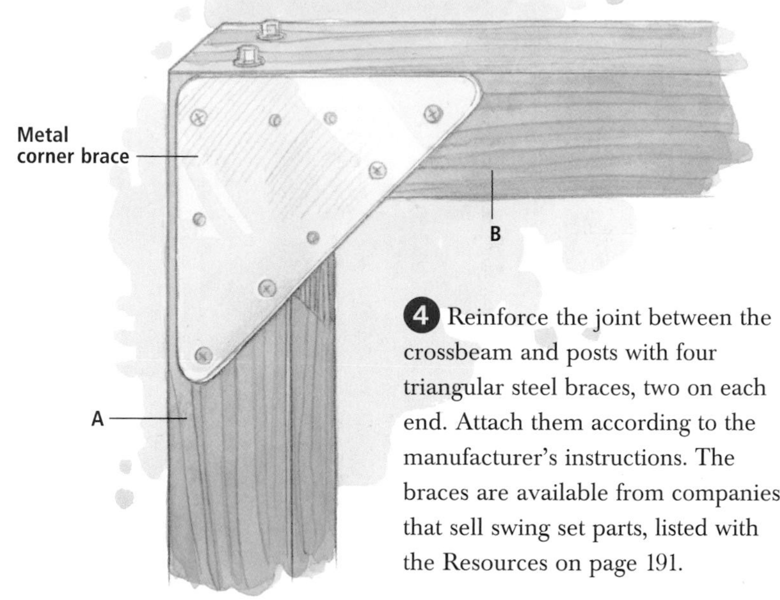

❸ Slip a washer on eaach 3/8×8-inch lag screw and drive a lag screw into each hole. (Make sure the lag screws and the rest of the fasteners are hot-dipped galvanized, especially in pressure-treated wood, where the preservatives cause rust. Hot-dipped fasteners are more corrosion resistant than electroplated fasteners.)

❹ Reinforce the joint between the crossbeam and posts with four triangular steel braces, two on each end. Attach them according to the manufacturer's instructions. The braces are available from companies that sell swing set parts, listed with the Resources on page 191.

Upper brace connection

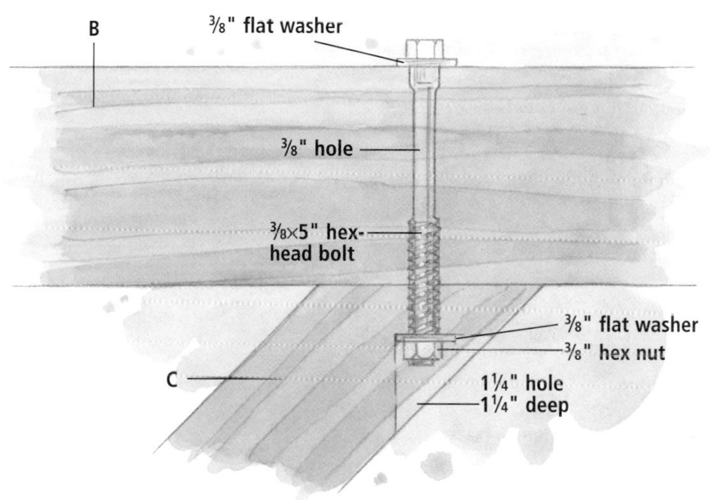

❺ Lay the top braces **(C)** in position. Use a 1 1/4-inch spade bit to drill a recess 1 1/4 inch deep where the bolts will go through the top braces and into the crossbeam and post, as shown in the drawing left. Then bore the 3/8-inch holes through the brace and crossbeam or post, centered in the recess. Slip washers over the heads of the 5-inch hex-head bolts and put them in the holes. Put a washer over the exposed end, slip on a nut, and tighten down with a ratcheting socket wrench.

Swing hangers

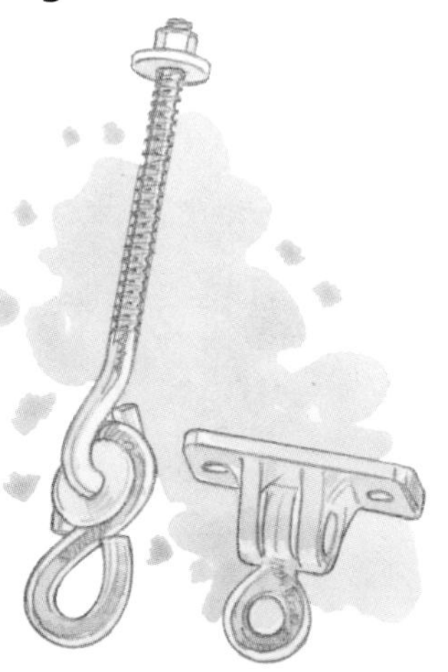

❻ Attach the swing hardware to the crossbeams. For standard swings, Consumer Product Safety Commission rules require at least 30 inches between posts and swings and 24 inches between adjacent swings. The hangers for a swing should be at least 20 inches apart. You can space them farther if specified by the manufacturer. If you are using a tire swing, it must be the only swing on the swing set.

❼ Use a rasp or router and bit to slightly round over all sharp corners. Follow up with coarse- and then medium-grit sandpaper to remove all the splinters.

Dig the postholes and erect the swing set

1 Select a level area in your backyard for the swing set. It should be shaded if possible, but the area to the front and rear of the swing must be free of obstructions for at least twice the height of the swing set, and there should be no obstructions within 6 feet of the sides. The swings should also be well clear of other play areas, including ball-playing areas, sandboxes, and slides.

2 Lay the assembled structure on the ground where you plan to erect it. Mark the posthole centers on the ground with spray paint, lime, or flour. Use a posthole digger to dig a hole 54 inches deep and 12 inches in diameter at each mark. Place 6 inches of gravel in each hole, and tamp it with the end of a 4×4 (see pages 180–183).

3 Cut four 18-inch wooden stakes from 1×3 and put them, along with four 8-foot 1×3 temporary braces, near the holes.

4 With some assistance, raise the swing set and stand the posts in the holes.

Digging postholes

Temporary braces

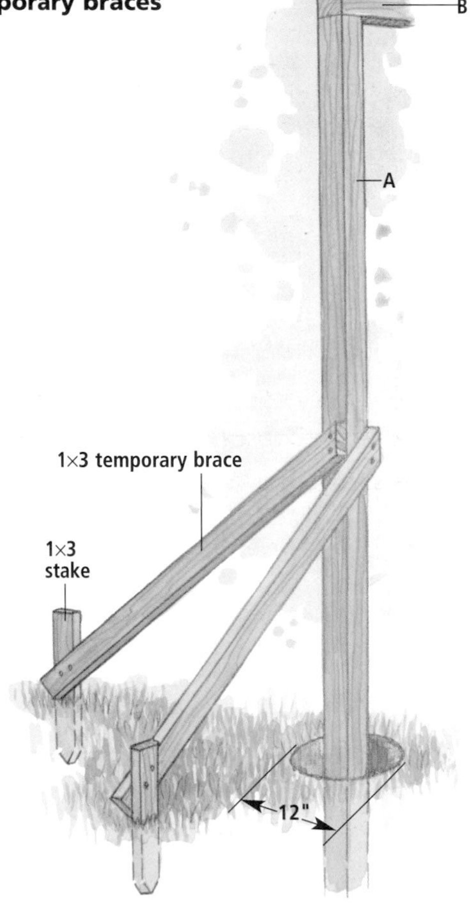

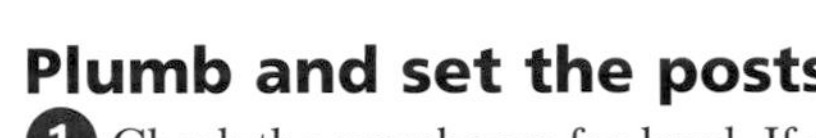

Plumb and set the posts

1 Check the crossbeam for level. If necessary, add gravel to the hole at the low end and tamp.

2 Use a level to plumb each post. Read the level on two adjacent faces of the 4×4 to make sure the posts are plumb both front to back and side to side.

3 Once the posts are plumb and the beam is leveled, attach two temporary braces to each post. Screw the braces to adjacent faces so they are 90 degrees to each other. Then drive the stakes into the ground and screw the braces to the stakes, checking to be sure the swing is still plumb and level as you go.

4 Mix premix concrete for the postholes. It will take about 3 cubic feet of concrete, or six 60-pound bags, to fill each 12-inch hole. Pour concrete around the posts and work a broom handle or piece of scrap wood up and down in the hole to remove any air pockets.

Double-check the posts and beam for plumb and level and make adjustments in the bracing if necessary. Variations of less than ½ inch in any direction are acceptable. Allow the concrete to set, then remove the stakes and temporary braces.

Lower brace connection

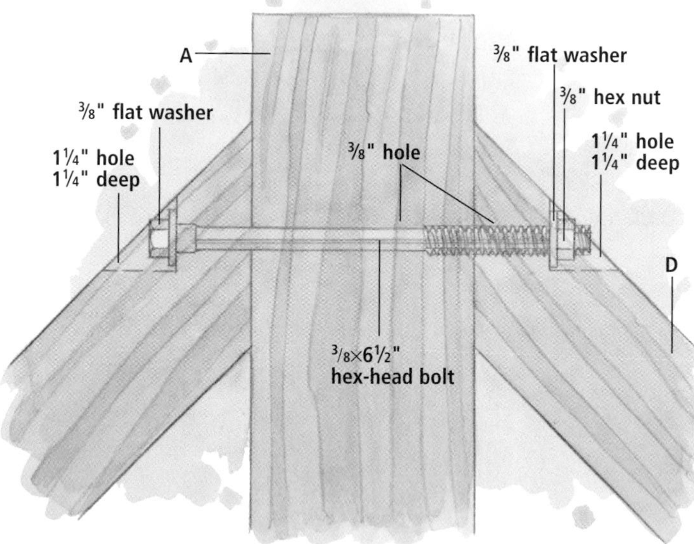

Install the foot braces and swings

1 Dig trenches 12 inches deep and perpendicular to the crossbeam for the bottom braces (**D**). Make the trenches just wide enough and long enough to receive the braces. Miter the ends of the bottom braces and attach them to the posts the way you did the top braces, using 6½-inch hex bolts.

2 Refill the trenches. Pack the soil firmly around the bottom of the braces. Level the area around the posts with soil or sand, if necessary.

3 Spread a layer of surfacing material, such as shredded rubber mulch, shredded bark mulch, wood chips, fine sand, or gravel to the depth specified on page 29.

4 Attach the swings to the hangers, following the manufacturer's instructions.

Buying Swings and Hardware

Suppliers offer a wide variety of swings and trapeze bars. Here's a quick guide to choosing what works best for you:

■ Do not use metal or wooden swing seats. Swing belts are softer and less likely to cause injury. If you prefer a flat seat, buy one molded from lightweight polyethylene.

■ Children under age 3 should use full-bucket swing seats, which have plastic front, back, and sides. Half-bucket seats have a chain or rope across the front. The seat bottom should be no more than 24 inches above the ground.

■ Trapeze bars are for older kids. They are typically made of zinc-plated steel. Sometimes they are coated with plastic. They are available with or without handles.

■ Tire swings need greater clearance than standard swings A tire swing must be mounted on its own swing set with no other swings. When the tire is held against the crossbeam, there must be a minimum of 30 inches between the tire and posts. A real auto or truck tire is heavy enough to hurt children, so buy a tire look-alike specifically made for swing set use. (See the suppliers listed in Resources on page 191.) Buoy balls are a variation on tire swings and require the same clearances and swing set construction.

■ Swing chains should be plastic coated to prevent pinched fingers. Coated chains are available in a variety of colors. Nylon rope is acceptable for hanging swings, but natural-fiber ropes, which can rot, are not.

■ Hang swings from hardware specifically made for the job and follow the manufacturer's directions for installation.

■ Clothing can catch on open S-hooks, presenting a strangulation danger. Use a galvanized spring clip to attach the chain to the hanger.

Swing Under Cover

Like the porch swing of bygone days, this is a comfy place for kids to while away a summer afternoon. And you don't need a porch for this freestanding swing. The trellis on each side provides support for climbing vines, and a fabric roof keeps harsh sun at bay. The swing seat is made of cotton canvas and plywood that's softened by a cushion.

Building the swing calls for skill in carpentry and sewing. The frame is made of wood and can be built by someone with intermediate woodworking skills and basic carpentry tools. Build with pressure-treated or other rot-resistant lumber, such as the dark heartwood of redwood or cedar. Choose boards that are straight and free of cracks and other defects. KDAT (kiln dried after treatment) lumber is usually worth the extra cost because it is less likely to warp as it dries.

Most of the sewing is long, straight seams with either a straight or a zigzag stitch. If you can handle a simple set of curtains, you have the skills needed. If you prefer to do less sewing, the instructions show nonsewing alternatives for certain steps; they're located just below the applicable step.

Swing exploded view

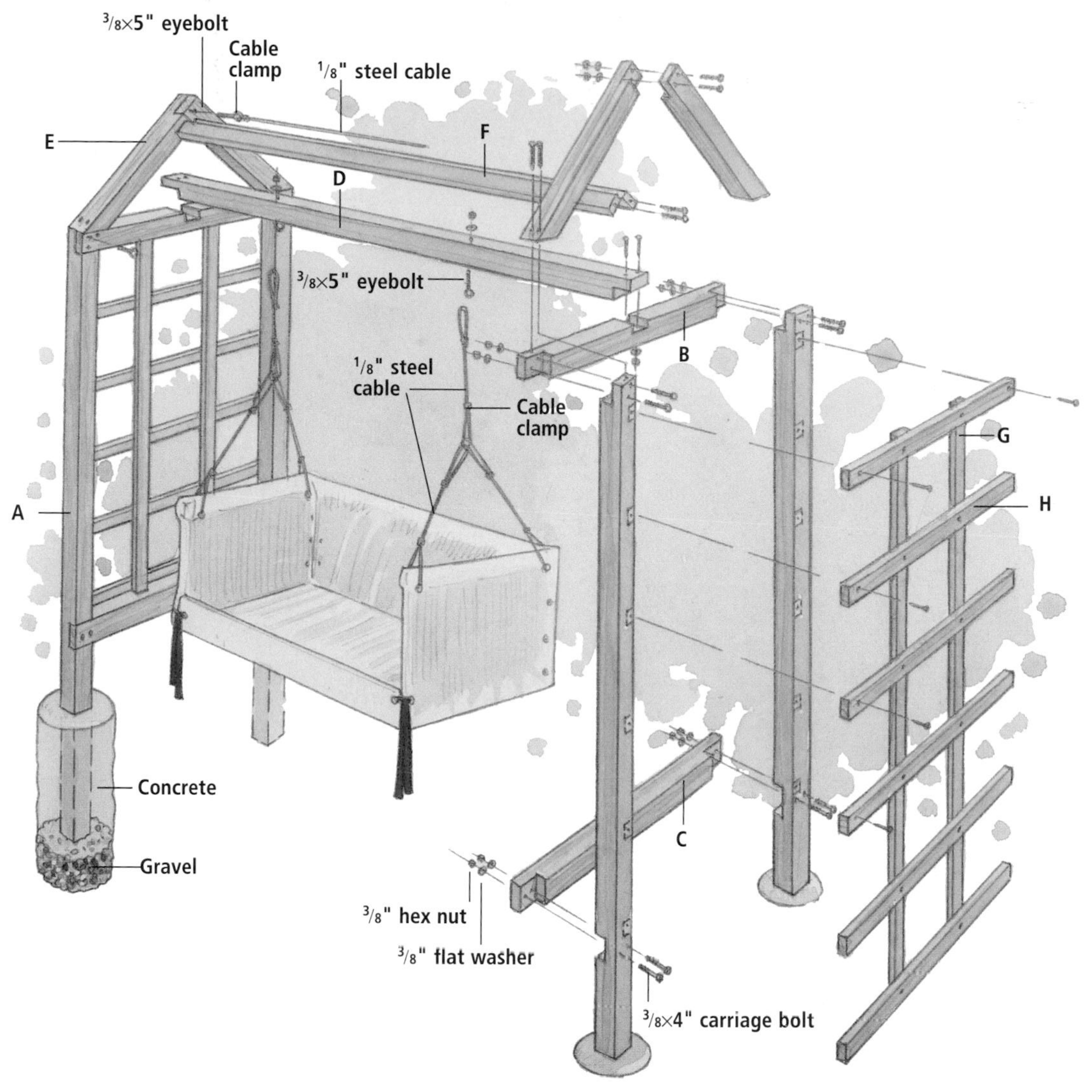

FRAME MATERIALS LIST

QUANTITY	PART	DESCRIPTION	FINISHED SIZE
4	A	POSTS	$3\frac{1}{2}$×$3\frac{1}{2}$×96"
2	B	TOP BEAMS	$3\frac{1}{2}$×$3\frac{1}{2}$×36"
2	C	CROSSBEAMS	$3\frac{1}{2}$×$3\frac{1}{2}$×36"
1	D	SWING BEAM	$3\frac{1}{2}$×$3\frac{1}{2}$×85"
4	E	ROOF BRACES	$3\frac{1}{2}$×$3\frac{1}{2}$×$25\frac{1}{2}$"
2	F	ROOF BEAMS	$\frac{3}{4}$×$3\frac{1}{2}$×78"
4	G	LATTICE STRINGERS	$\frac{3}{4}$×$1\frac{1}{2}$×$56\frac{1}{2}$"
12	H	LATTICE SLATS	$\frac{3}{4}$×$1\frac{1}{2}$×$32\frac{1}{2}$"
20	$\frac{3}{8}$×4" CARRIAGE BOLTS WITH FLAT WASHERS AND NUTS		
	4" DECK SCREWS		
	$1\frac{1}{4}$" DECK SCREWS		
2	$\frac{3}{8}$×5" EYEBOLTS WITH WASHERS AND NUTS		
	POLYURETHANE GLUE OR EXTERIOR WOOD GLUE		
	CONCRETE MIX FOR FOUR POSTHOLES		
	CRUSHED ROCK OR GRAVEL		
	PRIMER AND PAINT OR STAIN AND WOOD FINISH		

SWING UNDER COVER (CONTINUED)

SWING MATERIALS LIST

NOTE: CANVAS CLOTH SUITED FOR OUTDOOR USE IS AVAILABLE. IT IS USUALLY MADE OF POLYESTER OR A POLYESTER BLEND. COTTON DUCK CLOTH MAY REQUIRE DRY CLEANING, AND ITS HEAVIER WEIGHT MAY MAKE IT MORE DIFFICULT TO WORK WITH.

QUANTITY	PART	DESCRIPTION	FINISHED SIZE
1	I	CANVAS FABRIC FOR SEAT	90×27"
1	J	CANVAS FABRIC FOR BACK	55×23"
1	K	CANVAS FABRIC FOR FRONT FLAP	51×9"
4	L	PRINT FABRIC FOR TIES	45×9"
1	M	3/4" WOOD DOWEL	45"
2	N	1" WOOD DOWEL	19½"
1	O	½" PLYWOOD	50½×21½"
	SPOOL OF MATCHING THREAD		
	WATER-ERASABLE FABRIC-MARKING PEN (TO MARK GROMMET HOLES)		
	GROMMET OR EYELET KIT (SEE SIDEBAR ON PAGE 73)		
22	METAL GROMMETS OR EYELETS, 7/16" OR ½" WIDE (MAY BE INCLUDED IN THE KIT)		
4	LENGTHS OF 1/8" STEEL CABLE, 31" LONG		
2	LENGTHS OF 1/8" STEEL CABLE, 20" LONG		
12	CABLE CLAMPS		
2	METAL RINGS, 1½" INSIDE DIAMETER		

SWING CUSHION MATERIALS LIST

QUANTITY	PART	DESCRIPTION	FINISHED SIZE
2	R	CUSHION TOP AND BOTTOM (DECORATOR FABRIC)	52×23"
2	S	CUSHION ENDS (DECORATOR FABRIC)	4×23"
2	T	CUSHION SIDES (DECORATOR FABRIC)	4×52"
	SPOOL OF MATCHING THREAD		
	BATTING, AT LEAST 23" WIDE AND 3 1/8 YARDS LONG		
	FOAM RECTANGLE (CUT BY FABRIC STORE), 22×51"		
	FIRM-HOLD UPHOLSTERY SPRAY-MOUNT ADHESIVE		

CANOPY MATERIALS LIST

NOTE: COTTON TICKING—THE STRIPED FABRIC TRADITIONALLY USED FOR PILLOW AND MATTRESS COVERS—IS RECOMMENDED FOR THE CANOPY BECAUSE IT IS DURABLE AND PROVIDES GOOD SHADE. TICKING IS NOW AVAILABLE IN PATTERNS. A LIGHTER-WEIGHT FABRIC MAY BE USED AND WILL ADMIT FILTERED SUNLIGHT.

QUANTITY	PART	DESCRIPTION	FINISHED SIZE
3	P	CANOPY (TICKING FABRIC)	36×52"
3	Q	TAB MATERIAL (TICKING FABRIC)	2½×52"
	SPOOL OF MATCHING THREAD		
3	LENGTHS OF 1/8" STEEL CABLE, 76" LONG		
6	3/8×5" EYEBOLTS		
6	CABLE CLAMPS		

Build the frame

1 Cut the pieces to the lengths given in the Frame Materials List. The roof braces (**E**) are cut with 45-degree miters on one end. Often 4×4 posts have small splits at the ends. If the posts are split at both ends, cut off the split portion at the end that will be exposed.

Marking a half-lap

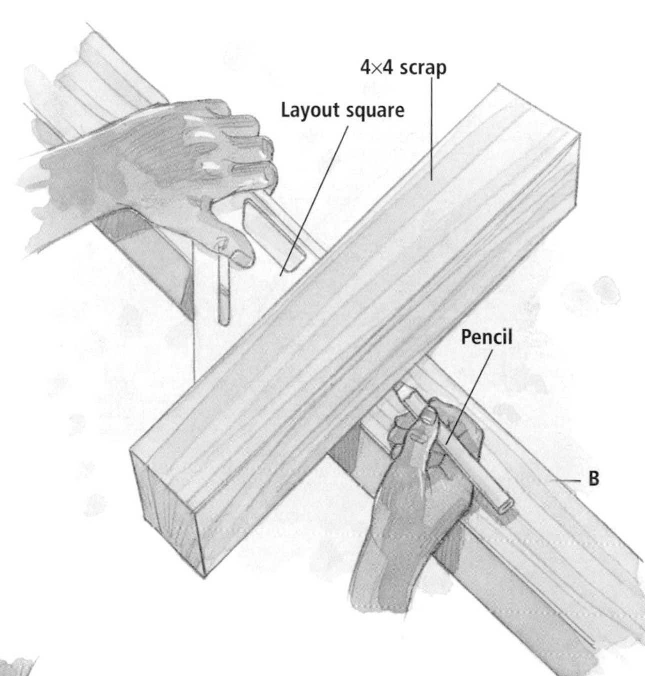

2 Lay out the notches for the half-lap joints in the 4×4 posts (**A**) and top beams (**B**). Lay out the center notches on the top beams too, by placing a scrap of 4×4 over where you'll cut the notch, as shown in the drawing above. Use a layout square to make sure the scrap is perpendicular to the top beam, then mark along each edge of the scrap with a pencil.

Cutting a half-lap

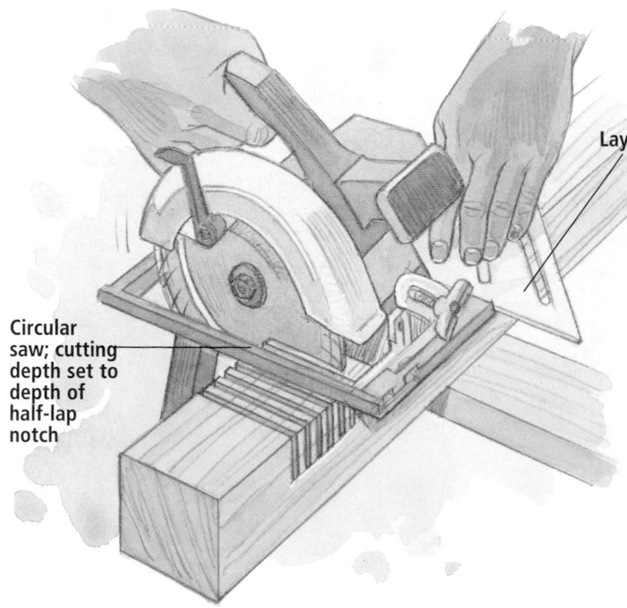

3 If you have never made a half-lap joint, practice on scrap pieces. Adjust your circular saw blade so it cuts exactly halfway through the board. Cut along the waste side of the layout line, then cut a series of kerfs about 3/8 inch apart in the waste area. Keep the saw's base flat on the board all the time you are cutting, and use a square as a saw guide. (A tablesaw or radial-arm saw also works well for making these cuts.)

4 Tap the kerfed area with a hammer to remove most of the material. Then use a chisel to clean out the joint and make the bottom fairly smooth. Start by holding the chisel with the bevel facing down. You may need to tap with a hammer occasionally, but for the most part you can cut away the wood without using a hammer. See that there are no raised portions in the middle of the notch. Dry-fit the pieces together to make sure they fit.

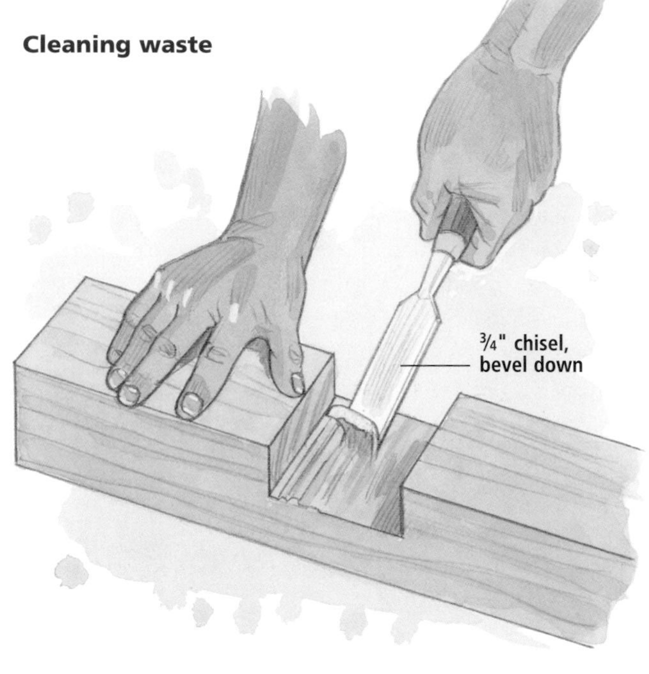

5 Apply primer or wood sealer to the wood as desired. Be sure to apply plenty of sealer to the cut ends and notches. You may apply finish paint or primer at this point, then apply a second coat after the structure is assembled.

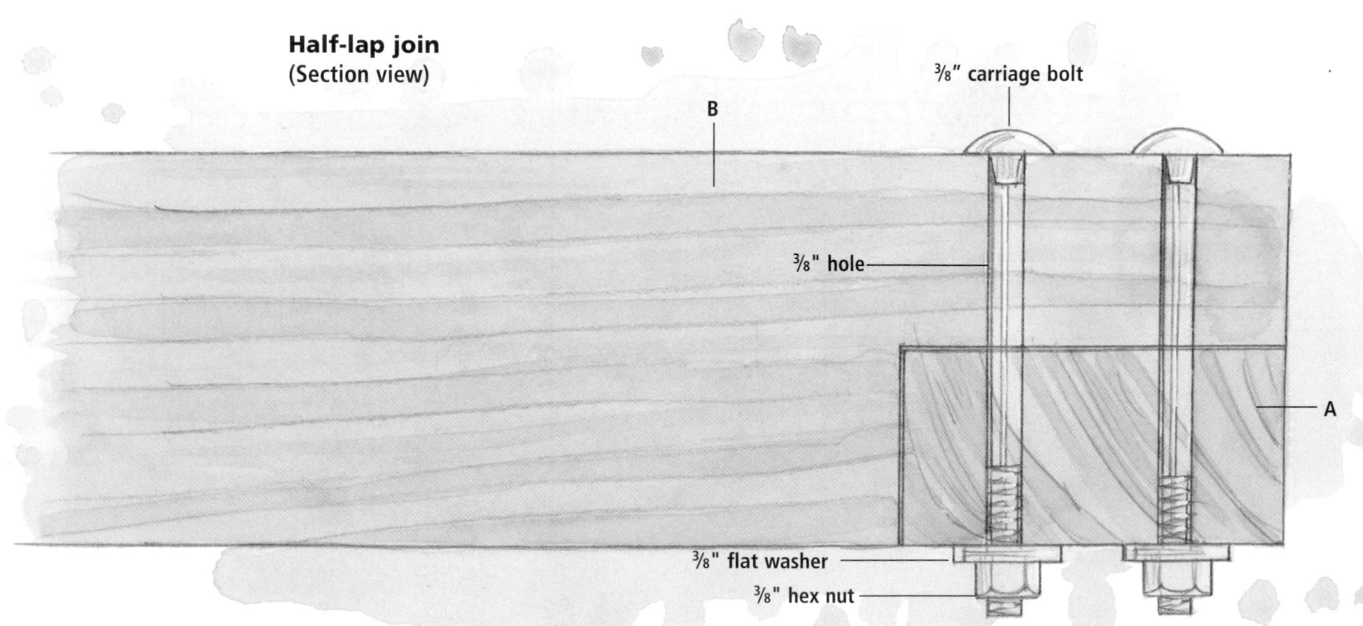

6 Working on a flat surface, assemble the swing frames with parts **A**, **B**, and **C**. Drill holes and fasten together the swing frames with 3/8-inch carriage bolts as shown above. Check that the pieces are square with each other as you work.

❼ Lay out four postholes in a rectangle as shown right. (For more on laying out posts, see pages 180–183.) Dig each hole 30 inches deep, or below the frost line, whichever is deeper. Pour about 6 inches of gravel into the bottom of each hole and pack it down with the end of the 4×4. Place the frame assemblies in the holes and make sure they are plumb, level from front to back, and the correct distance apart. You may need to adjust the height of one or more holes by adding gravel. Brace the assemblies with 1×4 temporary supports fastened to stakes in the ground. Lay a 2×4 across the top of the two frames and check with a level to ensure the frames are at the same elevation. Once the frames are plumb and level, mix concrete and pour into each hole. Allow the concrete to cure for two or more days.

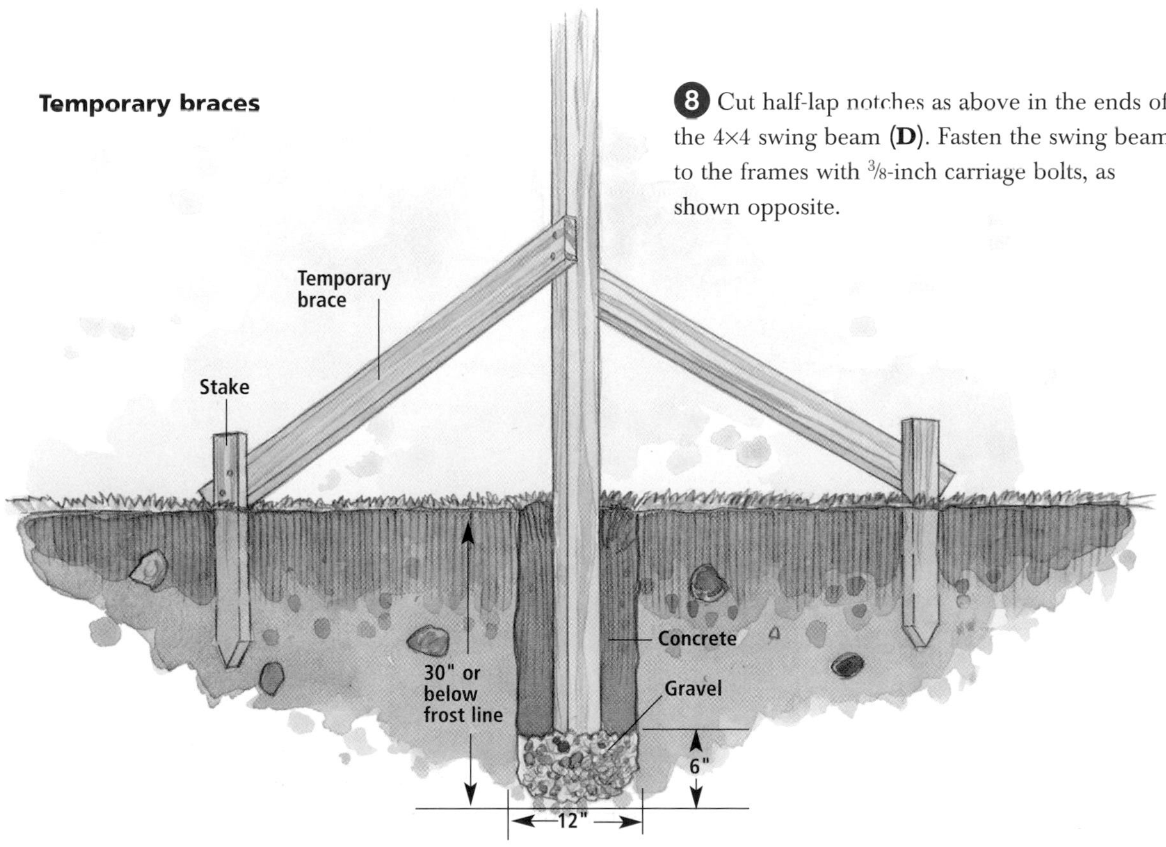

❽ Cut half-lap notches as above in the ends of the 4×4 swing beam (**D**). Fasten the swing beam to the frames with ⅜-inch carriage bolts, as shown opposite.

9 Mark and cut half-lap joints in the square ends of each roof brace **(E)**. Drill holes for the carriage bolts. Loosely bolt each pair of braces together at a 90-degree angle, then attach the mitered ends to the top of the swing frame assemblies with 4-inch deck screws, as shown in the exploded view on page 65. Tighten the bolts where the roof braces meet. Attach the roof beams **(F)** between the roof braces, angling them as shown below.

Roof structure

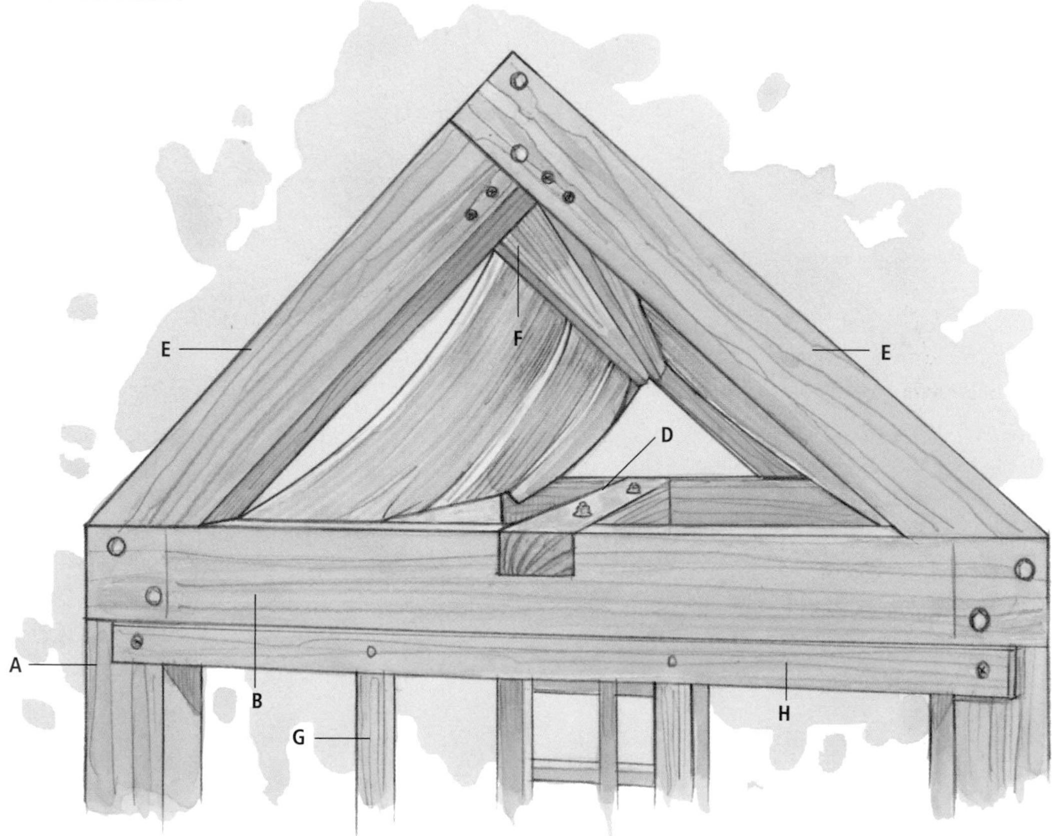

10 To make the lattice panels, place the stringers **(G)** about 9¾ inches apart on a flat surface. Align the ends with a framing square. Fasten a lattice slat **(H)** to each end of the stringers with 1¼-inch deck screws and glue, then space one every 9½ inches along the stringer. Position the assembled trellises on the outsides of the frame assemblies and drive 1¼-inch deck screws through the slats to fasten the lattice to the posts.

11 Drill ⅜-inch holes in the swing beam **(D)** to accept the eyebolts for the canvas swing. Also drill holes in the roof braces **(E)** to accept the eyebolts for the canopy. Position the holes so the eyebolts will suspend the roof's top tabs at the peak of the roof braces. Attach eyebolts with washers and nuts. Wait to drill holes for suspending the bottom tabs of the canopy until you've constructed it.

Glossary of Terms

■ **Press under:** Make a crease along the edge of the fabric, wrong sides together, and press with an iron.

■ **Raw edge:** The edge of the fabric with loose threads.

■ **Right side/wrong side of fabric:** The right side has the pattern (or brighter color), and the wrong side is the reverse side.

■ **Seam allowance:** The distance between the seam line (the line made by sewing) and the raw edge of the fabric.

■ **Selvage:** The edge on either side of a length of fabric, finished to prevent fraying, meant to be trimmed or removed when sewing.

■ **Sew together:** For this project, sew with right sides together using ½-inch seam allowances unless otherwise noted.

Making the canvas swing

1 Measure and cut the canvas into three pieces: one 90×27-inch rectangle for the seat and its sides (**I**); one 55×23-inch rectangle for the swing back (**J**); and one 51×9-inch strip for the front (**K**), as shown right.

2 Sew the backpiece (**J**). On each 23-inch edge of the backpiece, press under ½ inch, then fold and press under another 2 inches. Sew along the inner pressed edge ⅛ inch from the edge.

3 Make the dowel pocket for the backpiece (**J**) by pressing under 1 inch on one of the 55-inch edges, and then folding and pressing under another 4 inches. Sew ⅛ inch from the inner pressed edge and 2 inches from the outer pressed fold.

Canvas pieces

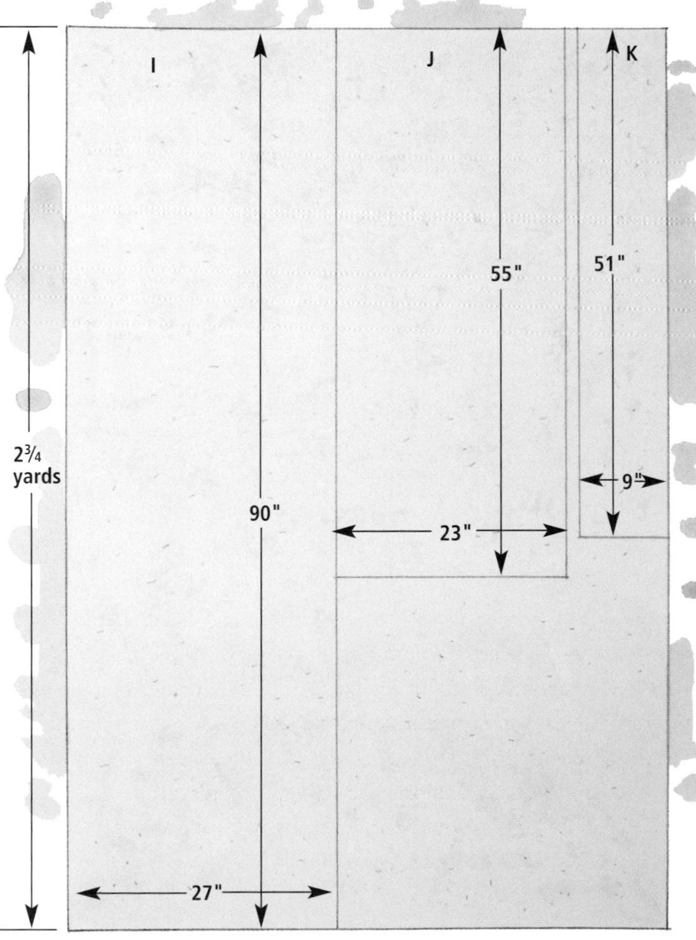

SWING UNDER COVER (CONTINUED)

4 Prepare the seat/sides piece (**I**): On each 90-inch edge of the seat/sides piece, press under ½ inch, then fold and press under another 2 inches.

Sewing the seat

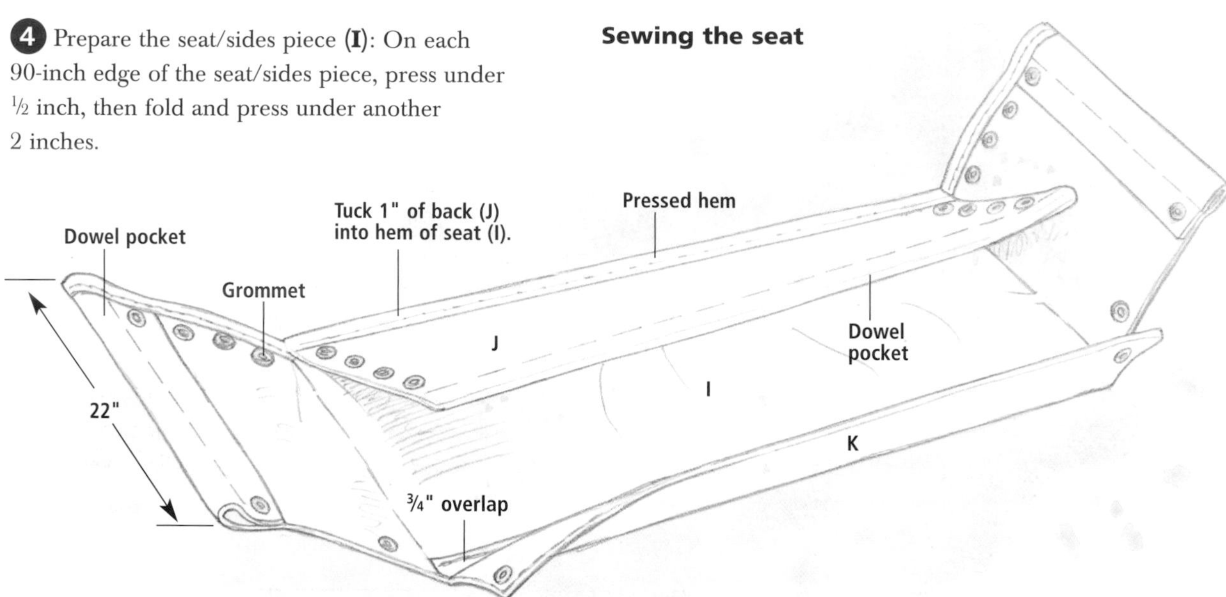

5 Sew the backpiece (**J**) to the seat/sides piece (**I**). Start by putting the wrong sides together and centering the backpiece on the seat/sides piece. Tuck 1 inch of the raw back edge into the pressed hem in the seat/sides, as shown above. Pin in place. Sew ⅛ inch from the inner pressed edge of the hem, catching the backpiece in the stitching. Fold the back away from the seat/sides piece and sew through all layers ¼ inch from the outer pressed edge of the hem. This second seam reinforces the back's connection to the seat.

6 Make the side dowel pockets by pressing under 1 inch, then folding and pressing under another 4 inches on each short edge of the seat/sides (**I**). Sew ⅛ inch from the inner pressed edge and 2 inches from the outer pressed fold. Close one end of each side dowel pocket by sewing ⅛ inch from the front edge of the pocket.

7 Sew the front piece (**K**). Fold the front strip in half lengthwise with right sides together. Sew short edges together using a ½-inch seam allowance. Turn right side out; press seams. Place the front on the seat (**I**) with the open edge overlapping the seat by ¾ inch. Sew through all layers ⅛ inch and ⅝ inch from the outer pressed edge of the seat hem. (Two seams add strength to the seat.)

8 Lay out the grommets, as shown above. Make the marks with a water-erasable fabric-marking pen to show the outline of the grommets. Exact spacing isn't crucial, but make sure that when the back (**J**) and seat (**I**) are in their final position, the marks for the back grommets align with the marks on the sides. Make sure that the marks on the front (**K**) align with marks on the front edge of the sides (**I**) too. Insert the dowels into the back pocket and side pockets before closing the pockets with grommets. Apply the grommets as explained in Setting the Grommets on the opposite page.

Corner ties

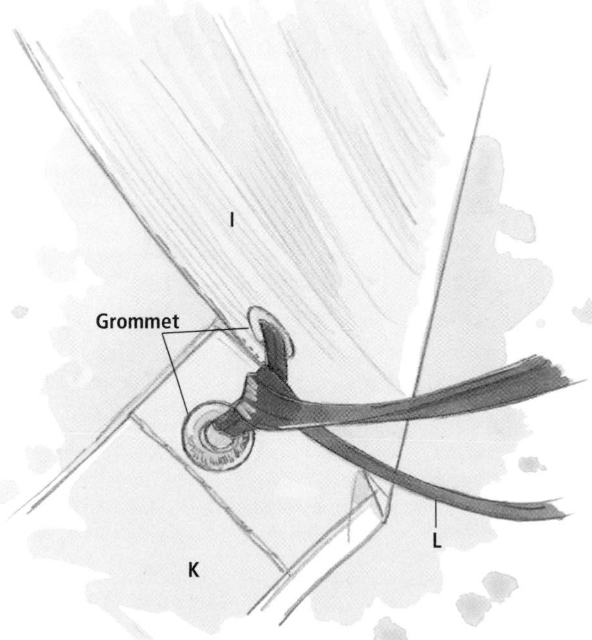

9 Make the ties **(L)** by cutting four 2×45-inch strips from ¼ yard of print fabric. Fold the strips in half lengthwise and press. Unfold the strips and fold in the long edges to meet at the pressed center fold. Fold in half lengthwise and press again, enclosing the raw edges. Machine-stitch close to the open long edges. From the strips, cut two 18-inch-long ties for the front corners of the canvas swing and eight 5-inch-long ties for the back corners. Thread a tie through each corresponding pair of grommets; tie and knot the ends as shown in the Corner Ties drawing.

To minimize sewing: Substitute lengths of ribbon or shoelaces for the ties. You'll need 76 inches of sturdy, nonfraying ribbon, cut as indicated in Step 9 above.

Setting the Grommets

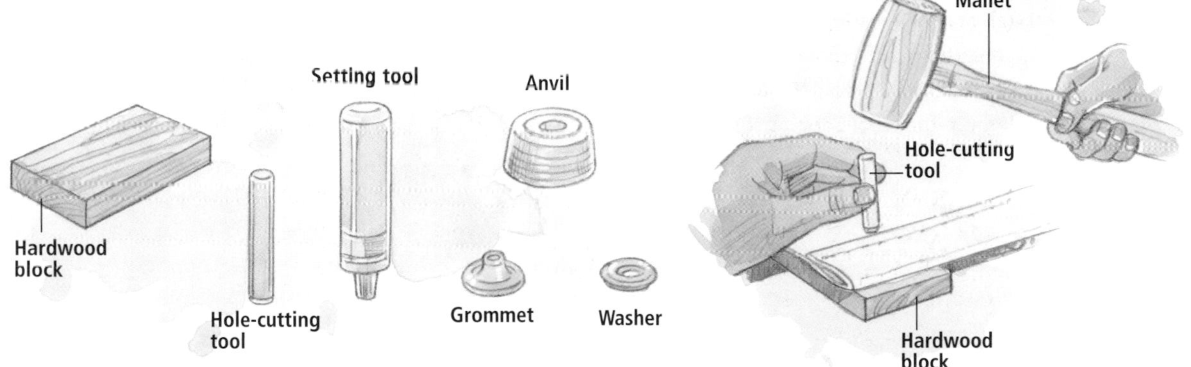

1 To cut a hole in the fabric, place the fabric on a piece of hardwood. Line up the hole-cutting tool over a mark indicating where a grommet is to be applied. Strike the tool with a wooden or plastic mallet.

2 Position the grommet with its post up, as shown, on the anvil that comes with the kit. Place the fabric, right side facing down, on top of the grommet/anvil, and check to be sure the grommet shaft is coming up through the hole in the fabric.

3 Slip a washer over the grommet shaft, with the curved side facing up and the teeth facing down toward the wrong side of the fabric. Press gently until the washer is stable.

4 Center the setting tool with its nose inserted through the hole in the washer. Holding the setting tool steady, strike with a wooden or plastic mallet two or three times, rotating the setting tool a quarter turn after each strike.

5 Check whether the grommet and washer fit tightly to the fabric. If necessary, reposition the setting tool and strike again.

SWING UNDER COVER (CONTINUED)

10 Cut the plywood **(O)** and make the cushion (see Making the Cushion, page 76). Place the plywood on the seat **(I)** and the cushion on the plywood.

11 Thread the cable. Start by running a 31-inch length of steel cable through a cable clamp and through the back grommet on one side of the swing. Feed the cable back through the clamp and tighten the nuts. Thread another 31-inch cable through the front grommet and repeat the process. Thread the unclamped ends of both cables through a clamp, then through a 1½-inch metal ring. Feed each cable through a clamp and tighten the nuts. Repeat on the other side of the swing.

Hanging the swing

12 Attach the cable to the swing structure by threading a 20-inch cable through a clamp and through each metal ring. Loop the end back through the clamp and tighten the nuts. Loop the unclamped end through a clamp, through the eye of a corresponding eyebolt screwed into the beam of the swing structure, then through a clamp and tighten. Repeat on the other side.

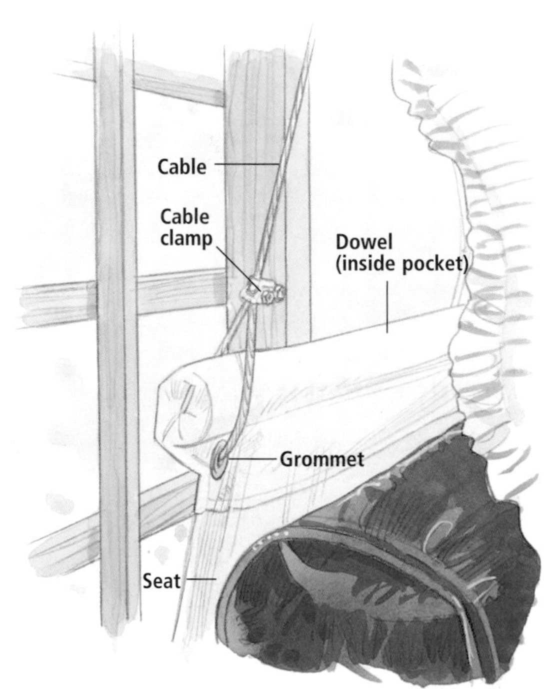

Cutting the canopy pieces

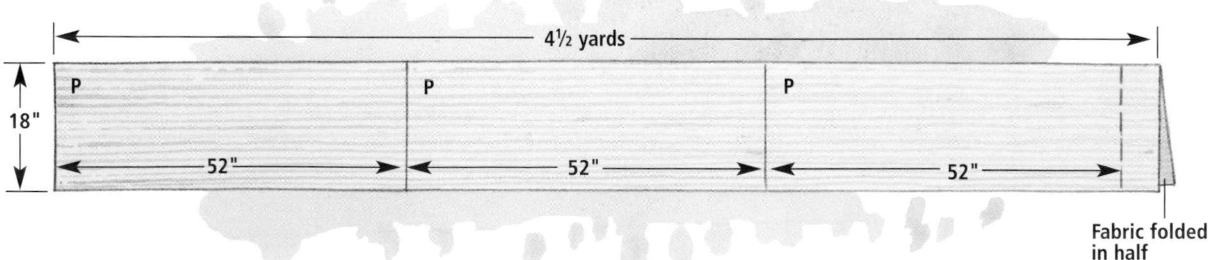

Sewing the canopy

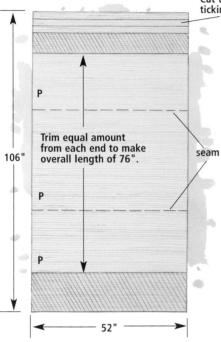

Cut three 2½" strips from leftover ticking to make tabs. (See Step 4.)

P

Trim equal amount from each end to make overall length of 76".

106"

seam

P

P

52"

Making the canopy

1 Cut three 52-inch-long pieces of ticking fabric using the entire (36-inch) width of the fabric **(P)**, as shown opposite page, bottom. Trim any selvages.

Making the canopy

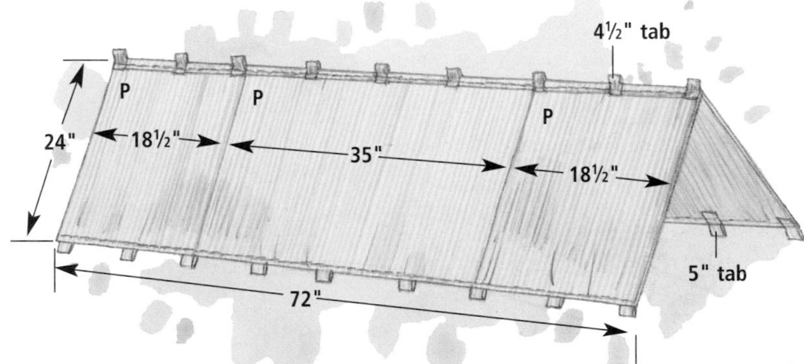

Cutting the cushion pieces

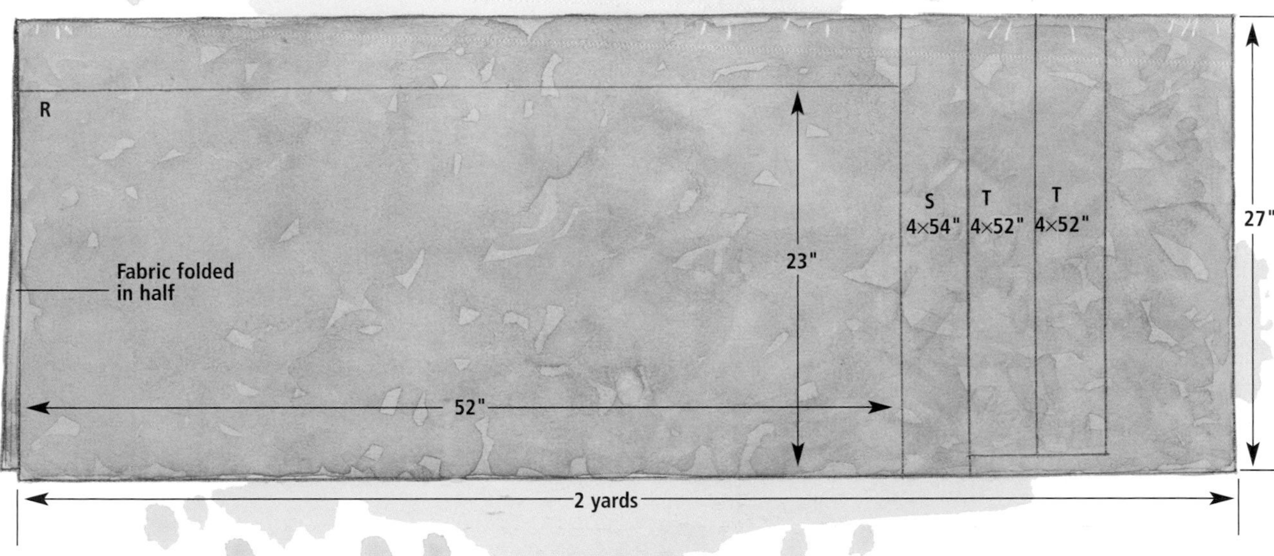

2 Pin, then sew the ticking pieces **(P)** together along the 52-inch edges, as shown in the Sewing the Canopy drawing on page 75. Finish seam allowances (to prevent fraying) by zigzag-stitching the raw edges together and pressing to one side. Trim the assembled canopy fabric, which measures 106 inches wide, to a width of 76 inches, removing equal amounts from each side edge. (Do not trim the 52-inch length). Set aside the fabric you cut off; you'll use it for the tabs (Step 4).

To minimize sewing: Instead of ticking, use a sheet or tablecloth cut to the finished size of 106×76 inches.

3 To finish the side edges, press under 1 inch twice on each 52-inch edge. Sew 1/8 inch from the inner pressed edges. Fold the canopy fabric in half, wrong sides together, aligning the raw edges; press along the fold to mark what will be the top of the canopy.

MAKING THE CUSHION

1 Measure and cut the fabric: From the decorator fabric, cut two 23×52-inch rectangles for the cushion top and bottom **(R)**, two 4×23-inch boxing strips for the sides **(S)**, and two 4×52-inch boxing strips **(T)**. Cut a piece of batting large enough to wrap around the foam.

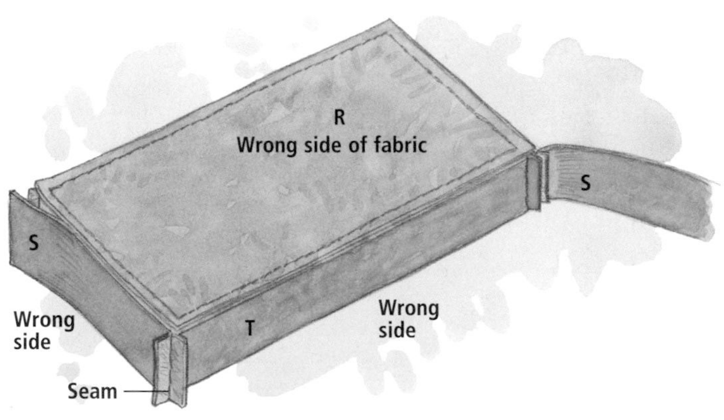

2 Use spray-mount adhesive to attach the batting to the foam; trim excess batting.

3 Sew together the short (4-inch) ends of the boxing strips, alternating the 23-inch-long **(S)** and 52-inch-long **(T)** strips to make one long, narrow strip.

4 Connect the side to the top **(R)**. Start by pinning the boxing strip to the top rectangle of the cushion fabric, positioning the seams at the corners. Sew the strip to the top.

5 Pin and sew the boxing strip to the cushion's bottom rectangle piece **(A)** in the same way, except that one long edge should be left open for turning.

6 Turn the cushion cover right side out and insert the batting-covered foam cushion. Hand-stitch the opening closed. (You will take out this seam occasionally to wash the cushion fabric.)

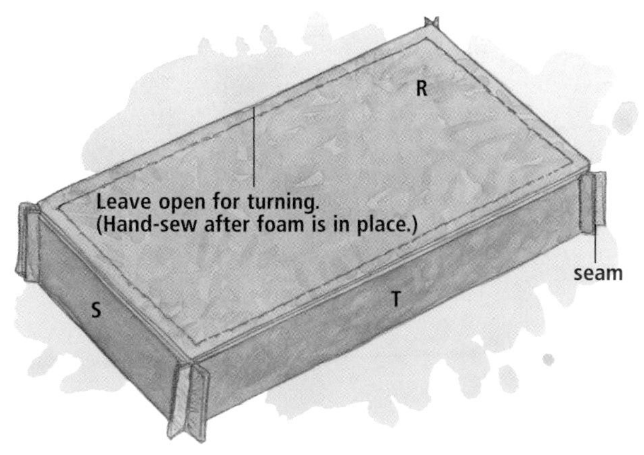

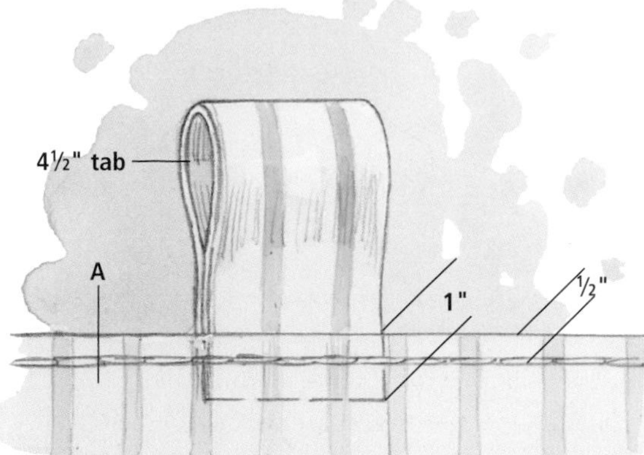

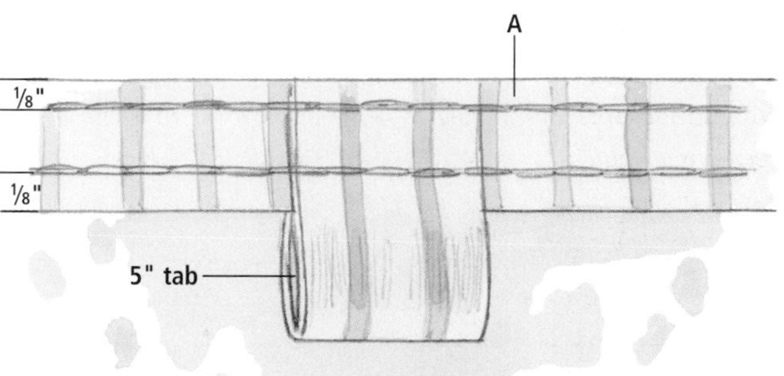

4 From the set-aside ticking fabric, cut three 2½×52-inch strips to make the tabs **(Q)**. Zigzag-stitch one long edge of each strip. Press under ⅝ inch on each unfinished long edge and then ¾ inch on each zigzag-finished edge. Sew down the center of the strips through all layers. From the strips, cut nine 4½-inch-long tabs for the folded top edge and eighteen 5-inch-long tabs for the bottom edges.

5 Attach the tabs to the top edge of the canopy. Start by pressing under ½ inch on the short edges of the 4½-inch-long tabs, then press each tab in half. Evenly space the tabs over the folded top edge of the canopy with 1 inch extending beyond the fold; pin in place. Sew ½ inch from the folded edge of the canopy, catching the tabs securely in the stitching.

6 Hem the bottom edges of the canopy and add tabs: Press under 1 inch twice on each 72-inch edge of the canopy bottom. Press each 5-inch-long tab in half. Evenly space nine tabs along each bottom hem, as shown in Making the Canopy (see page 75), tucking ½ inch of the tab in the hem; pin in place. Sew ⅛ inch from the inner pressed edge of the hem, catching the tabs in the stitching. Press the tabs down over the hem and sew ⅛ inch from the outer pressed edge of the hem.

To minimize sewing: Substitute grommets for the tabs along the bottom edges of the canopy. Press the bottom edges as indicated in Step 6, then sew two seams along each bottom edge: the first ⅛ inch from the fold, and the second ⅛ inch from the hem edge. Space nine grommets evenly between the two seams.

7 Hang the canopy from the swing structure. Begin by threading 76-inch lengths of steel cable through the tabs at the top and bottom of the canopy. Loop each end of the top cable through the eye of a corresponding eyebolt in the swing roof braces, then through a clamp; tighten the clamp with a wrench.

8 With the canopy in place, determine the placement of four additional eyebolts, which will suspend the bottom two steel cables of the canopy from the top beams as shown in the Exploded View (page 65). Drill pilot holes, then screw in the eyebolts. Loop the ends of each bottom cable through the eye of a corresponding eyebolt, then through a clamp; tighten with a wrench.

A Kid's Retreat

Yesterday it was a pirate ship. Today it's a medieval castle. Tomorrow—who knows? A great play structure lets your children's imaginations run wild. This retreat allows for numerous activities and is big enough to handle a crowd.

Even better, you can change it as your kids grow. When they're little tykes, they'll love the sandbox, and you can hang bucket-style swings from the crossbeam. As they get older, you can swap the baby swings for flat seats or sling-style models. You could also remove a few balusters and add a slide as an escape route from the tower. Or put a climbing wall on the facade. Whatever you do, your kids will get plenty of exercise for their growing bodies and their creativity as they sail their retreat across the expanses of their imaginations (and your yard).

Retreat exploded view

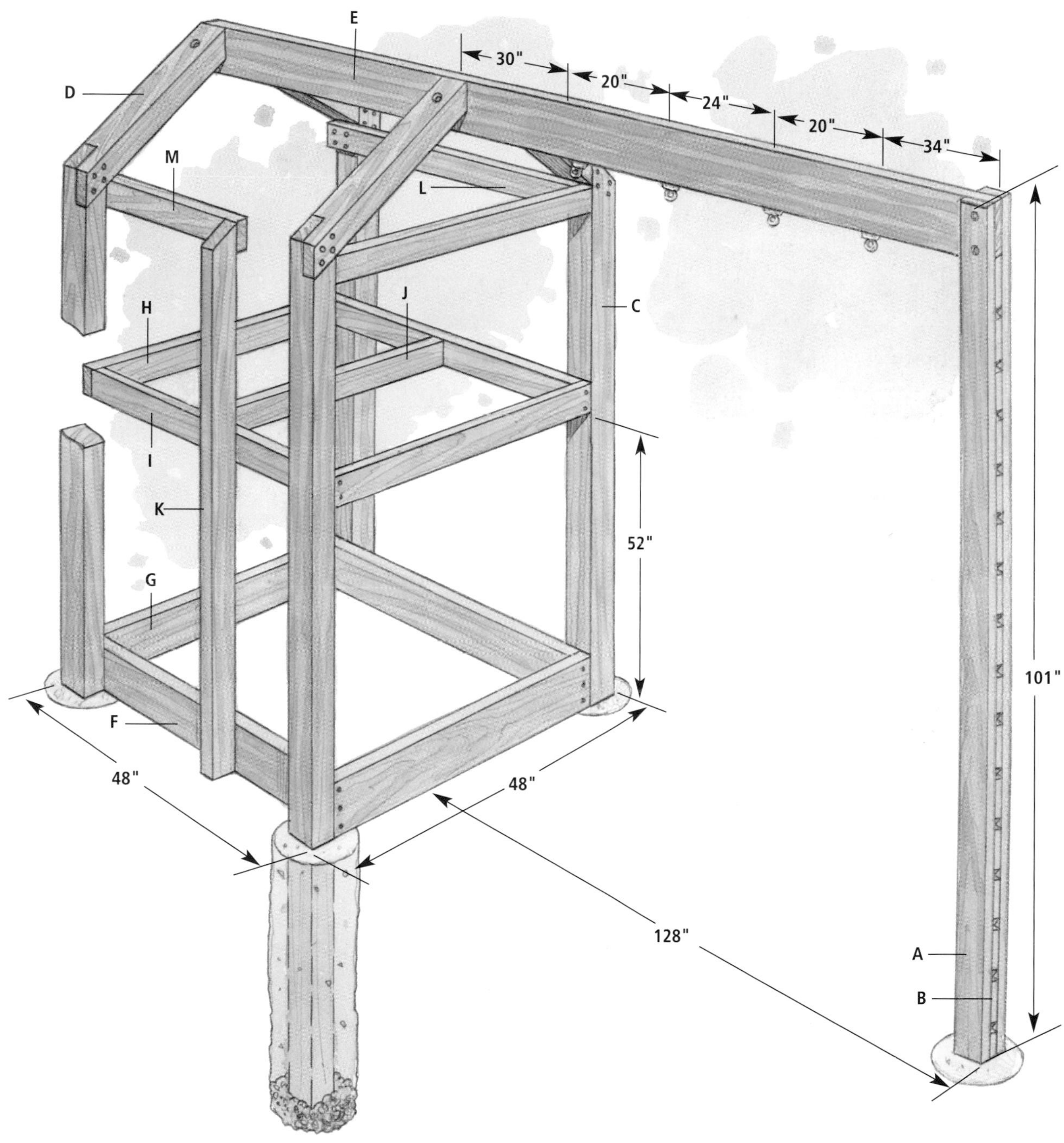

MATERIALS LIST

QUANTITY	PART	DESCRIPTION	FINISHED SIZE
2	A	OUTER END SUPPORT POST PIECES	1½×3½×144"
1	B	INNER END SUPPORT POST PIECE	1½×3½×136¾"
4	C	CORNER POSTS	3½×3½×132"
4	D	RAFTERS	3½×3½×33½"
1	E	RIDGE BOARD	1½×7¼×176"
2	F	SANDBOX SIDES	1½×7¼×45"
2	G	SANDBOX SIDES	1½×7¼×41"
2	H	PLATFORM JOISTS	1½×3½×41"
2	I	PLATFORM JOISTS	1½×3½×45"
1	J	PLATFORM JOIST	1½×3½×38"
1	K	LADDER STRINGER	1½×3½"× CUT TO FIT
1	L	HANDRAIL	1½×3½×82½"
1	M	HANDRAIL	1½×3½"× CUT TO FIT
1	N	HANDRAIL	1½×3½×41"
5	O	LADDER RUNGS	1½×3½×15"
8	P	RUNG SUPPORTS	1½×3½×11⅞"
10	Q	FLOORBOARDS	1½×3½×48"
1	R	FLOORBOARD	1½×4¾×48"
18	S	BALUSTERS	1½×1½×31½"

QUANTITY	PART	DESCRIPTION	FINISHED SIZE
1	T	THRESHOLD	1½×5½×48"
1	U	FACADE	¾×48×92¼"
SUPPLIES:			
		1½", 2½", AND 3" RUST-RESISTANT SCREWS	
		7D RUST-RESISTANT BOX NAILS	
		16D RUST-RESISTANT CASING NAILS	
2		½×6" CARRIAGE BOLTS WITH WASHERS AND NUTS	
2		½×5" CARRIAGE BOLTS WITH WASHERS AND NUTS	
		½ CUBIC FOOT OF GRAVEL	
12		60-POUND BAGS OF CONCRETE (GRAVEL MIX)	
		EXTERIOR PRIMER AND PAINT	
		FABRIC FOR ROOF	49¼×63"*
6		¼" GROMMETS	
		6-MIL PLASTIC	
		SAND	

*DIMENSIONS BEFORE HEMMING

SHOPPING LIST

ALL OF THE MATERIAL USED (EXCEPT THE PLYWOOD) SHOULD BE ROT RESISTANT. CHOICES INCLUDE PRESSURE-TREATED LUMBER, CEDAR, REDWOOD, OR OTHER ROT-RESISTANT SPECIES.

QUANTITY	SIZE	PARTS
3	2"×4"×12'	A, B
5	4"×4"×12'	C, D
1	2"×8"×16'	E
2	2"×8"×8'	F, G
12	2"×4"×8'	H, I, J, K, L, M, N, O, P, Q
1	2"×6"×12'	R, T, V
18	2"×2"×3'	S
1	¾"×4"×8' EXT. PLYWOOD	U
2	2"×4"×8'	FOR USE AS TEMPORARY SPACERS
6	1"×2"×8'	FOR USE AS BRACES

Make the uprights

1 Start with the three 12-foot 2×4s **(A, B)**. These will be screwed face to face to form the end support post for the swing set. Before you assemble them, cut one 2×4 to 136¾ inches. This piece will be sandwiched between the two longer pieces creating a notch for the ridge board **(E)**. The shorter piece also has a series of V-notches cut in each edge for decoration as shown right. The notches are 1½ inches wide and ¾ inch deep and are spaced 6 inches on center along 8 feet of the piece. (Most of the rest is buried in the ground.) Cut the notches with a jigsaw.

End support post

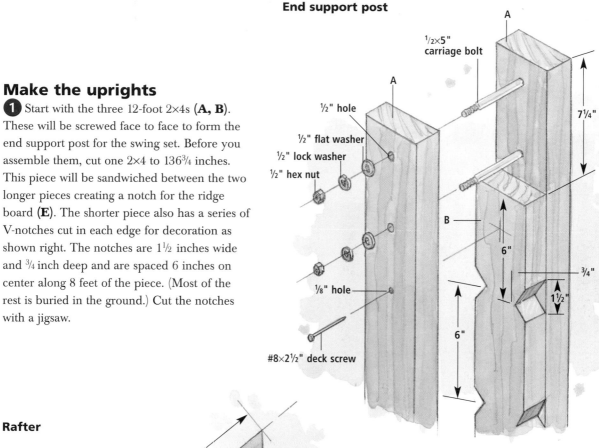

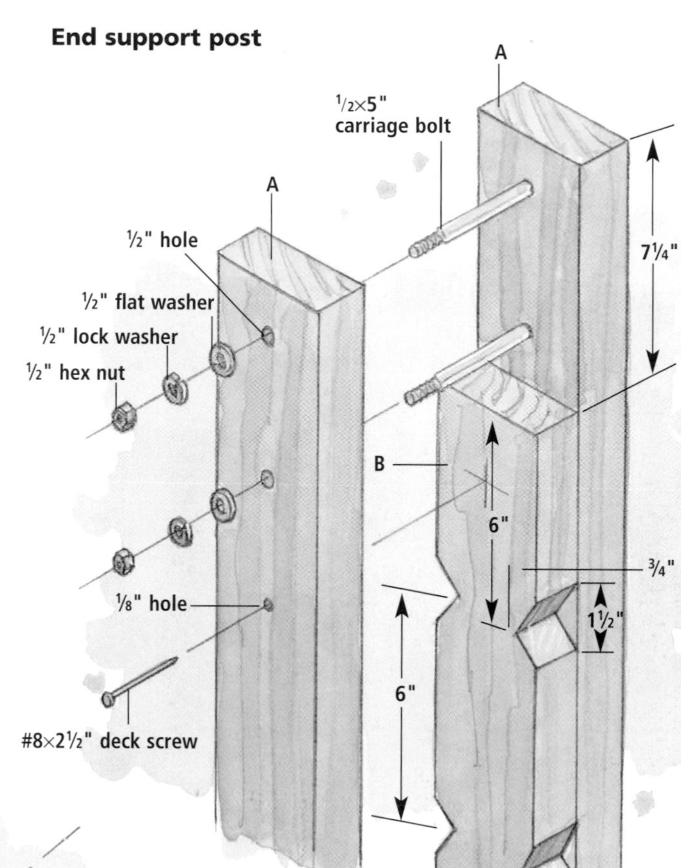

Rafter

2 Stack the three 2×4s so that the notched piece is between the two longer pieces. Fasten the outer pieces to the center one with 2½-inch rust-resistant screws. Predrill the holes with a ⅛-inch drill bit to avoid splitting the wood. Space the screws about 6 inches apart down the center of each outer piece.

3 Cut four of the 4×4 posts to 127 inches long for the corner posts **(C)**. Cut the remaining 4×4 into four 34-inch pieces for the rafters **(D)**. Cut one end of each corner post and both ends of each rafter at a 50-degree angle as shown left.

4 Join the corner posts to the rafters with half-lap joints as shown right. To cut the half-laps, set the blade on your circular saw to cut halfway through the 4×4s. Lay out the notches as shown. Make the shoulder cuts by cutting across the pieces parallel to the angled cuts you made in Step 3. Then make the cheek cuts by cutting along the layout lines on both sides of the pieces. This will leave a small section uncut. Finish the cut with a handsaw. Clean up the cheeks with a sharp chisel.

Half-lap joint

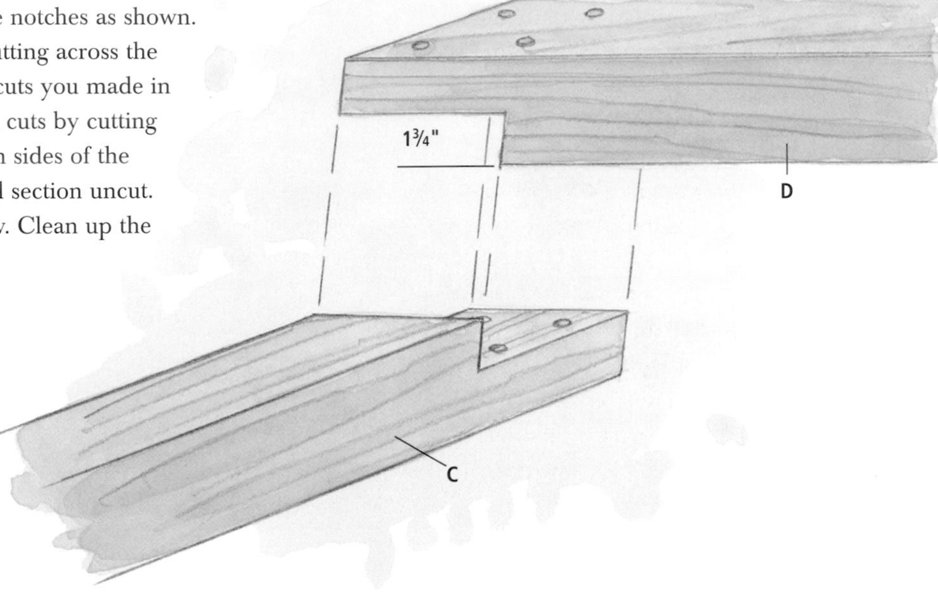

5 Screw one rafter to each corner post with four 3-inch rust-resistant screws. Predrill the holes with a ⅛-inch drill bit to avoid splitting the wood.

Making the shoulder cut

Making the cheek cuts

Dig the holes and set the posts

1 Decide approximately where you want the retreat. Tie a piece of mason's line around a 16d nail and drive it into the ground to mark the location of the end support post. Stretch the string out about 15 feet and drive a second nail into the ground to hold the line taut. Lay out the locations of the corner posts by using a framing square as shown right. Drive nails into the ground to mark the center of each post. (See pages 180–183.)

2 Spray-paint 12-inch-diameter circles on the ground to mark the five holes. The circles should be centered on the marker nails. With a posthole digger, dig the holes 54 inches deep. As you dig, pile the dirt on a plastic tarp to make cleanup easier.

3 Line each hole with 6 inches of gravel and pack it with a tamper or the end of the 4×4 so that it won't settle.

4 Position two of the post/rafter assemblies on the ground opposite each other. Place a piece of 2× material between the tops of the rafters to space the rafters for the ridge board. Then adjust the posts until they are 41 inches apart. Cut one of the extra 2×4s in half and screw the pieces to the posts as temporary spreaders as shown right. Repeat with the second set of post/rafter assemblies.

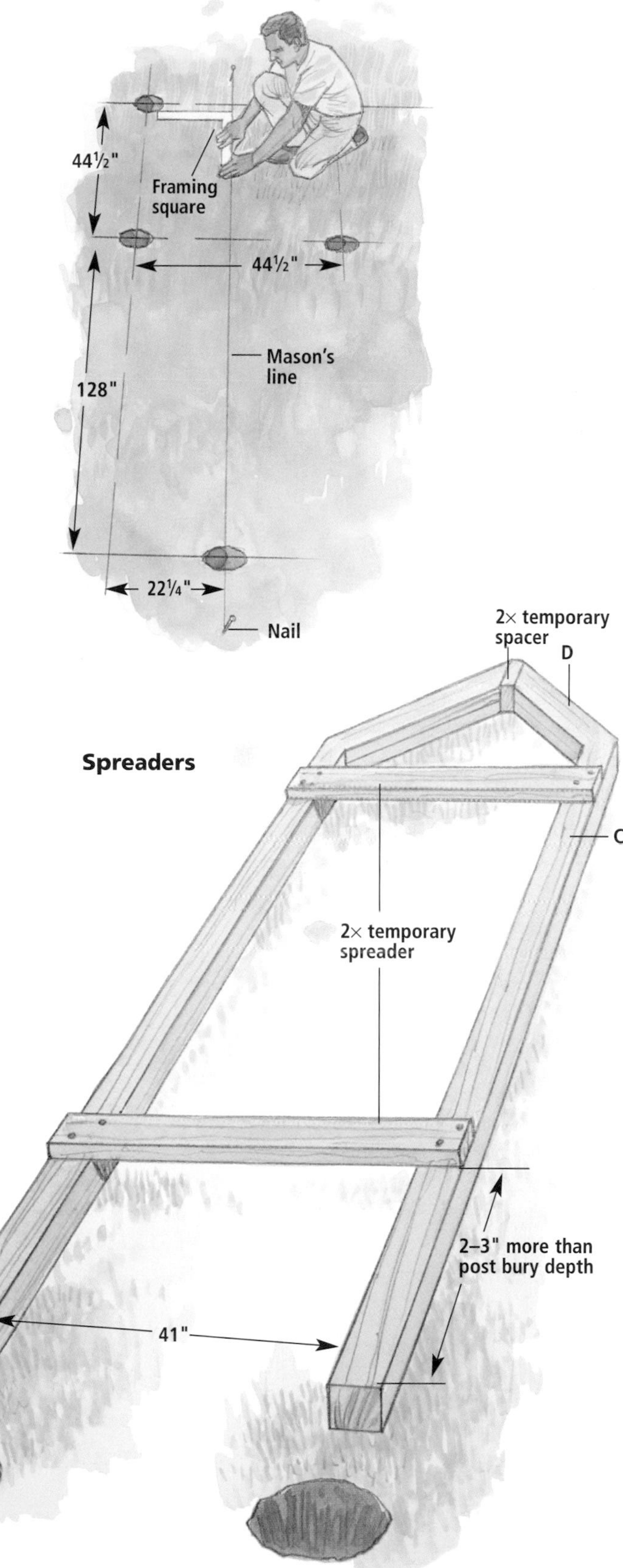

Setting the frames

5 With a helper, stand the post/rafter frames up in their holes. Check two adjacent faces to be sure they are plumb (vertical) and brace them as shown right. Also put the end support post in its hole and brace it plumb.

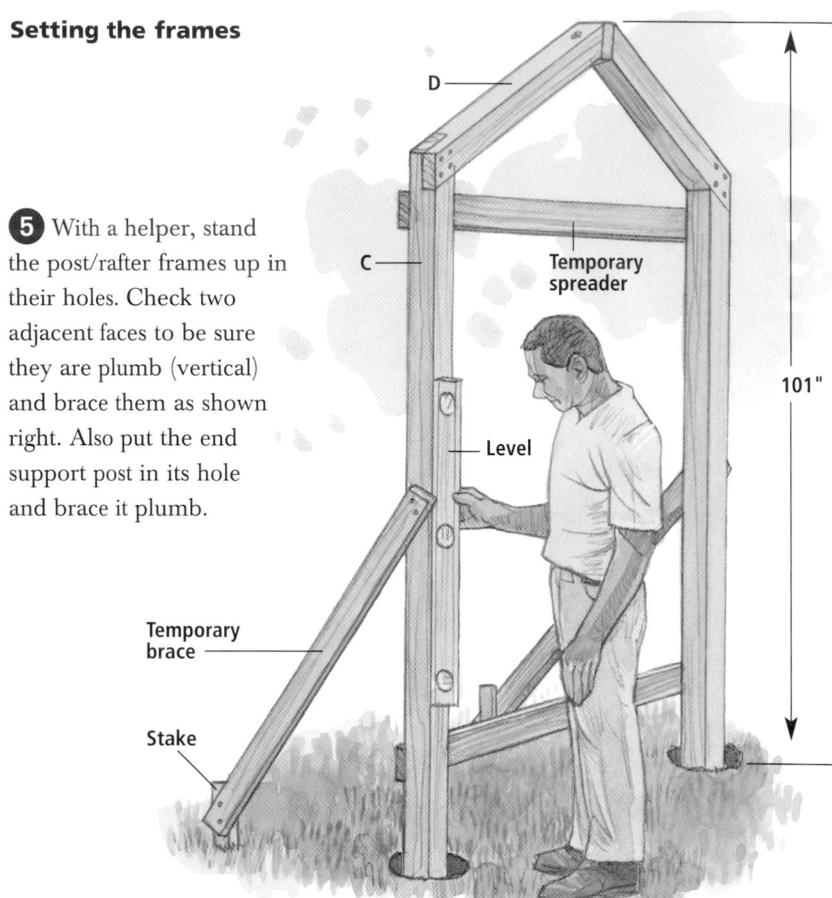

6 Lay out the position of swing hangers on the ridge board. For standard swings, the Consumer Product Safety Commission calls for at least 30 inches between posts and swings and 24 inches between adjacent swings (see page 79). The hangers for one swing should be at least 20 inches apart. Allow more room if specified by the hardware manufacturer. A tire swing requires a special hanger and must be the only swing on the set.

Boring straight holes

7 When you drill the holes for the mounting hardware, make sure the holes don't angle off to the side or to the front and back. Put a combination square on the ridge. As you drill, keep the drill parallel to the blade of the square to keep the hole straight. Have a helper watch from the end of the ridge board to make sure the hole is straight in that direction too.

8 Bolt the hangers in place with washers, lock washers, and nuts, or as directed by the manufacturer.

9 Working on ladders, have your assistant help you lift the ridge board (**E**) into position. Hold it there and place a level on top to make sure the board is level as shown right. If the ridge board isn't level, screw it temporarily to the rafters and end post with two 3-inch screws at each joint. Remove the braces and add gravel to the holes until the ridge is level. Reattach the braces.

Checking for level

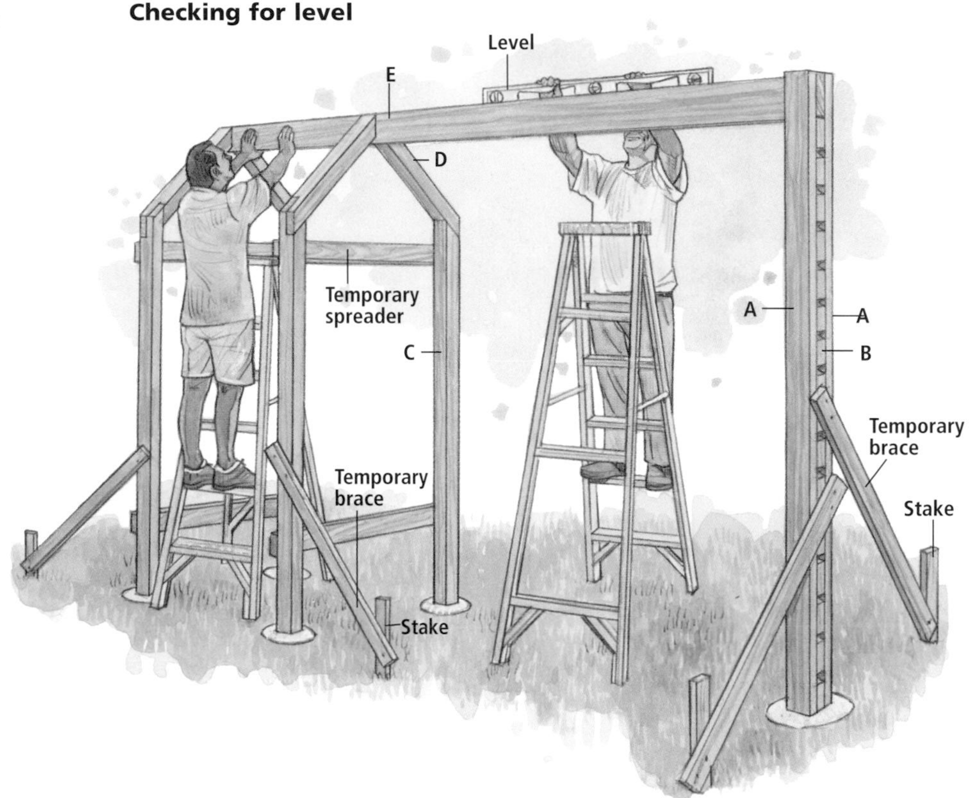

Carriage bolt detail

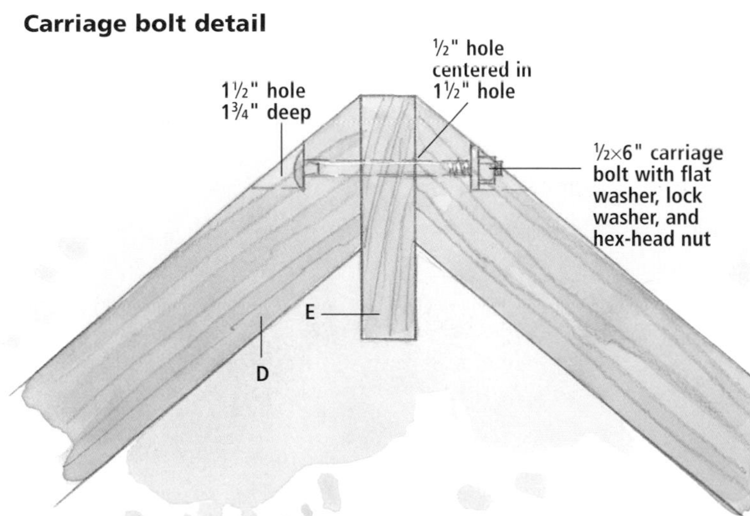

10 Screw or tack the ridge board in place with a few nails, still working from the ladders. Then drill holes for the carriage bolts that will secure it to the verticals as shown in the drawings on page 81. Bore 1½-inch holes 1¾ inches deep with a spade bit. Then drill ½-inch diameter through holes, starting in the dimple left by the point of the spade bit.

11 Mix concrete and fill the holes around all five posts. As you fill the holes, poke a scrap of wood up and down in the concrete to eliminate any gaps and air pockets. Trowel the concrete around each post to smooth the surface.

Add the horizontal framing

1 Check the distances between the four corner posts. Measuring from outside corner to outside corner, the posts should all be 48 inches apart. If they aren't, adjust the lengths of some of the pieces.

2 Cut the platform joists **(H, I)** to length. Two of the joists **(H)** should be 3 inches shorter than the outside dimension between the posts. The other two joists **(I)** should fit in between the posts as shown in the Retreat Exploded View drawing on page 79.

3 Hold one of the long joists **(I)** in place between two of the posts, positioned 52 inches above the ground. Level it, then screw it in place leaving a 1½-inch space at either end as shown right.

Attaching the joists

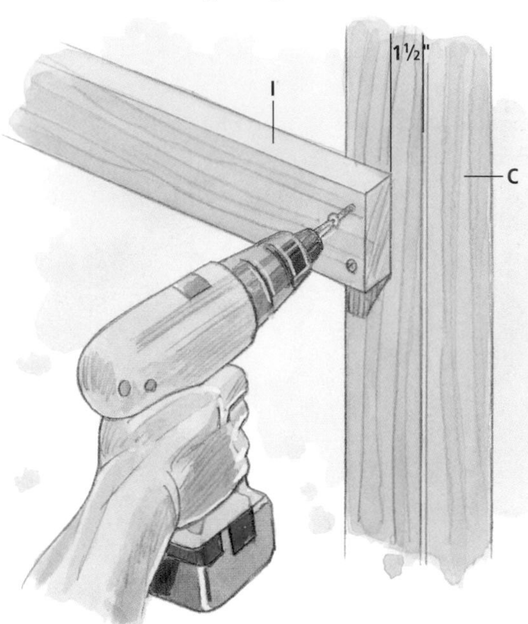

Attaching the final joists

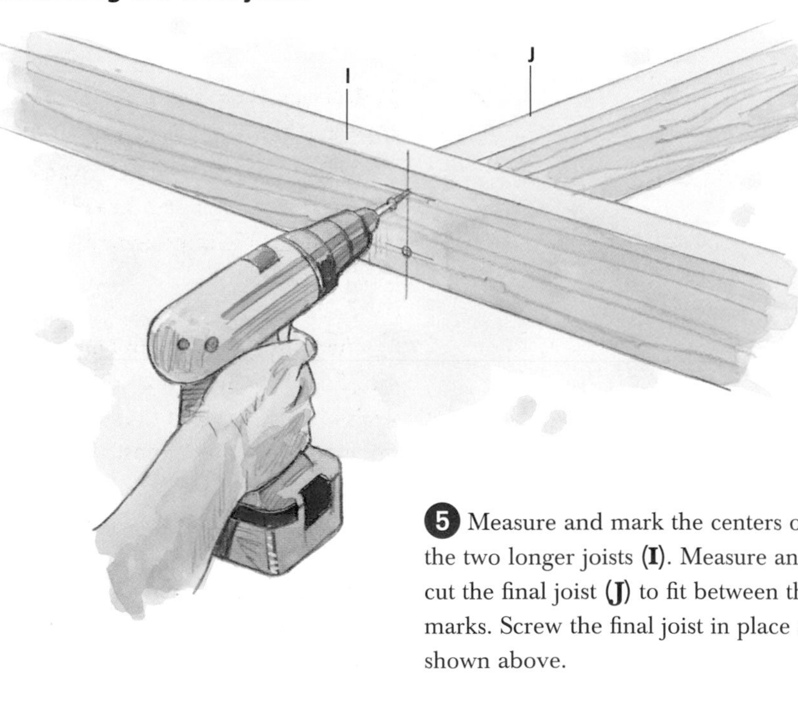

4 Screw the shorter joists **(H)** to the ends of the joist you just installed, making sure they are level. Level and install the fourth joint.

5 Measure and mark the centers of the two longer joists **(I)**. Measure and cut the final joist **(J)** to fit between the marks. Screw the final joist in place as shown above.

6 Repeat the process to install the sandbox sides **(F, G)** at ground level. Also attach the two handrails **(L, N)** near the tops of the posts as shown on page 79.

7 Cut the ladder stringer **(K)** to length so it reaches from the ground to the height of the post where the handrail will be attached. Cut the top of the stringer at a 50-degree angle to match the slope of the rafters. Screw the stringer to the sandbox side and the platform joist as shown right. Make sure the stringer is plumb and that the space between the post and the stringer is 15 inches at both the top and bottom before driving in the screws.

8 Cut the short handrail **(M)** so it reaches from the corner post to the stringer. Screw it in place.

Installing the stringer

Installing the rungs

Adding the rungs, decking, and balusters

1 Cut the ladder rungs **(O)** to fit between the stringer and the corner post. Also cut the rung supports **(P)** to 11⅞ inches long.

2 Start the ladder by positioning a rung flush with the bottom of the sandbox side. Toenail the rung to the stringer and the corner post. Screw two rung supports in place on top of the first rung. Then add the second rung on top of the supports and toenail it in place as shown left. Work your way up to the top of the ladder in this manner.

Final assembly

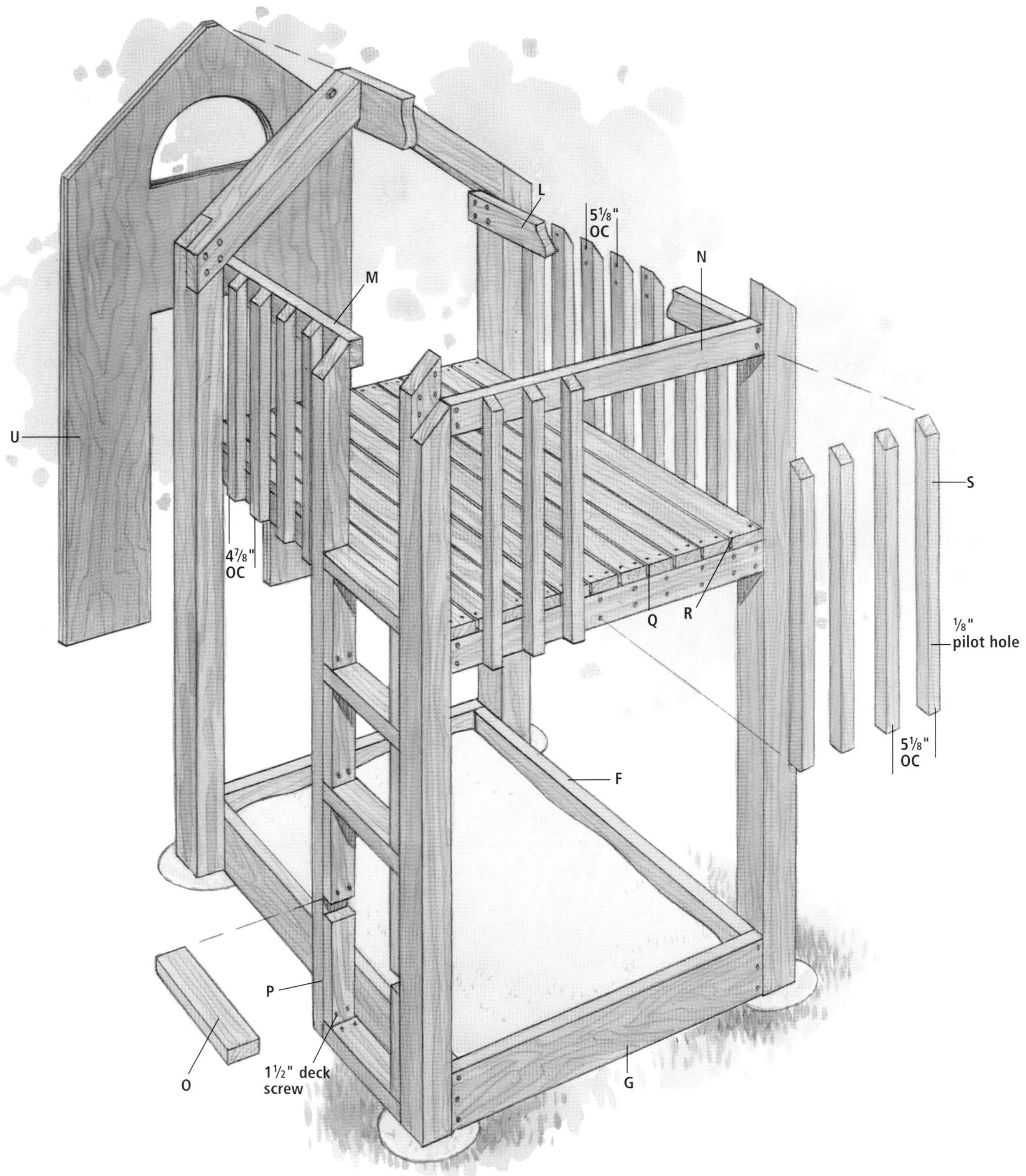

Using nails as spacers

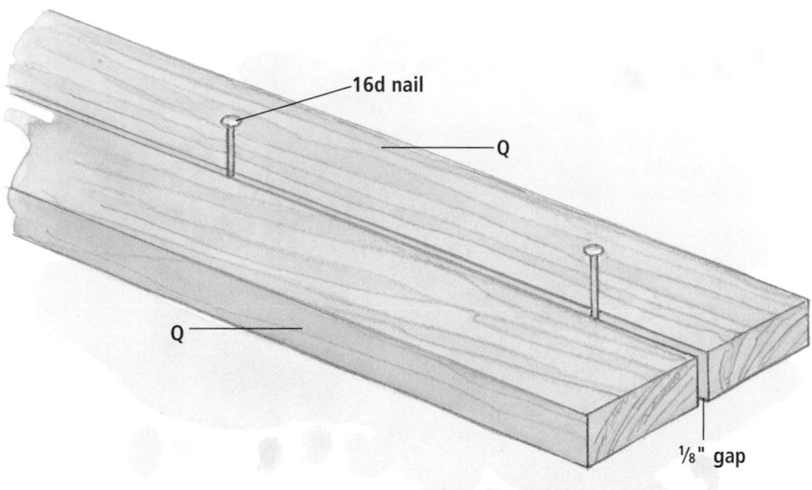

Installing balusters

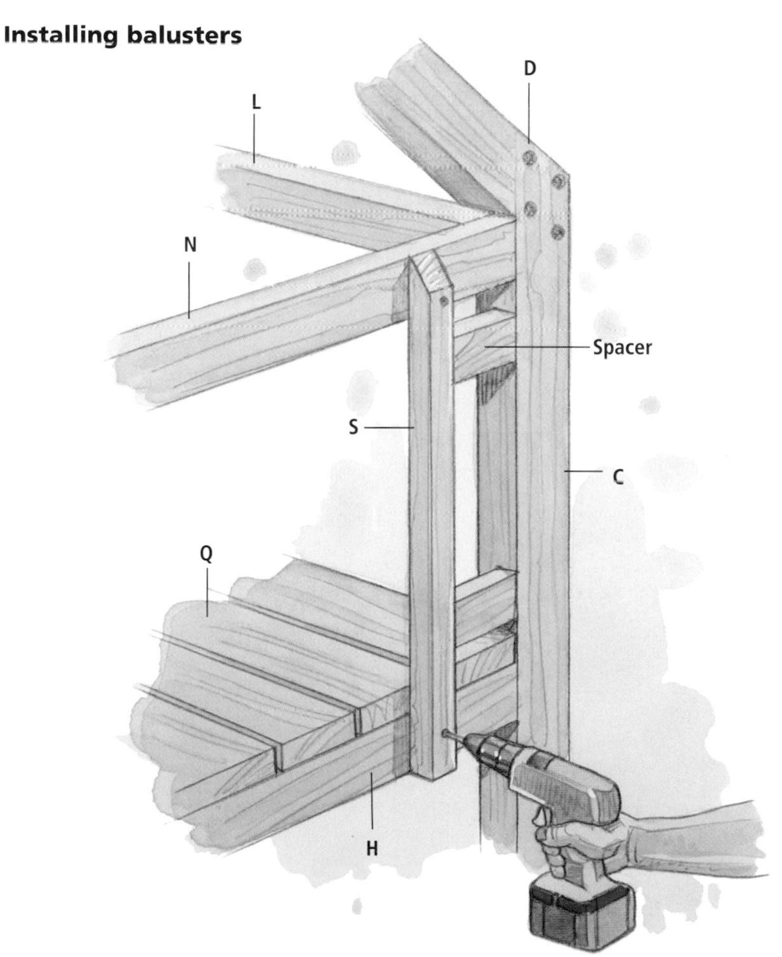

3 Measure to double-check the length of the floorboards (**Q, R**), and cut them to length. Screw them in place on top of the joists, leaving a ⅛-inch gap. An easy way to maintain this spacing is to trap 16d nails between the pieces as you install them as shown left. You'll probably need to rip the final floorboard (**R**) to width before you can fit it in place.

4 Measure the required length of the balusters (**S**); the measurements may vary from the length shown because of construction variations. Cut them to length, cutting one end to a 50-degree angle. Cut two spacers 3⅝ inches wide to help place the balusters 5⅛ inches apart on center (OC) on the two sides where the balusters run from post to post. Make two more spacers 3⅜ inches long to space them at 4⅞ inches OC adjacent to the ladder.

5 Put the spacers in between the post and the first baluster. Drill pilot holes, then screw the baluster in place as shown left. Install the rest of the balusters, using the spacers to keep the spaces consistent.

A KID'S RETREAT (CONTINUED)

Add the facade

1 Cut the threshold (**T**) to length. Notch the ends to fit around the corner posts as shown right. Screw the threshold in place on top of the sandbox side.

2 Lay out the doorway and the window openings on a 4×8 sheet of exterior plywood (**U**). Use the measurements shown below. Cut out the openings with a jigsaw, first drilling a ½-inch-diameter hole in one corner of the window so you have a place to start sawing. Smooth the edges of the cutouts with sandpaper.

Threshold

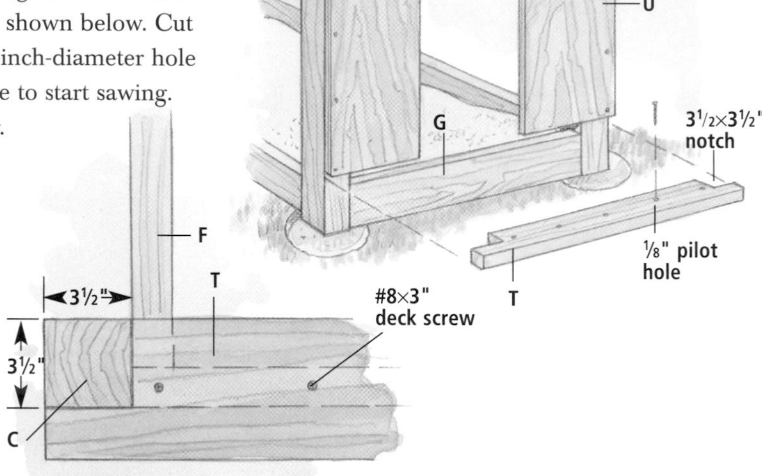

Facade

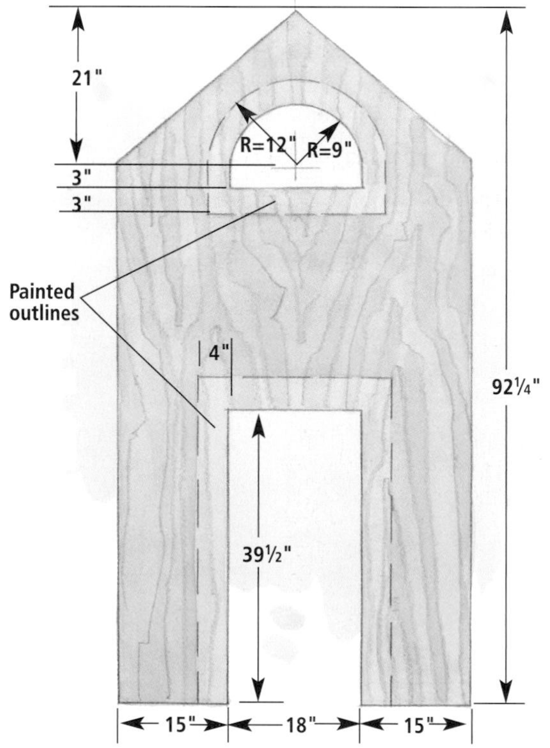

3 Set the facade in position on top of the threshold. Screw it in place temporarily (one screw on each side should do the trick), then climb up on the platform and trace the rafters onto the backside of the plywood. Take the facade down and cut along the lines.

4 To help keep rot at bay, prime and paint the bottom edge of the facade before you install it permanently. When the paint is dry, put the facade back on the threshold and screw it in place.

Sanding the Facade

5 If the edges of the facade overhang the sides of the posts, sand them flush with a belt sander as shown right. At the same time, round over the edges slightly to help prevent splinters.

6 Prime and paint the facade. When the paint dries, lay out the door and window outlines as shown above and paint them a contrasting color.

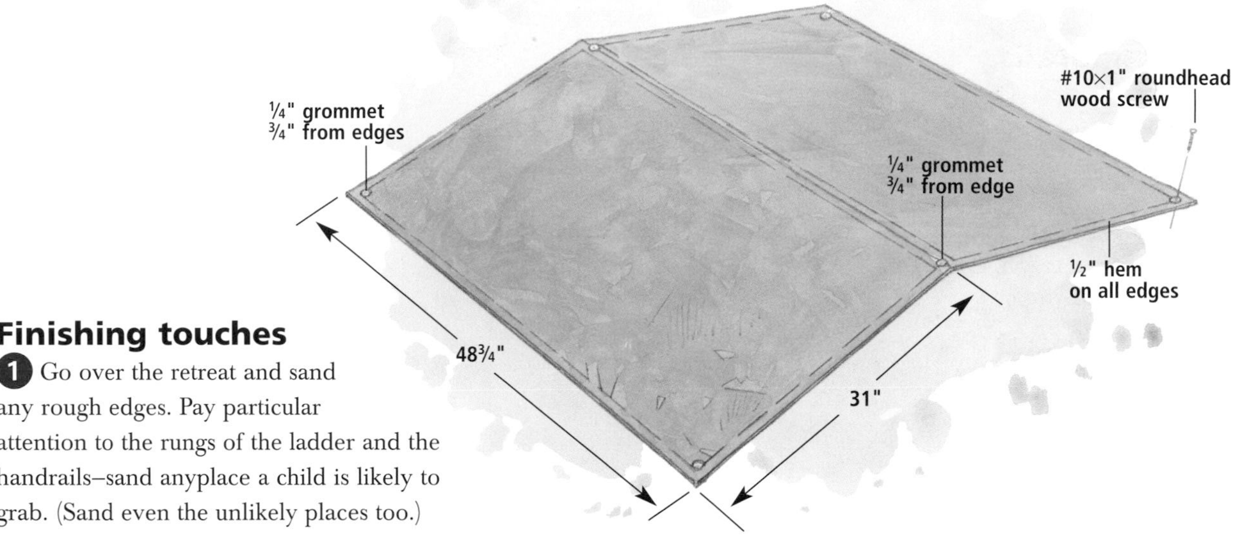

Finishing touches

❶ Go over the retreat and sand any rough edges. Pay particular attention to the rungs of the ladder and the handrails–sand anyplace a child is likely to grab. (Sand even the unlikely places too.)

❷ Fill the sandbox with play sand–you'll need several hundred pounds.

❸ Add a canvas (or synthetic) roof to the platform. A local awning shop can make up the roof as shown above. Screw the roof to the retreat through the grommets around the edges.

❹ Hang the swings. You can get swings that are approved for safety from the suppliers listed in Resources, page 191. Sling or belt seats are the most popular; if you'd like a flat seat, get a lightweight polyethylene seat from one of the suppliers. Wood and metal seats can cause injury if they hit someone.

How Can the Kids Help?

Although construction of this retreat should be left to skilled adults, there are a few places where your kids can help out. Start by showing them where to dig the holes for the posts.

If you have two drills, use one to drill the pilot holes and let responsible youngsters drive in the screws with the other. Many older children will be happy to drive screws for you all day long. If they have trouble sinking the screws all the way home, have them rub a little wax (an old candle works great) on the threads. The screwdriver can slip out of the screw head with great force, and often at about eye level. You and the child should both wear safety glasses.

As you work, take the time to clean up the sawdust and scraps and dispose of them immediately. Some treated lumber leaves hazardous residue, so it is best to keep children away from scraps and sawdust.

High-Rise Playhouse

Every kid would like a place to call his or her own. Someplace to pretend or just daydream on a summer afternoon. It would sometimes serve as a hideout or a clubhouse, but it would always be a place to escape from chores and homework and the adult world. A place like that up in the air would be just about kid nirvana. And that's just what this project provides: a terrific playhouse on tall legs.

Building the playhouse is straightforward. It is framed much like a standard house–a really short house. Use pressure-treated lumber (or a naturally rot-resistant species of wood such as cedar or redwood) for the posts and floor joists. Composite decking material is great for the porch floor because it stands up to the weather and needs little maintenance. Everything else can be untreated wood as it will be painted or otherwise protected from the weather.

Exploded view

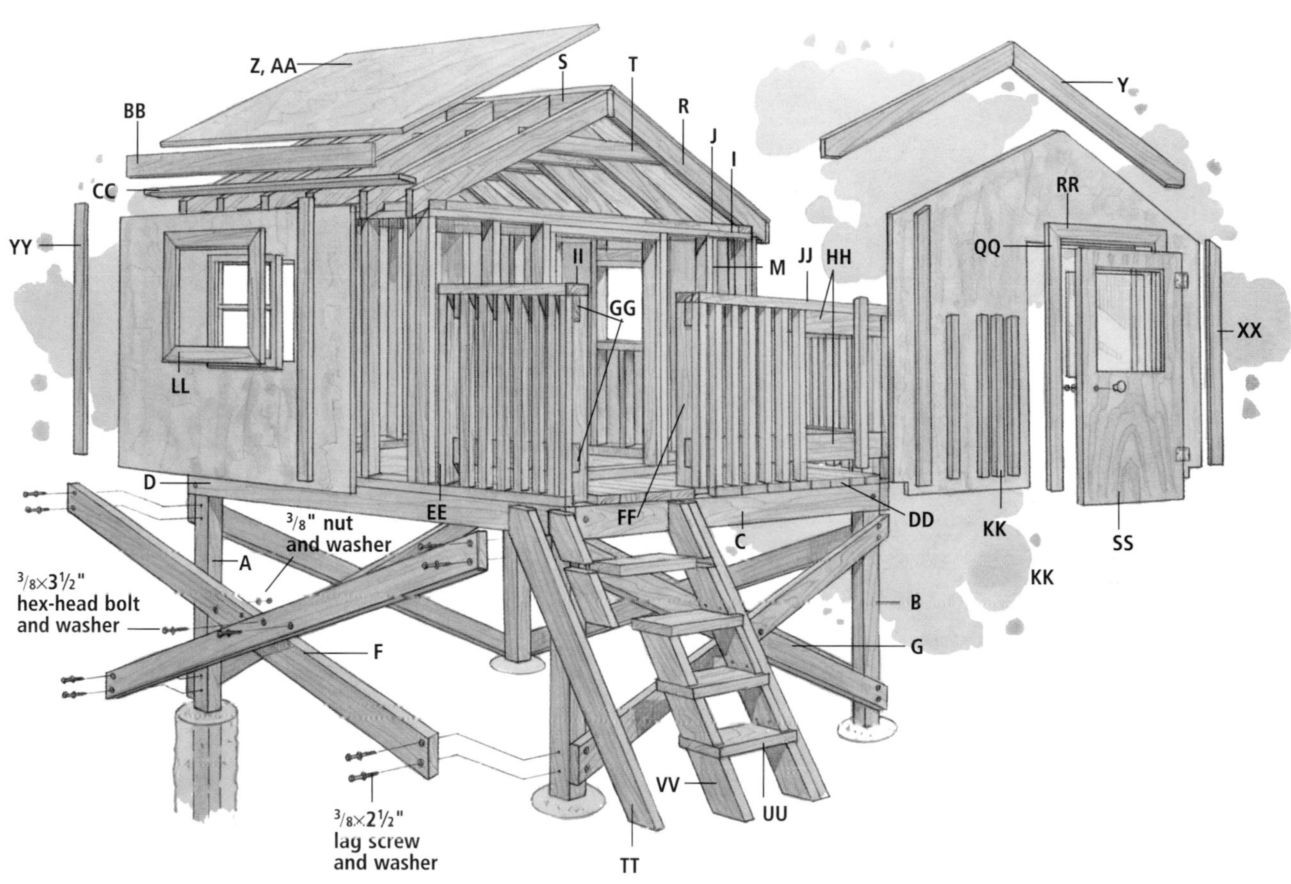

SHOPPING LIST

ALL MATERIAL SHOULD BE ROT RESISTANT.

QUANTITY	SIZE	PARTS
2	4"×4"×8'	A
2	4"×4"×12'	B
1	4"×4"×4'	FF
14	2"×6"×8'	C, E, II, JJ, UU, ZZ
2	2"×6"×10'	D
18	2"×4"×8'	I, J, K, L, O, Q, S, T, EE
14	2"×4"×10'	M, N, O, P, VV
9	2"×4"×12'	R, GG, HH, TT
27	2"×2"×3'	KK
4	1"×6"×12'	F

QUANTITY	SIZE	PARTS
4	1"×6"×10'	G
5	1"×6"×8'	BB, CC, MM
5	1"×6"×6'	Y, MM
17	1"×4"×6'	LL, QQ, XX
3	5/4"×5"×10' DECKING	DD
2	1/2"×1"×8'	OO, PP
3	3/4"×4'×8' A-C PLYWOOD	H, SS
8	5/8"×4'×8' SIDING	U, V
3	1/2"×4'×8' C-D EXT PLYWOOD	AA

HIGH-RISE PLAYHOUSE (CONTINUED)

MATERIALS LIST

QUANTITY	PART	DESCRIPTION	FINISHED SIZE
2	A	SHORT CORNER POSTS	3½× 3½× 108"
2	B	LONG CORNER POSTS	3½× 3½× 144"
2	C	SHORT RIM JOISTS	1½× 5½× 93"
2	D	LONG RIM JOISTS	1½× 5½× 120"
8	E	FLOOR JOISTS	1½× 5½× 93"
4	F	LONG BRACES	¾× 5½× 132"
4	G	SHORT BRACES	¾× 5½× 107"
2	H	FLOOR	¾× 48"× 80¾"
4	I	WALL PLATES	1½× 3½× 96"
2	J	WALL PLATES	1½× 3½× 89"
4	K	WALL PLATES	1½× 3½×73¾"
2	L	WALL PLATES	1½× 3½× 80¾"
22	M	WALL STUDS	1½× 3½× 56¼"
4	N	HEADERS	1½× 3½× 24"
6	O	WINDOWSILL/HEADER	1½× 3½× 24"
2	P	SHORT STUDS	1½× 3½× 22¾"
1	Q	SHORT STUD	1½× 3½× 30¾"
12	R	RAFTERS	1½× 3½× 65¾"
1	S	RIDGE BOARD	1½× 3½× 80¾"
6	T	COLLAR TIES	1½× 3½× 44"
4	U	FRONT/BACK SIDING	⅝× 48× 96"
2	V	SIDING	⅝× 48× 74½"
2	W	SIDING	⅝× 32¾× 74½"
4	X	FILLER PIECES	⅝× 5½× 6"
4	Y	RAKE BOARDS	¾× 5½× 68"
2	Z	ROOF SHEATHING	½× 48× 82¼"
2	AA	ROOF SHEATHING	½× 17¾× 83½"
2	BB	FASCIA BOARDS	¾× 5½× 82"
2	CC	SOFFITS	¾× 5½× 82"
17	DD	DECK BOARDS	1× 5½× 38½"
2	EE	THIN RAILING POSTS	1½× 3½× 41½"
1	FF	RAILING POST	3½× 3½× 41½"
4	GG	SHORT RAILS	1½× 3½× 35½"
2	HH	LONG RAILS	1½× 3½× 64"
2	II	SHORT HANDRAILS	1½× 5½× 37½"
1	JJ	LONG HANDRAIL	1½× 5½× 67½"
27	KK	BALUSTERS	1½× 1½× 36"
12	LL	WINDOW TRIM	¾× 3½× 31"
2	MM	DOOR JAMBS	¾× 5½× 55½"
1	NN	DOOR JAMB	¾× 5½× 26½"
2	OO	DOOR STOPS	½× 1× 55½"
1	PP	DOOR STOP	½× 1× 25½"
2	QQ	DOOR TRIM	¾× 3½× 58½"
1	RR	DOOR TRIM	¾× 3½× 33½"
1	SS	DOOR	¾× 26½"× 55½"
2	TT	LADDER STRINGERS	1½× 3½× 69½"
4	UU	LADDER RUNGS	1½× 5½× 21"
8	VV	RUNG SPACERS	1½× 3½× 12"
4	XX	FRONT AND BACK CORNER BOARDS	¾× 3½× 58½"
4	YY	SIDE CORNER BOARDS	¾× 3½× 54"
5	ZZ	DECK SUPPORTS	1½× 5½× 5½"
1 LB		#8×2½" RUST-RESISTANT SCREWS	
14		⅜×6" RUST-RESISTANT HEX-HEAD BOLTS WITH WASHERS AND NUTS	
12		60-POUND BAGS OF READY-MIX CONCRETE (GRAVEL MIX)	
8		⅜×3½" RUST-RESISTANT HEX-HEAD BOLTS WITH WASHERS AND NUTS	
8		⅜×2" RUST-RESISTANT CARRIAGE BOLTS WITH WASHERS AND NUTS	
36		⅜×2½" LAG SCREWS	
5 LBS		#8×2" RUST-RESISTANT SCREWS	
12		RAFTER/HURRICANE TIES WITH NAILS	
5 LBS		16D COMMON NAILS	
1 LB		8D COMMON NAILS	
80 SQ FT		15-POUND ROOFING FELT	
38'		DRIP EDGE	
80 SQ FEET		ASPHALT SHINGLES	
5 LBS		ROOFING NAILS	
2		HINGES FOR DOOR	
1		DOOR LATCH	
3		2×2' WINDOWS (BUY BEFORE FRAMING THE WALLS, THEN MAKE OPENINGS TO FIT WINDOWS.)	

Set the posts

1 Push a gutter spike or length of rebar into the ground to mark the center of one of the back posts **(A)**. Push another spike into the ground 89½ inches from the first to mark the second back post, as shown right. Tie a length of mason's line to the first spike and mark it 116½ inches from the spike. Tie a line to the second spike and mark it 147 inches from the spike. Push a third spike into the ground where the marks on the lines intersect to mark the center of the third hole. Repeat the process, reversing the measurements to locate the center of the fourth hole. (See pages 180–183.)

Corner post layout

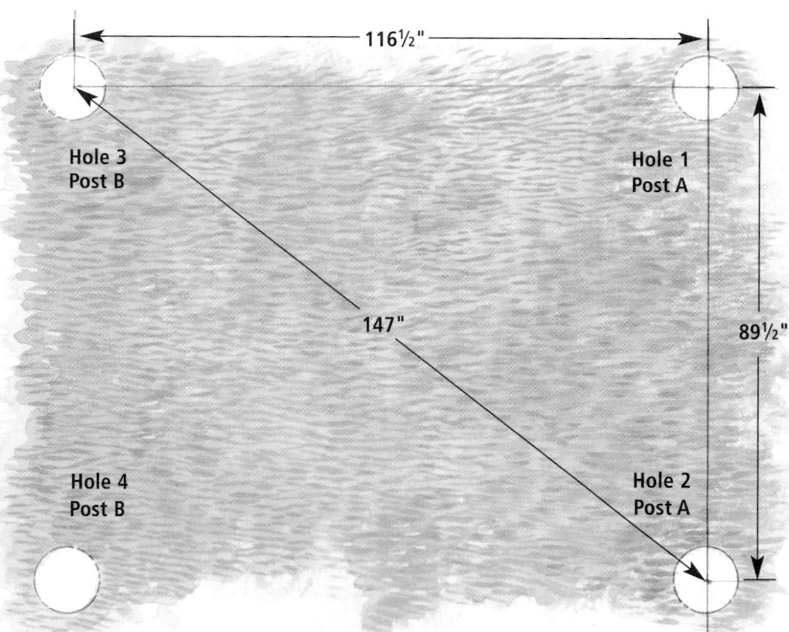

Bracing the posts

2 Mark a 12-inch-diameter circle around each nail with spray paint or flour. Dig the four 12-inch postholes 48 inches deep, or below the frost line, whichever is deeper. Stand the posts in their respective holes. The long posts **(B)** go in the front, but don't cut them to length yet. Brace the posts straight up and down (plumb) as shown left. The distance between the outsides of the posts should measure 93 inches from side to side and 120 inches from front to back. The short posts should measure 60 inches from top to ground.

Joist holes

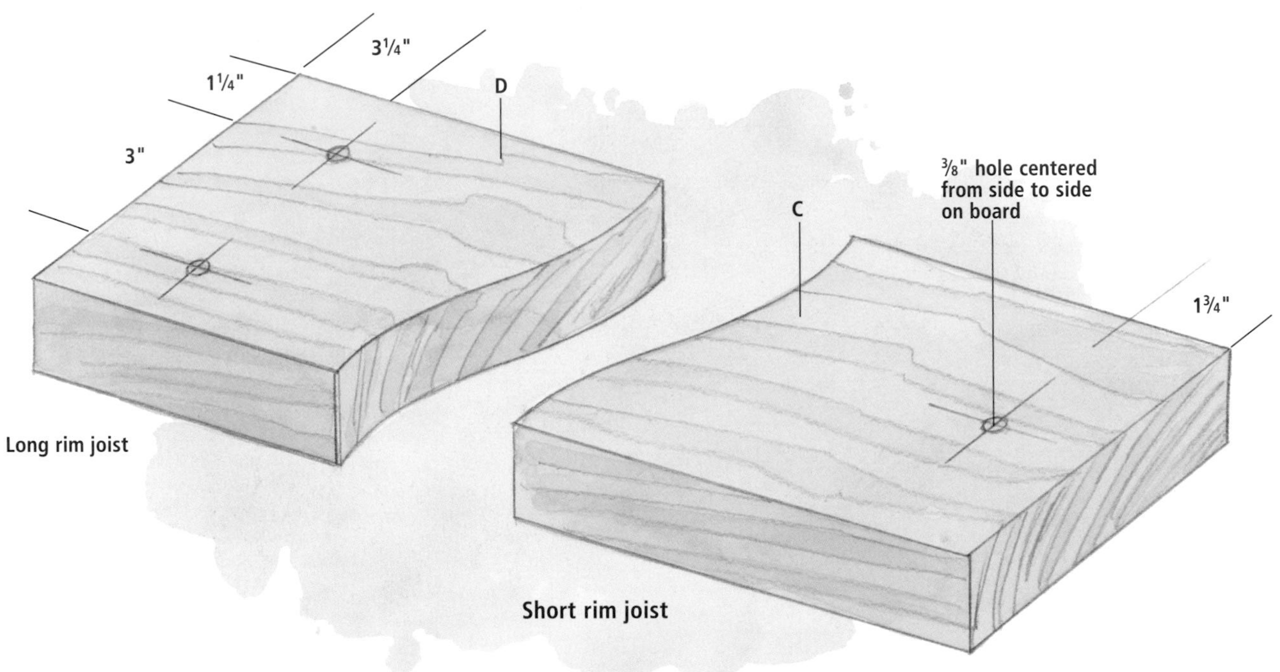

3 Cut the two short rim joists **(C)** to length. Drill a single ⅜-inch hole in each end of each piece. The holes should be centered from side to side and in 1¾ inches from the end as shown above. Have someone help you hold one of the pieces in place at the top of the two short posts. Check to be sure the joist is level, then screw it in place with 2½-inch screws. Once it is secure, put a ⅜-inch-diameter bit in the joist hole and bore through the post. Fasten each end permanently by slipping a washer over a ⅜×6-inch bolt, putting the bolt through the hole, adding a second washer, and then tightening a nut over the entire assembly.

4 Cut the long rim joists **(D)** to length. Drill two holes in both ends as shown. With a helper, hold one of the joists in position against the posts. One end should be even with the joist you just bolted in place. Raise or lower the other end until the joist is level. Screw it in place, then drill the holes through the post for the bolts and fasten it to the posts permanently. Repeat the process for the second long joist. Then position the final short joist between the two front posts and bolt it in place as before.

5 Before proceeding, use a level to make sure the posts are still plumb. Also measure across the diagonals to make sure the assembly is relatively square. (The assembly is square if the diagonal measurements are equal; they are close enough if they are within 1/8 inch.) Adjust as needed, then mix concrete and fill the holes.

6 When the concrete sets you can remove the temporary braces. These will be used as the crossbraces **(F, G)** in the final assembly. Hold them in place, crossed between the posts as shown right. Cut the ends at an angle to make them flush with the posts. Drill holes, then fasten the crossbraces to the posts with 3/8×2 1/2-inch lag screws and washers. Bolt the braces together at the middle with 3/8×3 1/2-inch hex-head bolts and washers. Flex the braces to overlap them.

Installing crossbraces

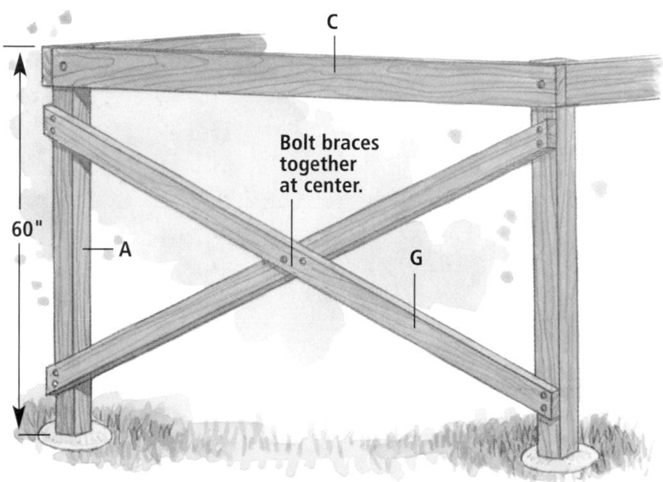

Front view

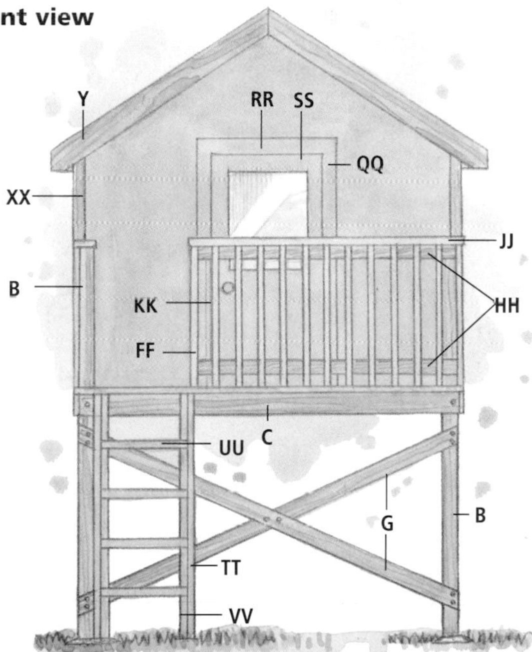

Side view

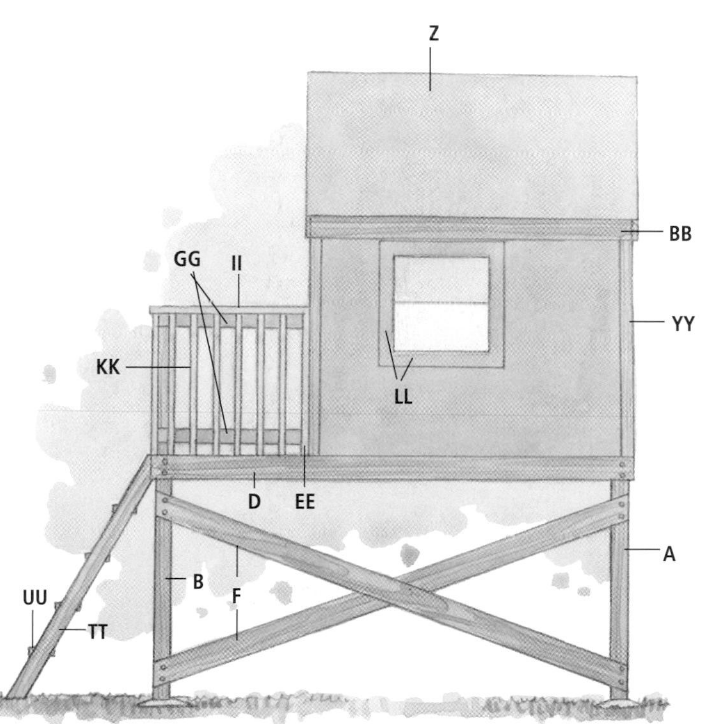

Framing the deck

1 Cut the floor joists (**E**) to fit in between the long rim joists. Nail them in place, following the spacing shown in the Deck Framing diagram right. Note that two of the joists almost touch each other: This gives the floor of the playhouse and the deck boards a surface on which to rest. Don't install the joist marked in the drawing until later; it would interfere with installing the sheathing.

2 Cut the plywood for the floor to length. Hoist the pieces up onto the platform and screw them to the joists.

Deck framing

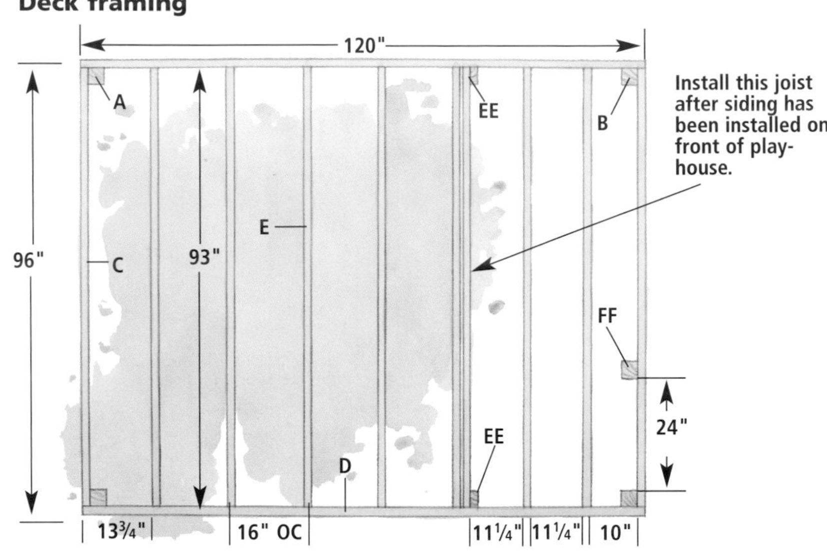

Frame the walls

1 Cut the wall plates (**I, J, K, L**), studs (**M**), headers and sills (**N, O**), and short studs (**P, Q**) to length. Put the pieces for the back wall (two of **I**, six of **M**, one **O**, and one **Q**) up on the deck. Nail the wall together while it's lying down flat on the floor. Use 16d nails, driving them through the plates and into the studs. Space the pieces as shown right. With a helper, stand the wall up and nail it in place across the back of the platform. The outside of the wall should be flush with the outside edge of the plywood floor. If the wall seems unstable, add a temporary diagonal brace along one side to help stabilize the assembly.

Back wall

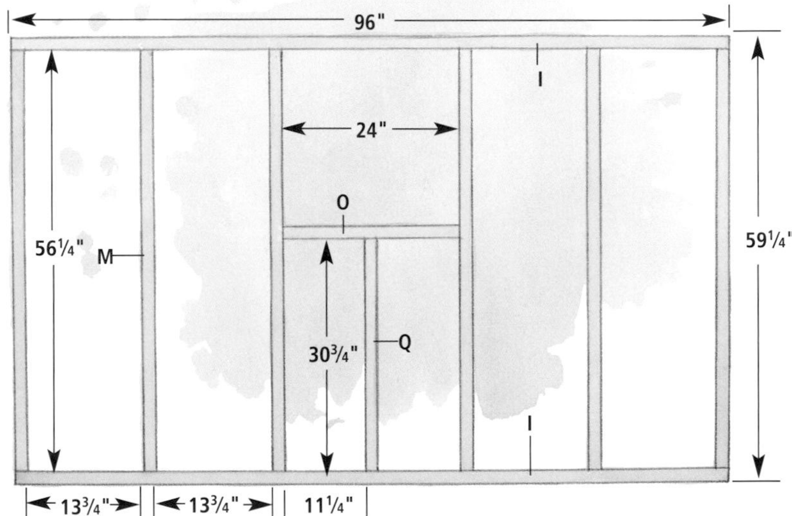

2 Put the pieces for one of the side walls (two of **K**, five of **M**, four of **N**, four **O**, and one **P**) on the floor. Nail two of the headers together to make the built-up header that goes over the window. (Buy the window first, and then frame the opening to match the manufacturer's specifications.) Then nail the wall together as shown opposite. Stand the wall up adjacent to the back wall. Nail it to both the back wall and the deck. Repeat for the second side wall.

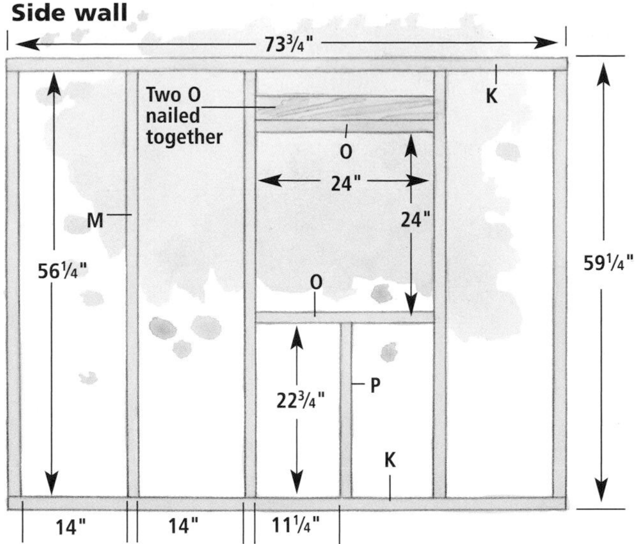

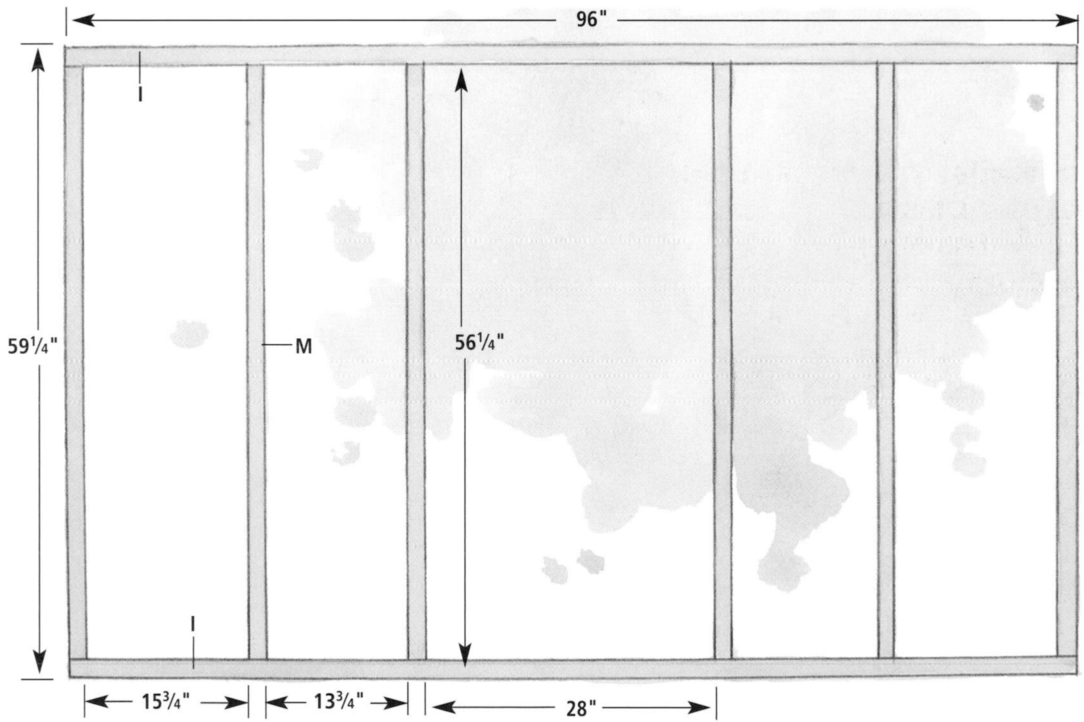

3 Assemble the pieces for the front wall on the platform (two of **I** and six of **M**). You'll have to assemble this wall turned 90 degrees from its actual orientation as it is slightly wider than the space is. Nail the pieces together as shown above. Stand the wall up and nail it in position.

4 Add the remaining four wall plates (**J, L**) to the top of the wall assembly. This helps hold the walls together at the corners. Nail the plates (**L**) along the side walls first (the plates should lap the front and back walls). Then install the final two plates (**J**) along the front and back walls. Use 8d nails to make the connections.

Frame the roof

1 Cut the rafters **(R)** about 2 inches longer than specified. Cut the ridge board **(S)** and the collar ties **(T)** to length. Cut a pair of rafters to the dimensions shown right. If you have one, make the angled cuts with a power mitersaw. Start cutting the notch with a circular saw, then finish the cuts with a jigsaw or handsaw. Test the pair of rafters for fit. Make any necessary adjustments, then use those rafters as patterns for cutting the remaining five pairs.

Rafter detail

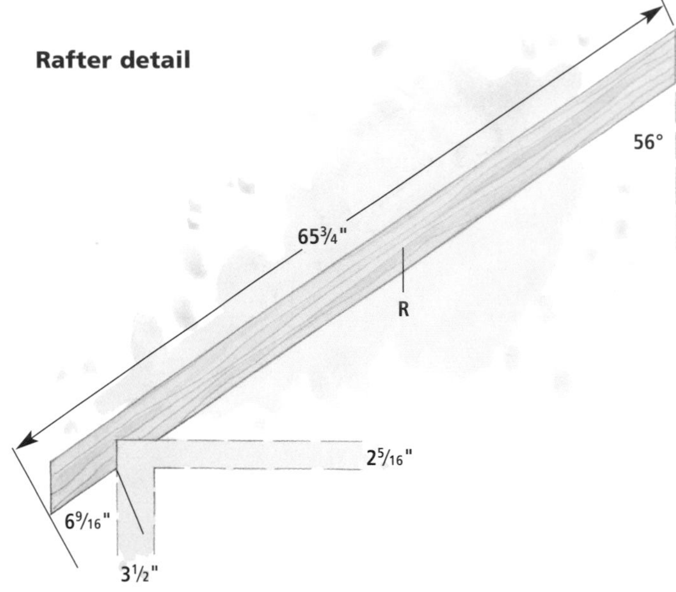

Roof framing side view

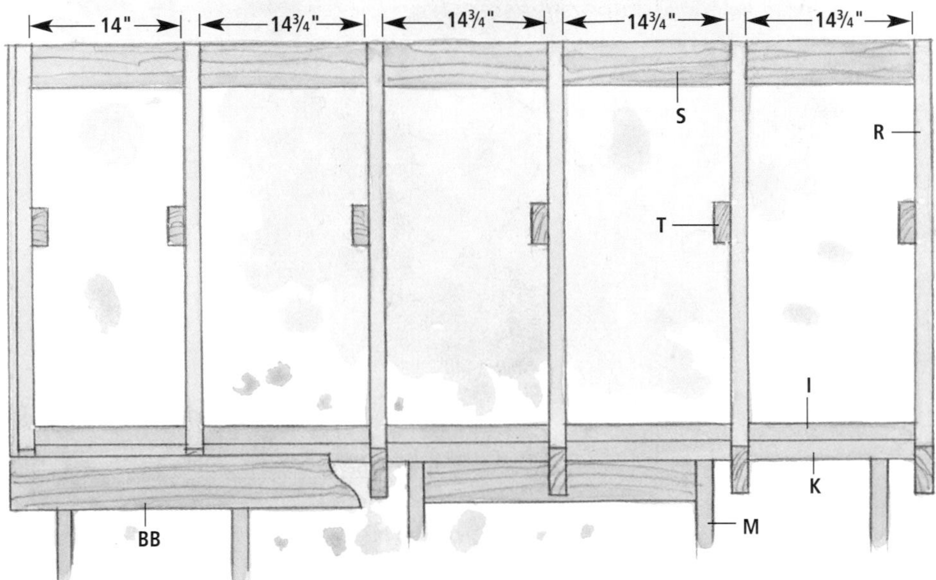

2 Have helpers hold the rafters in place as you fasten them to the walls. Position the first one flush with the back wall. Nail it to the plate. Prop the opposing rafter in position with the ridge board trapped in between. The opposite end of the ridge can rest on the front wall. Nail the second rafter to the plate. Repeat the process with the rafters at the front wall, boosting the ridge board into position. Nail the top ends of the rafters to the ridge board and the lower end to the wall top plates.

3 Fill in the rafters in between, spacing them according to the dimensions above. Complete attaching the roof by nailing hurricane clips to the rafters and top plates.

4 Use 8d nails to fasten the collar ties to the sides of the rafters as shown below and above. These will help keep the walls from bowing outward under the weight of the roof. Place the collar ties toward the back of the house on all rafters except those at the back end.

Roof framing end view

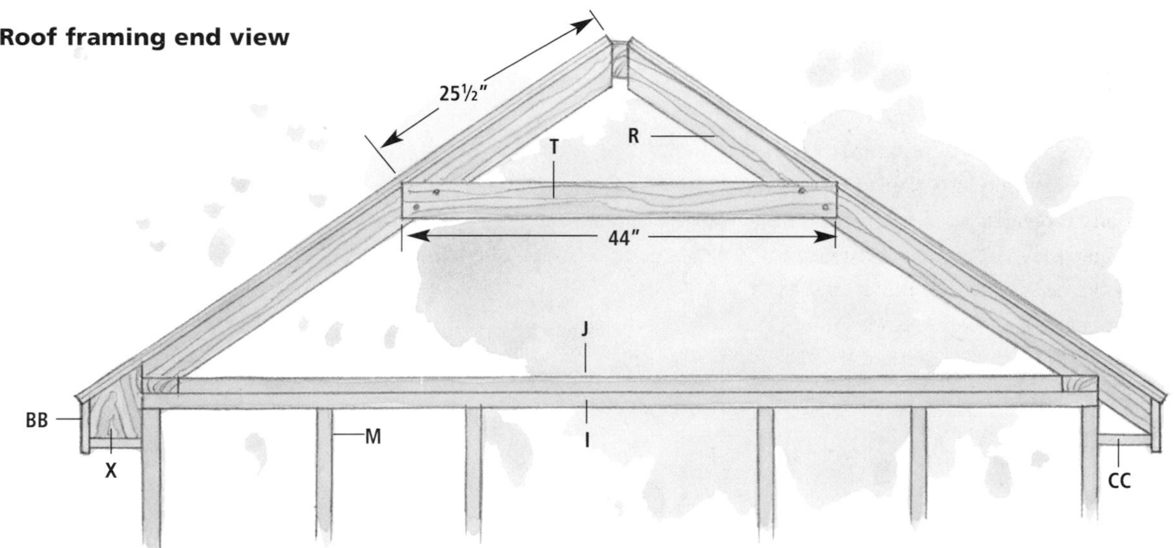

Install the siding

1 The siding on the front and back of the playhouse runs from just below the plywood floor to the roof peak. To make siding installation easier, screw a piece of scrap wood about 3 feet long to the back rim joist and the joist at the front of the playhouse as shown right. This piece of scrap should be about 2 inches down from the topside of the floor. Rest one piece of siding on this scrap with one side flush with the corner of the playhouse. Have a helper trace the roof angle and the window opening on the backside of the siding.

2 Remove the siding and cut along the rooflines with a circular saw. Also make the cuts for the window opening. Set the siding back on the scrap and screw it to the studs. Repeat the process with the other three pieces of siding on the front and back.

Temporary support

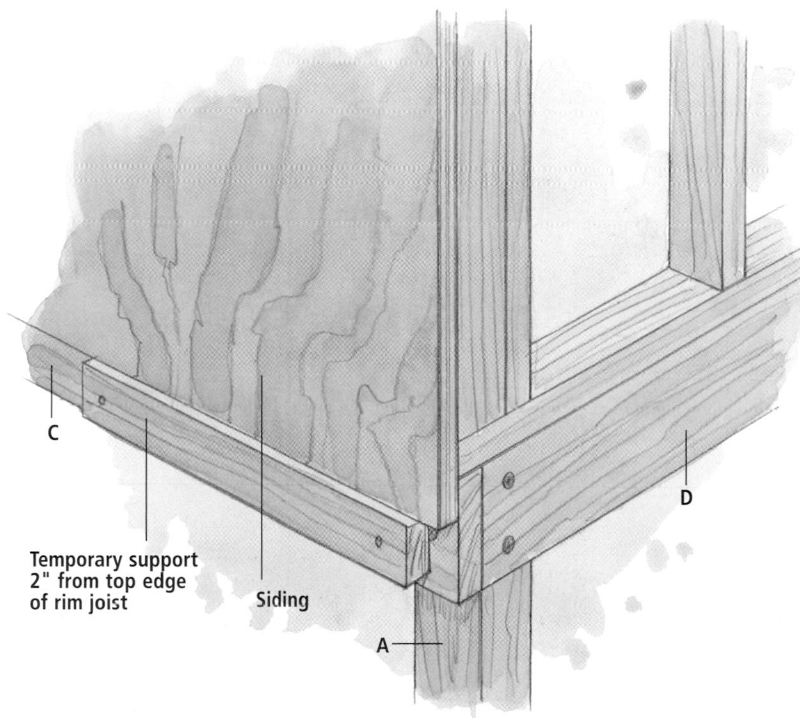

3 The siding butts against the underside of the rafters on the side, so it isn't as easy to use the scrap as a positioner. Fortunately, the pieces aren't as long and are therefore lighter. Cut the pieces to length (and width in two cases). Have a helper hold the pieces in position while you screw them in place.

4 Cut the fascia boards (**BB**) and the soffit pieces (**CC**) to length. They should be 1¼ inches longer than the distance from one outside rafter to the other. Nail the fascia board to the ends of the rafters with 8d finish nails, leaving a ⅝-inch overhang at each end.

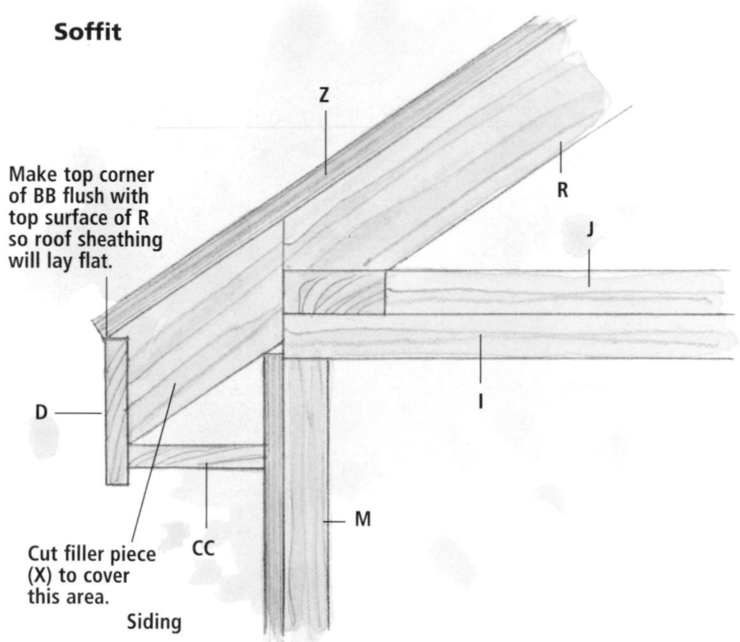

5 Slip the soffit in place behind the fascia board as shown left. Fasten it in place with 8d finish nails driven through the face board and screws driven through the siding from inside the playhouse.

6 Cut the filler pieces (**X**) from scraps of siding. The pieces should close off the ends of the soffit. Screw the pieces to the sides of the rafters.

7 Cut the rake boards 2 inches longer than specified, then trim the top ends at the same angle you used for the rafters. Hold the pieces in place and trace around the fascia board and soffit to mark the pieces for length. Cut along these layout lines. Screw the rake boards in place on the front and back of the playhouse, flush with the top edge of the siding. (These boards will nearly cover the filler pieces.)

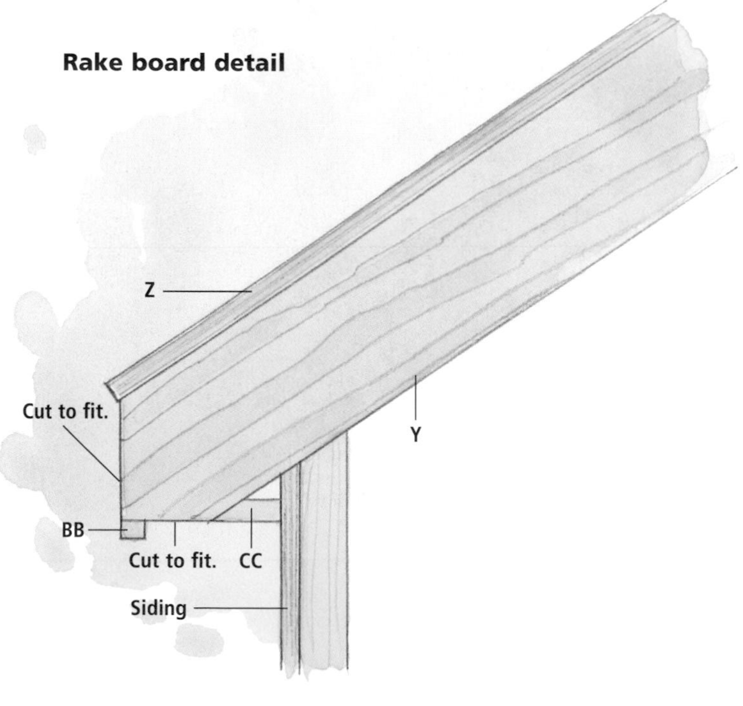

Finish the roof

1 Cut the roof sheathing **(AA)** to length (and width for two of the pieces). The pieces should be long enough to completely overlap the rake boards at each end. Nail the pieces to the rafters with 8d common nails spaced about 8 inches apart.

2 Roll tar paper out across the sheathing. Start at the lower edge of each side, then overlap the first piece with the second as you work you way up to the peak. Hold the paper in place with a few roofing nails. Nail the drip edge around all the exposed edges of the roof as shown in the Drip Edge drawing right.

3 Follow the installation instructions that come with the shingles. Generally a starter row of shingles is installed along the bottom edge of the roof with the mineral-covered tabs either cut off or pointed up toward the peak. The first course of shingles lays right on top of the starter row with the tabs pointed down. For the second course, cut half a tab off the length of the first shingle. (Cutting off part of the tab offsets the joints between the first course and the second, creating a more watertight roof.) The course is completed with full shingles.

Subsequent courses are installed with tabs pointed down. From the second course up, no course begins with a shingle the same length as the one below it. Follow the manufacturer's instructions that come with each bundle of shingles to cover the ridge with a series of single tab pieces bent over the peak.

Drip edge

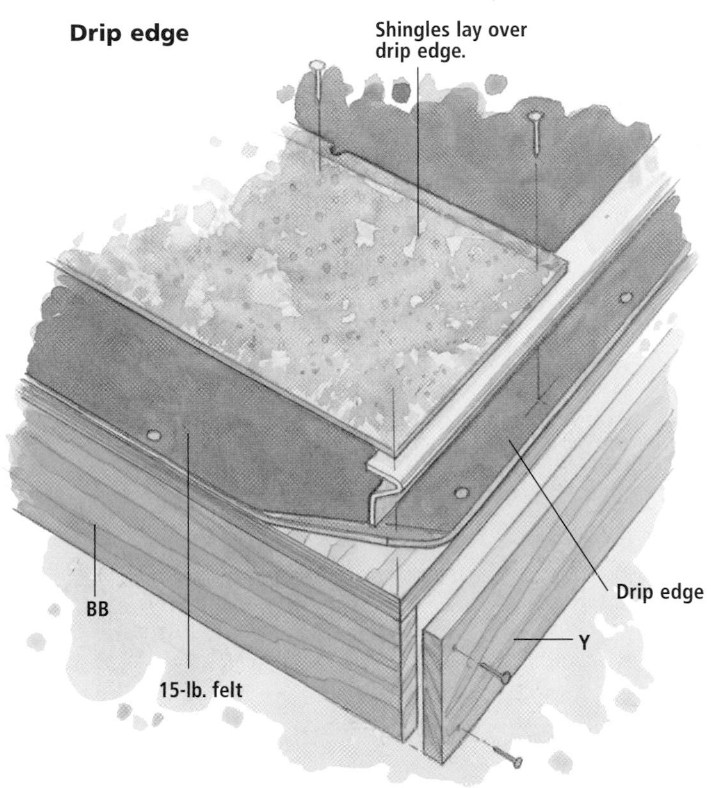

Installing shingles

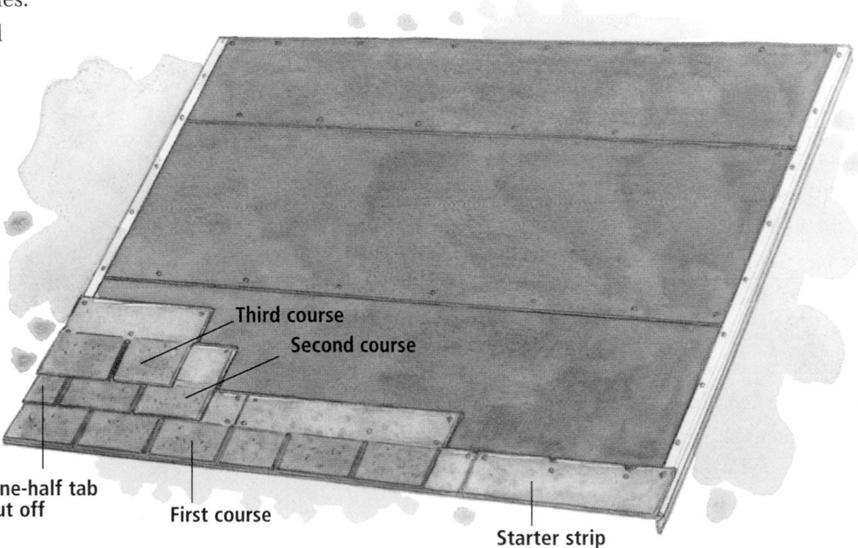

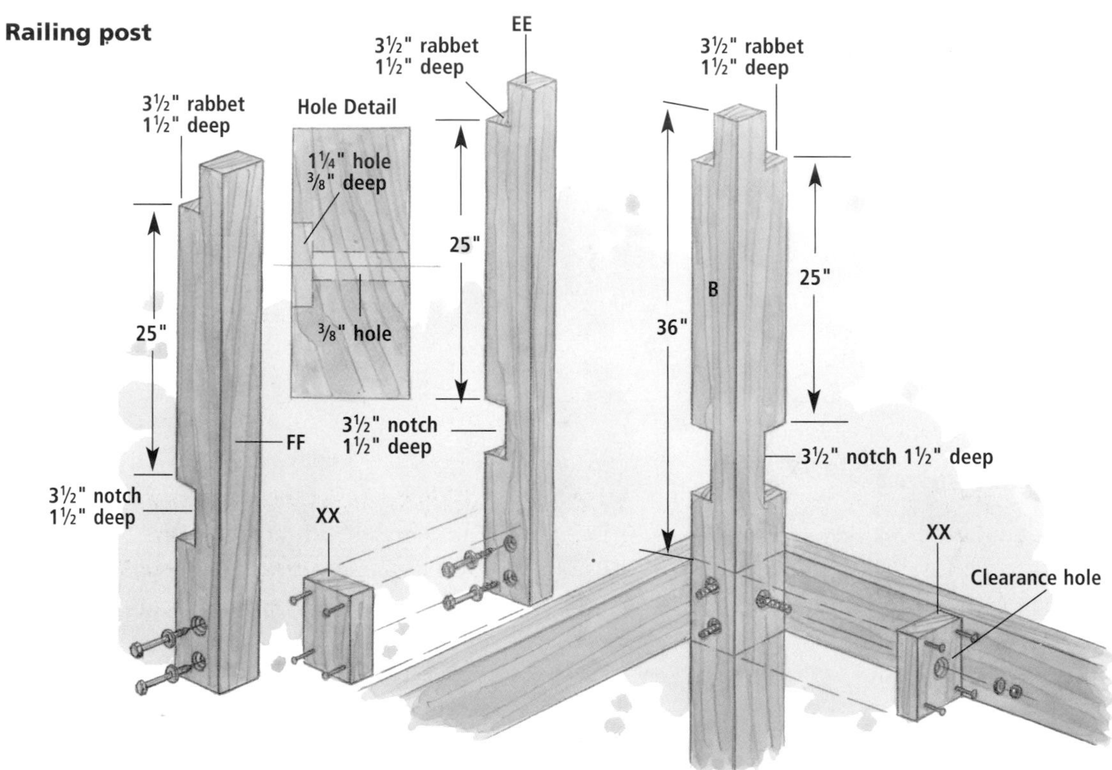

Install the deck

1 Install the final joist (the one you set aside earlier). Position it about ½ inch away from the siding at the bottom of the front wall.

2 Cut the railing posts **(EE, FF)** to length. Drillcounterbores 1¼ inches wide by ⅜ inches deep in the thinner posts **(EE)** as shown in the Hole Detail drawing above then drill holes for ⅜-inch lag bolts centered in the counterbores. Hold one of the posts in place and measure its height in relationship to the top surface of the joists. Mark the same distance on the front corner posts and cut them to match.

3 Notch the posts to house the railings. There are five posts: two thin ones that go against the house **(EE)**, the two front corner posts **(B)**, and the post next to the stairs **(FF)**. Start cutting by setting your circular saw to cut 1½ inches deep. Clamp the thin railing posts **(EE)** together. Make three shoulder cuts as shown right and located as shown opposite. Make matching cuts in the corner post **(B)** that is nearest the ladder. Make the cuts in the corner post **(B)** that is farther from the ladder on the two outside faces of the post.

4 To complete the lower notches, make a series of cuts through the waste, then clean up the area with a sharp chisel. To complete the upper notches, reset your saw to make its maximum-depth cut and cut in from the ends of the boards. This will leave the waste attached by a small bit of wood. Cut through this with a handsaw.

Cutting the notches

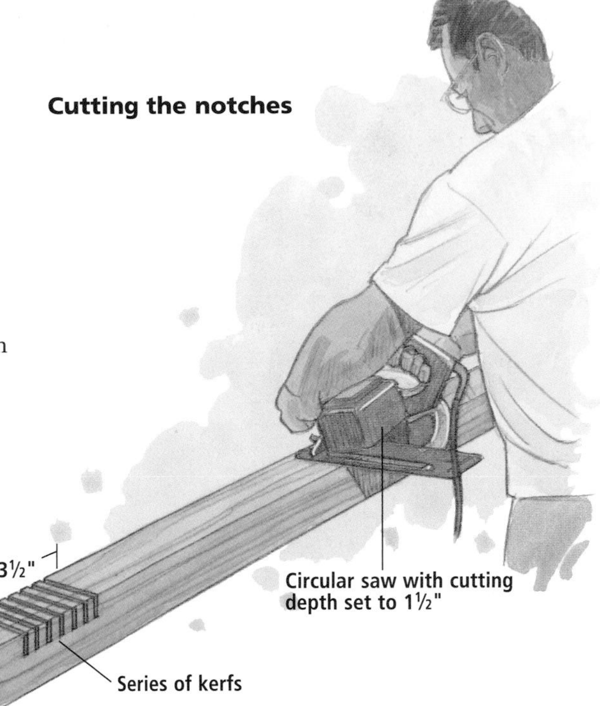

5 Bolt the railing post **(FF)** nearest the ladder to the joists with two 6-inch hex-head bolts. Attach the thin posts **(EE)** to the joists using lag screws, and then screw them to the house framing. Locate the posts as shown in the Deck Framing diagram on page 98.

Easing the edges

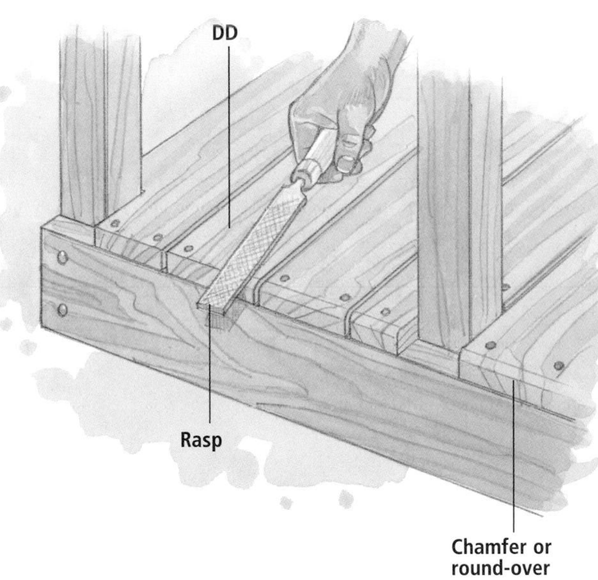

6 Cut five 5½-inch lengths of 2×6 supports **(XX)** to help support the deck boards where they are notched to go around the posts. Predrill holes, then screw these pieces to the railing posts and the corner posts. On the 4×4 posts, the blocks are attached to the side facing the playhouse. For the blocks on the two corner posts, first drill a hole through each block to accommodate the hex-head bolt that is holding the rim joist in place. The tops of the blocks should be flush with the top edges of the joists.

7 Cut deck boards to length. If you're using composite lumber, you'll find it cuts very much like real wood. The boards should reach from the outside edge of the front rim joist to about ½ inch in front of the front wall.

8 Notch the boards to fit around the various posts. Then screw the boards in place, leaving approximately a ⅛-inch gap in between the pieces. While you can drive screws into composite lumber without a pilot hole, predrilling generally works better and looks better. Use a file or a chisel to ease the edges of the pieces where the ladder will be as shown in the Easing the Edges drawing.

Complete the railing

1 Cut the rails (**GG, HH**) to fit in the notches in the posts. Install the shorter ones (**GG**) first, then fit the longer ones along the front of the deck. Screw the rails in place as shown right.

2 Cut the handrails (**II, JJ**) to length. Cut one end of the rail square and miter the other at 45 degrees so the ends can meet in a miter as shown below. Screw the rails in place on top of the posts.

Hand rail

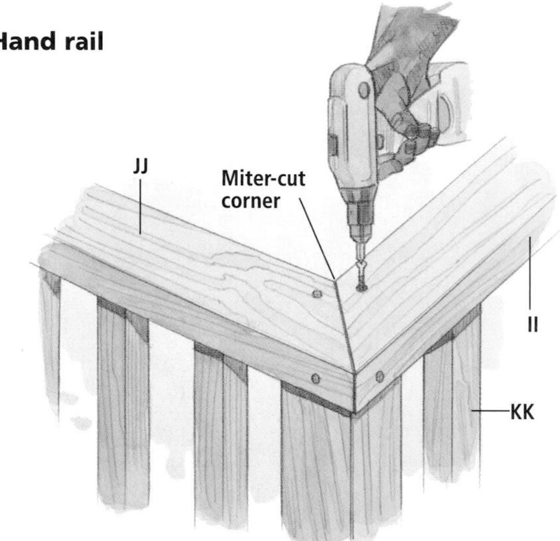

Rail Installation

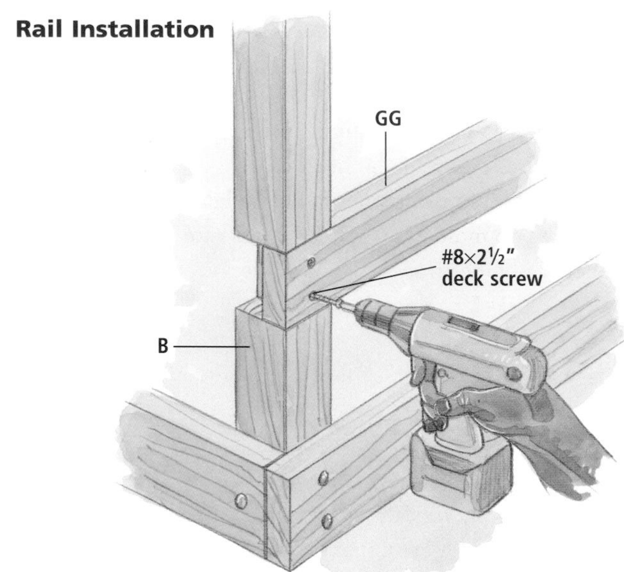

3 Screw the balusters (**KK**) in place along the rails, spacing them 3⅞ inches apart.

4 Screw the stringers to the joist in front of the opening in the railing, driving the screws in at an angle through the side of the stringer and into the joist

Make the ladder

1 Cut the ladder stringers (**TT**) to length, cutting a 30-degree angle at the top end of each as shown right.

2 Cut the rungs (**UU**) to length. Cut the eight spacers (**VV**) from 15-inch lengths of 2×4. Cut 30-degree miters at the top and bottom to make the spacers 12 inches long.

3 Screw a spacer to the bottom of each stringer, with a minimum of three screws each. Put a rung on top of the spacer and drive two screws through each stringer to hold it in place. Put spacers on top of the rung, screw them in place, and then screw the rung in place. Work your way up the ladder, alternately screwing in spacers and rungs.

Ladder detail

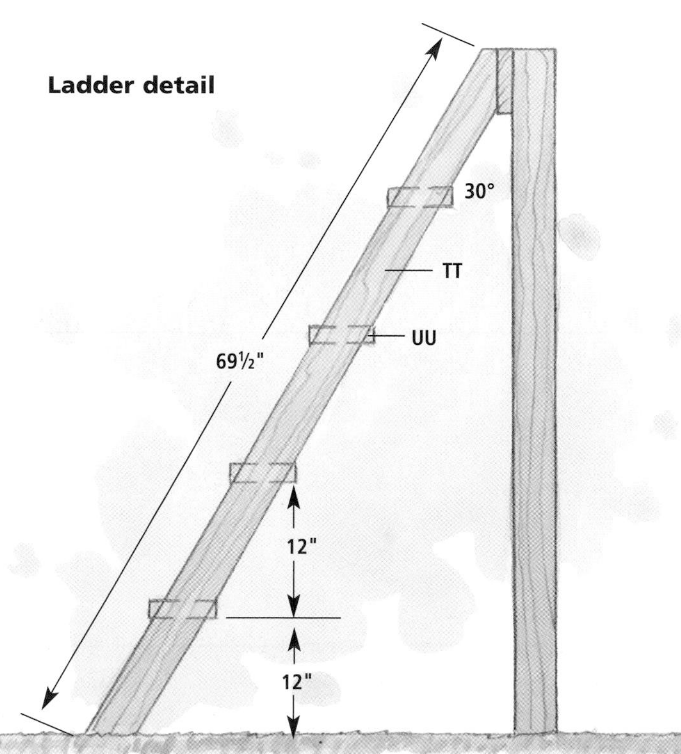

Install the windows and door

1 Fit the windows in their openings. Nail the flanges on the window frames to the siding surrounding the opening.

2 Cut the wood for the door jamb **(MM, NN)** to fit around the inside of the doorway as shown. Nail it in place with 8d finish nails. Cut the doorstop moldings **(OO, PP)** to fit around the inside of the jamb. Nail it in place, leaving a 3/4-inch recess for the door.

3 Cut the top of the front and back corner boards **(XX)** to follow the slope of the roof and then nail them to the corners with 8d finishing nails. Cut the top of the side corner boards **(YY)** to length and nail them to the four corners.

4 Cut the door **(SS)** to size from a piece of plywood. If you want, you can cut a window opening in it as well. Hinge the door to the door jamb. Install the latch to keep the door closed.

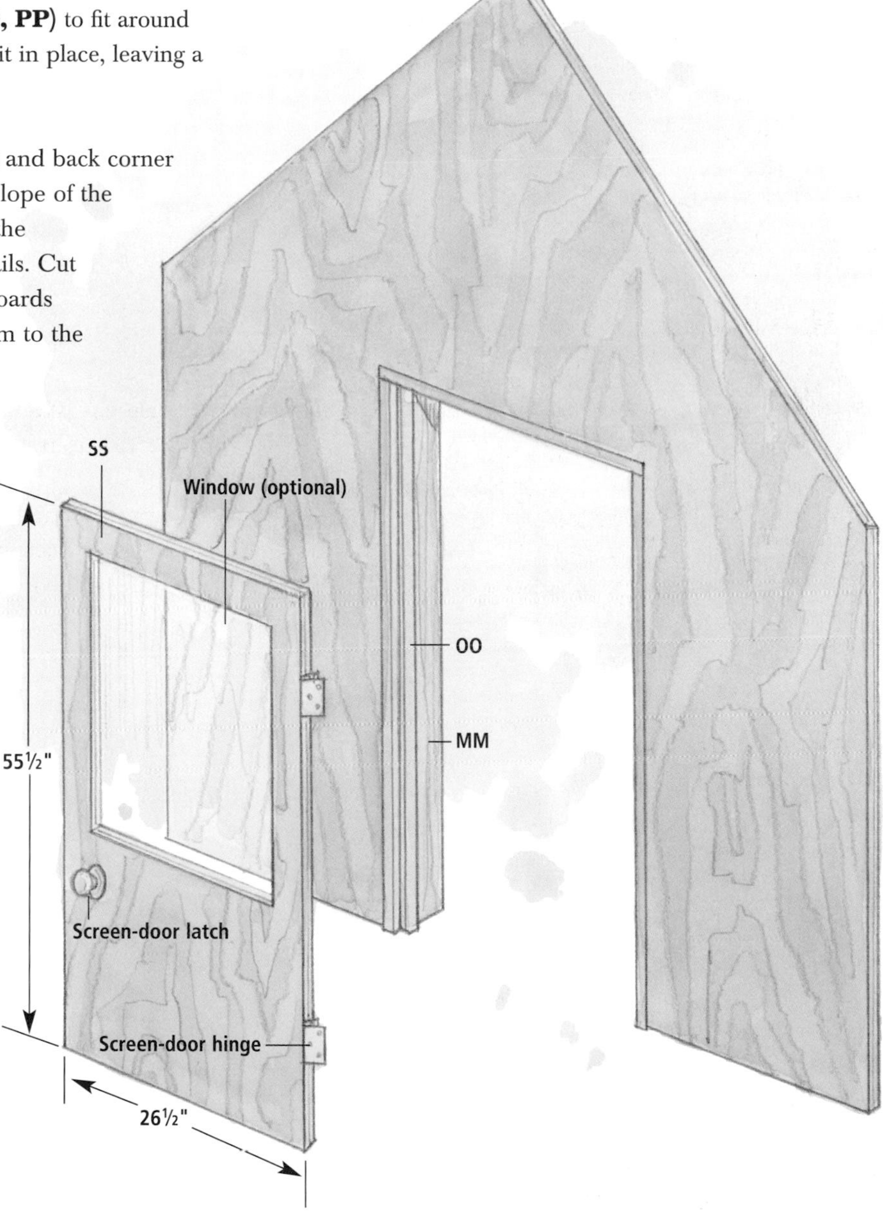

5 Cut the door and window trim **(LL, QQ, RR)** to frame the openings, mitering the corners where the pieces meet. Nail the pieces in place with 8d finish nails.

6 Paint the playhouse. You can insulate the ceiling and put up paneling inside for a more finished look.

Fort Frolic

This project combines a conventional swing set with with a fortlike tower that shelters a sandbox. The swing set is supported at one end by the fort tower. A tarp over the fort serves as a sunscreen and rain umbrella. With this kind of protection, outdoor play can go on come rain or shine.

Jack S. Bowser, who designed this playset, points out that the assembled playset will take up a fair chunk of the yard; you should make sure that your site can accommodate both. The fort's optional slide–which you buy rather than build–extends 8 feet as well, and you'll need additional room for landing clearance. You should place the structure on level ground so the joints of the subassemblies will square up.

Because of the height of the tower and the stress caused by the pendulum action of the swings, check from time to time that all the fasteners are secure. If you build the fort in a sandy soil that won't safely anchor the project, make the corner posts and swing set legs long enough to reach below the frost line, then dig holes for the posts and legs and set them in concrete. Adapt the dimensions given in the directions as necessary to accommodate this added length.

Exploded view

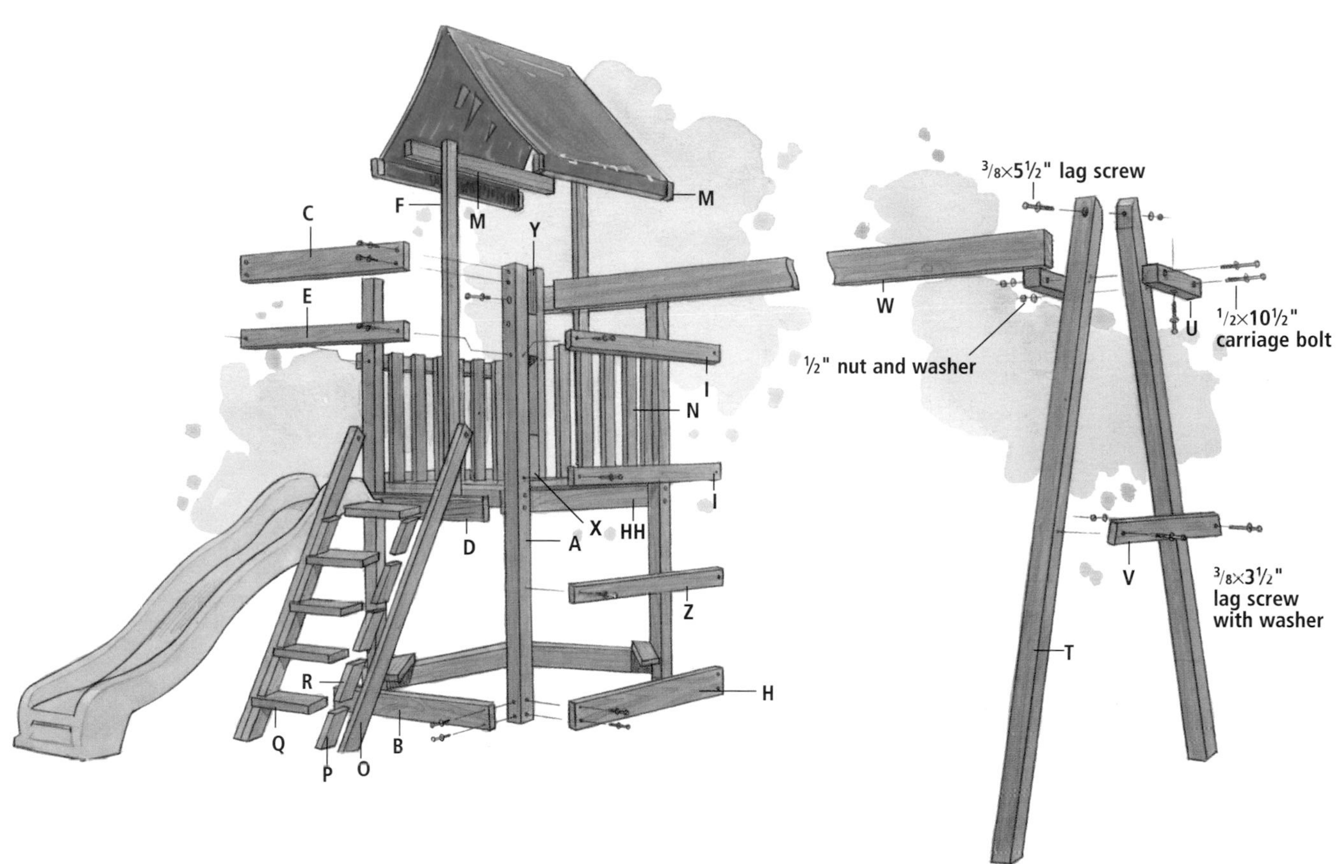

SHOPPING LIST

QUANTITY	SIZE	PARTS
1	4"×6"×12′	W
2	4"×4"×12′	T, U
5	4"×4"×8′	A, X, Y
11	2"×6"×10′	B, C, D, H, HH, J, L, Q, S
4	2"×4"×12′	E, F, G, I, O
6	2"×4"×10′	I, M, P, R, Z
2	2"×4"×8′	K, V
4	1"×6"×10′	N

FORT FROLIC (CONTINUED)

MATERIALS LIST

QUANTITY	PART	DESCRIPTION	FINISHED SIZE
FORT:			
4	A	CORNER POST	4×4×96"
2	B	LOWER FRONT/BACK FASCIA	2×6×51"
2	C	TOP FRONT/BACK FASCIA	2×6×51"
2	D	MIDDLE FRONT/BACK FASCIA	2×6×48"
2	E	FRONT/BACK SAFETY RAIL	2×4×48"
2	F	FRONT/BACK CENTER POST	2×4×83"
1	G	LOWER BACK SAFETY RAIL	2×4×48"
2	H	SIDE FASCIA (2)	2×6×60"
2	HH	DECK SUPPORT	2×6×60"
4	I	SAFETY RAILS	2×4×60"
9	J	DECK BOARD	2×6×48"
4	K	FILLER BOARD	2×4×19½"
6	L	STAKES	2×2×18"
3	M	TARP BOARD	2×4×60"
2	MM	CENTER DECK SUPPORT	2×4×60"
16	N	PICKET	1×6×30"
2	O	LADDER UPRIGHT	2×4×72"
2	P	BOTTOM STEP SUPPORT	2×4×9½"
5	Q	LADDER STEP	2×6×16¾"
8	R	STEP SUPPORT	2×4×9½"
2	S	SANDBOX SEAT	2×6×25"
SWING:			
2	T	LEG	4×4×115"
2	U	LEG BLOCK	4×4×19½"
1	V	CROSS MEMBER	2×4×65"
1	W	SWING BEAM	4×4×144"
2	X	MOUNTING BLOCK	4×4×12"
1	Y	MOUNTING POST	4×4×47½"
1	Z	SWING-SIDE SAFETY RAIL	2×4×60"

QUANTITY	DESCRIPTION
HARDWARE FOR FORT:	
54	⅜×3½" LAG BOLTS
54	⅜" FLAT WASHERS
4	¼" FLAT WASHERS
216	3" DECK SCREWS
64	2" DECK SCREWS
1	TARP, APPROXIMATELY 51×97"
HARDWARE FOR SWING SET:	
3	½×10½" CARRIAGE BOLTS
2	½×9" CARRIAGE BOLTS
5	¾" FLAT WASHERS
5	½" FLAT WASHERS
5	½" LOCK WASHERS
5	½" NUTS
2	⅜×3½" LAG BOLTS
3	⅜×5½" LAG BOLT
4	⅜×10" LAG BOLT
9	⅜" FLAT WASHERS
6	*5" GALVANIZED SWING HANGERS
12	⅜" FLAT WASHERS
6	SPRING CLIPS
3	SWINGS WITH COATED CHAIN

*IF 5" ARE UNAVAILABLE, USE 6" HANGERS AND CUT OFF TOP ONCE INSTALLED TO AVOID RISK OF INJURY.

Counterbores, Clearance Holes, and Pilot Holes

Every lag bolt in this project requires three holes. The first one is a recess (called a counterbore) in the piece of wood that the bolt goes through. This puts the head of the bolt below the surface to protect kids against cuts and scrapes. The second hole, centered in the counterbore, is a clearance hole the same diameter as the bolt. The third hold is the pilot hole, drilled into the piece of wood the lag bolt threads into. It is slightly smaller than the clearance hole, allowing the lag bolt threads to grab the wood.

Directions for drilling the holes occur in the appropriate steps. Except where noted in this project, counterbores are 1⅛ inches in diameter and ⅜ inch deep, clearance holes are ⅜ inch in diameter, and pilot holes are ¼ inch in diameter.

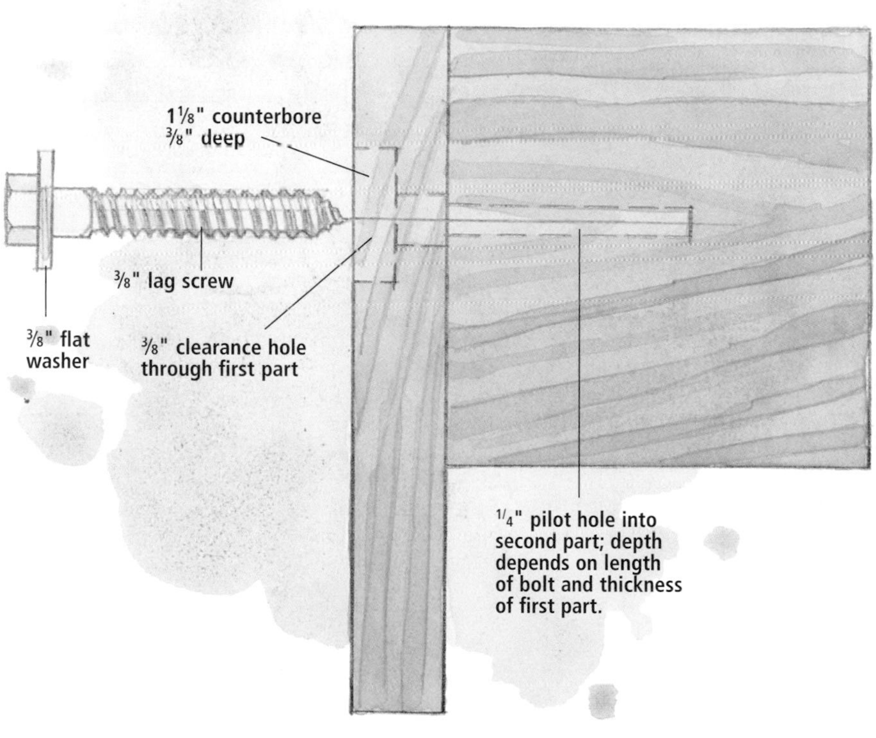

Assemble the front panel

1 The front and back panels are the same, except that the back panel also has a lower safety rail (**G**) and four pickets (**N**) added later. Raising the panels shows the location of the extra rail on the back panel. The Exploded View drawing on page 109 and the Front and Back Panels drawing right show how all the parts fit together. Cut all the pieces of the project as shown in the Shopping and Materials Lists, but don't cut any angles on any of the pieces yet.

2 On a flat surface, place two corner posts (**A**) 48 inches apart. Measuring from the bottom of each post, mark off distances of 1/2 inch, 48 1/2 inches, and 78 3/4 inches. Position the lower front fascia (**B**) across the lower end of the posts with its bottom edge at the 1/2-inch mark and with an overhang of 1 1/2 inches at each end. Check that the fascia is square with the posts and that the posts are 48 inches apart on the outside.

3 Counterbore and drill two holes through the fascia and into the post below. Start by drilling a 1 1/8-inch-diameter hole 3/8 inch deep for each of the bolts using either a spade bit or Forstner bit. Center a 3/8-inch-diameter hole in the center mark left by the bit and drill through the fascia. Hold the fascia in place and drill a 1/4-inch hole centered in the clearance hold 2 inches into the post. Attach the fascia with 3/8×3 1/2-inch lag bolts and flat washers.

Front and back panels

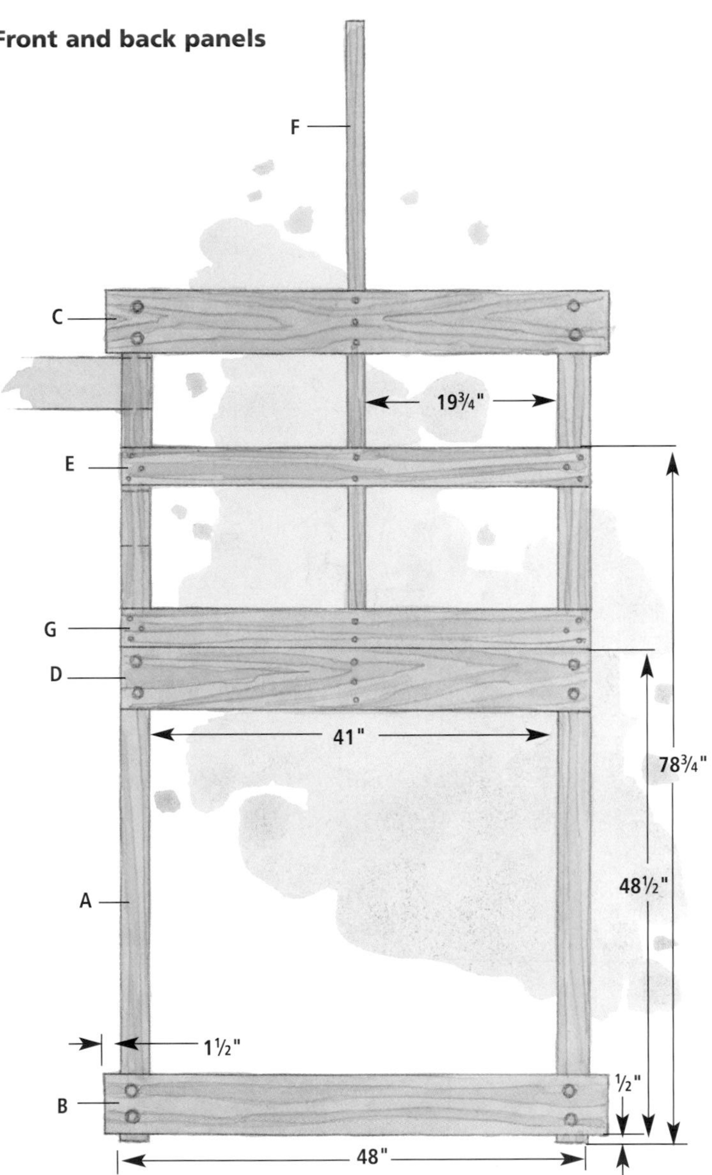

Drill the Counterbores and Clearance Holes at the Same Time

You can save time by drilling the counterbores all at once and then drilling the clearance holes through them before beginning assembly.

Set aside the pieces indicated in the drawing, then drill the counterbores and clearance holes as indicated. All the counterbores in these boards are 1⅛ inches in diameter and clearance holes are ⅜ inch in diameter (see page 111).

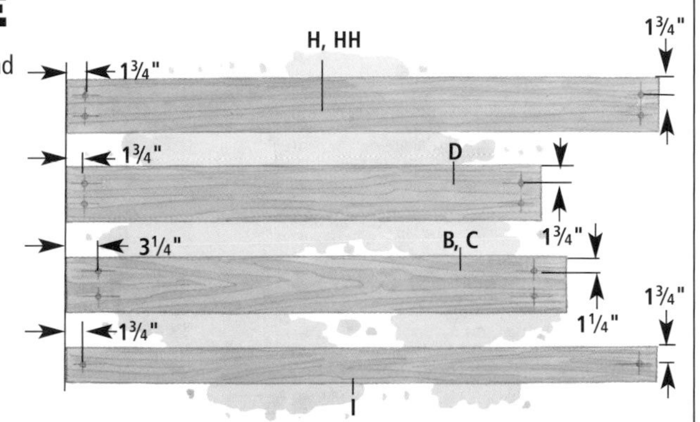

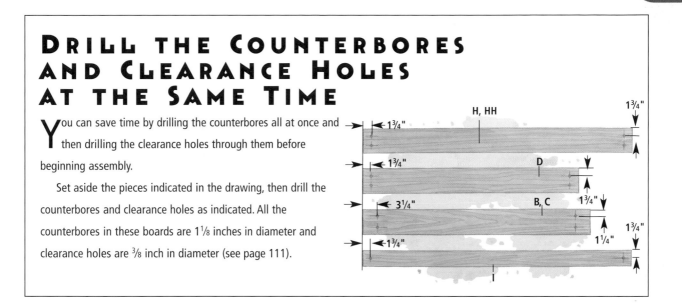

4 Position the top front fascia **(C)** across the other end of the posts, with its upper edge flush with the post tops. Again check that the fascia is square and the posts are 48 inches apart, then attach as in Step 3.

5 Position the middle front fascia **(D)** across the posts with its upper edge at the 48½-inch mark and attach as in Step 3.

6 Position the front safety rail **(E)** across the posts with its upper edge at the 78¾-inch mark and attach it to both posts with three 3-inch deck screws, arranging them in a triangle as shown on the Front and Back Panels drawing. To minimize the chance of splitting the wood, drill ⅛-inch pilot holes first.

7 Put the front center post **(F)** midway between the corner posts and against the back of the safety rail **(E)**. Align the bottom of the center post flush with the bottom of the middle fascia. Check that the space between the facing surfaces of the center post and adjacent corner post is 19¾ inches. Attach the center post with 3-inch deck screws: three in the top fascia, two in the safety rail, and three in the middle fascia.

Assemble the back panel

1 Assemble the back panel the same way you did the front. Add the lower back safety rail **(G)**, positioning it on top of the middle back fascia **(D)**. Attach it with six 3-inch deck screws in the pattern used for the front safety rail. Attach the back center post the same way you attached the front center post, driving an additional two screws into the back safety rail.

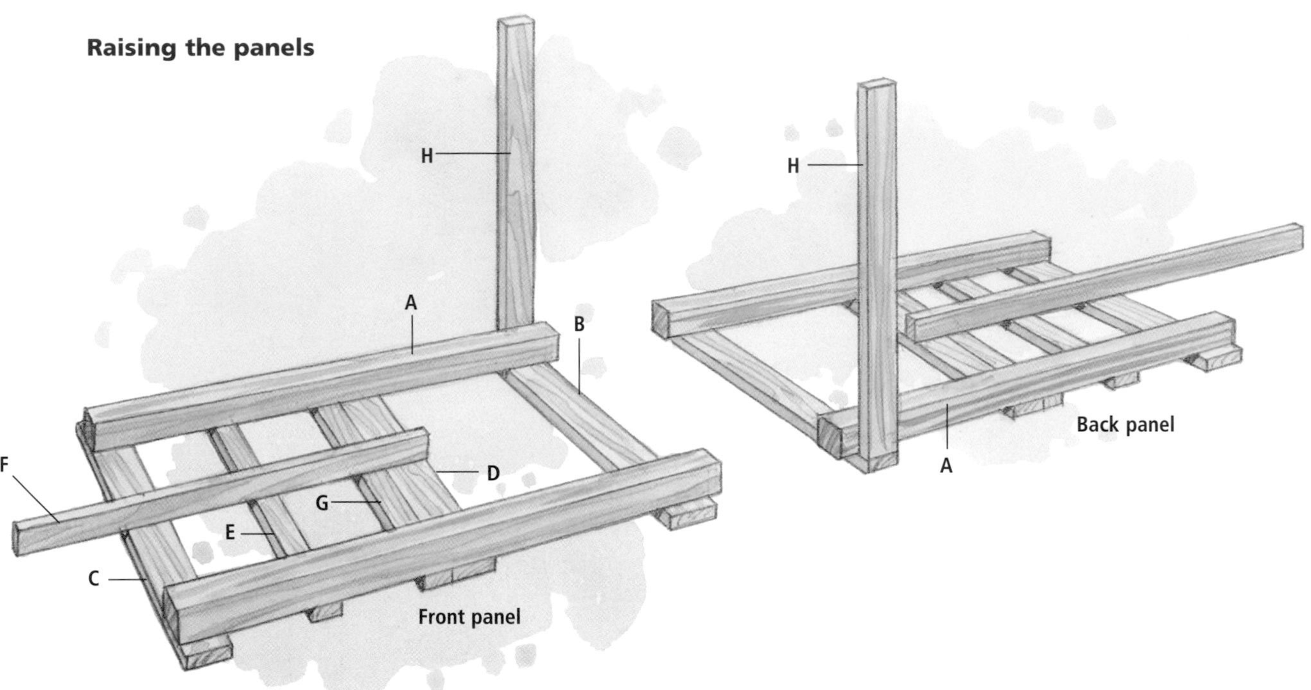

Raise the panels to construct the fort

1 Place the front and back panels on a flat surface with the fascias on the underside and the tops of the center posts pointing in opposite directions, as shown above. Position a side fascia (**H**) at the bottom of either side of the front panel so that it rests squarely and flush against the 1½-inch overhang created by the lower front fascia.

2 Counterbore and then drill ⅜-inch diameter holes through the fascia, then drill ¼-inch diameter holes into the posts, as before. Attach the side fascia with two ⅜×3½-inch lag bolts and ⅜-inch flat washers. For the back panel, attach a side fascia to the corner post on the other side, as shown above.

3 With a helper, stand both panels upright. Join them by attaching the free ends of the side fascia boards to the other panel, using lag bolts as described above. The side fascias should be square and flush against the 1½-inch overhang at the bottom of the panels.

4 Position both deck supports (**HH**) with their top edges 47 inches from the bottom of the posts, placing them on the inside of the corner posts as shown left. Attach them with two lag bolts through the ends into the corner posts, as you did on the side fascias.

5 Position the top edge of the lower side safety rail (**I**) 50½ inches from the bottom of the corner posts, on the outside of the corner posts. Attach it to the front and back panels with a lag bolt at each end, as described above for the side fascias. The lower edge of the piece should be flush with the top of the deck support (**HH**).

Side view

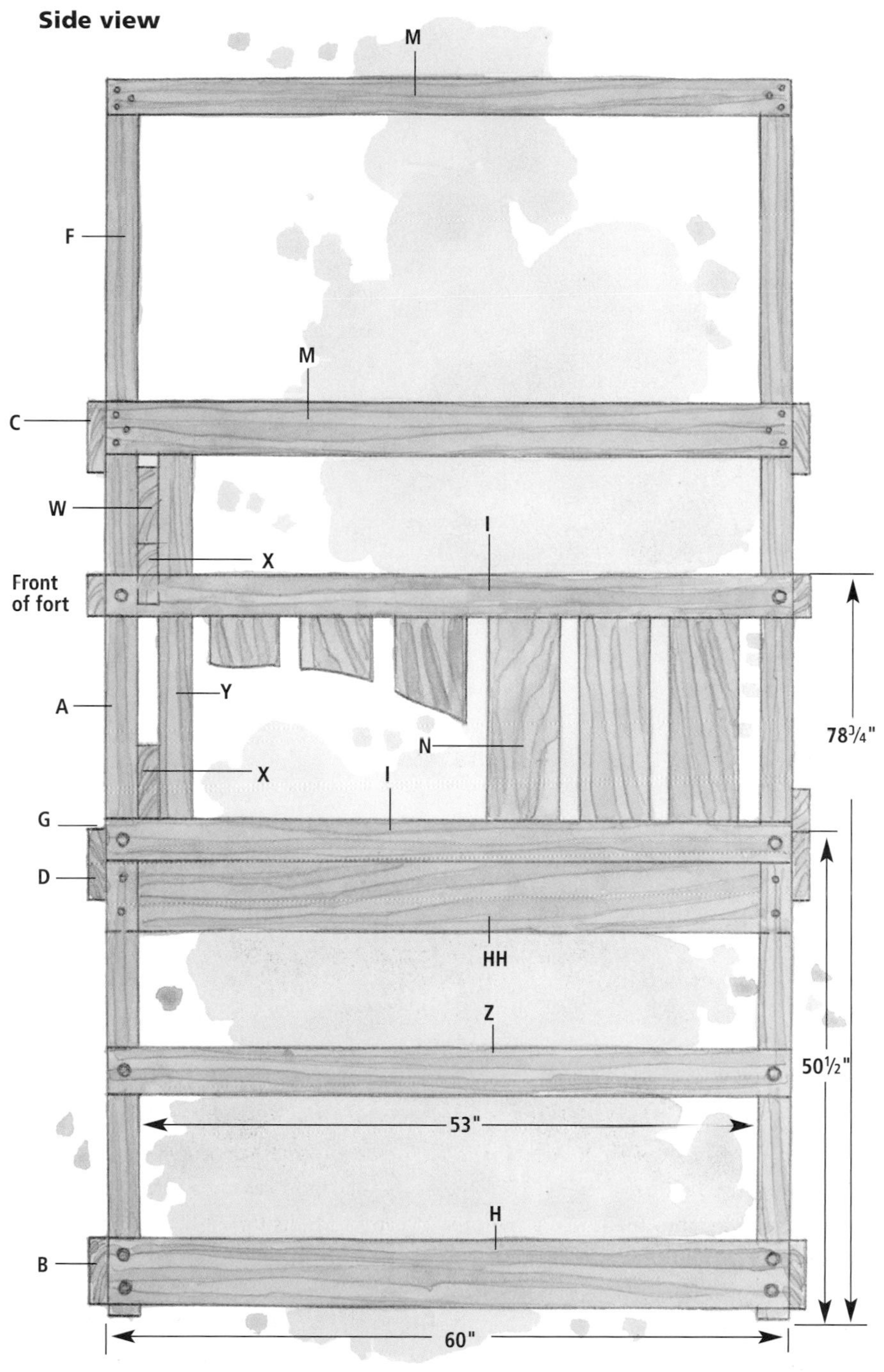

Assemble the ladder

1 Lay a ladder upright **(O)** on a flat surface.

2 Place a bottom step support **(P)** at the bottom end of the ladder upright with the angled end toward the top of the upright. Align the edges and bottom with the upright and secure with four 3-inch screws.

3 Place a step support **(R)** against the ladder upright and 1½ inches away from bottom step support, using a ladder step as a spacer. Align the support with the edges of the upright and secure with four 3-inch screws. Continue placing supports until there are four supports on the upright. Make sure the supports are exactly as shown at right.

4 Repeat the process to build the second ladder upright. Double check against the drawing to make sure that you aren't making two left sides or two right sides of the ladder.

5 Place one ladder upright on a flat surface with the supports facing up. Place the ladder steps **(Q)** in the diagonal grooves created by the step supports. Place other ladder upright, with the supports down, over the ladder steps. Align the edges of the step with the edges of upright. Attach the steps from the outside of the upright using two 3-inch screws for each step.

6 Flip the ladder over and align the edges of the step with the edges of the other upright. Attach the steps from the outside of the upright using two 3-inch screws for each step. Attach the top step once the ladder is attached to the fort.

7 Attach the ladder uprights to the center post and corner post with three 3-inch deck screws for each side. Make sure that the top step is even with the top of the middle fascia. If the ground is slightly uneven, you may need to trim the top of the ladder to get it at the right height.

Ladder

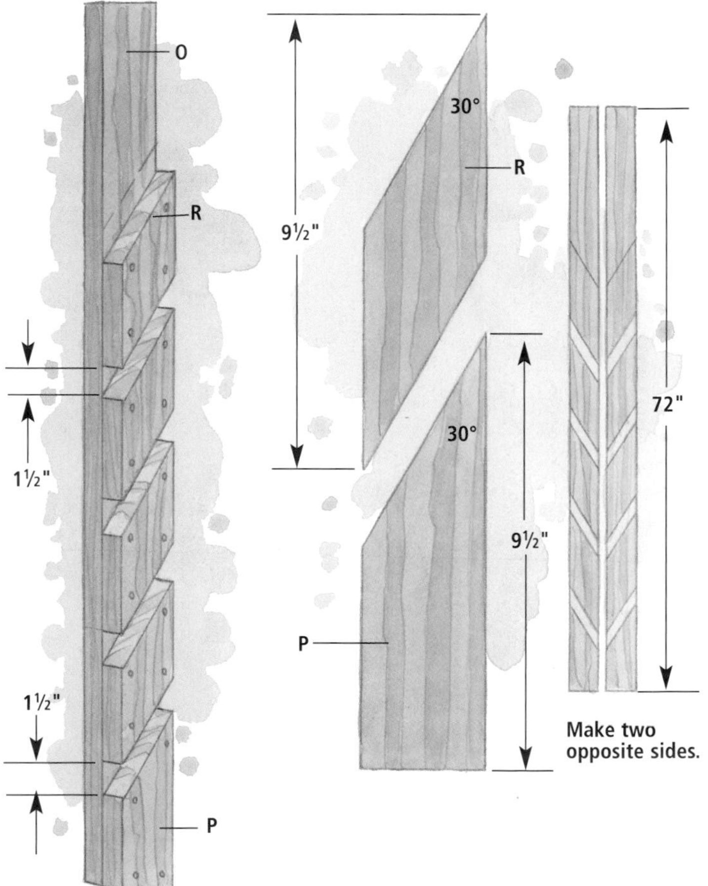

Add the deck

1 Lay the nine deck boards **(J)** across the two deck supports **(HH)** already in place, but do not attach them. Add the other two deck supports **(MM)**, running them under the deck boards and attaching them to the center posts **(F)** using three 3-inch deck screws for each joint. Place four filler boards **(K)** between each corner post and the adjacent center post, as shown below. Attach each filler board with one 3-inch deck screw at each end; to minimize the chance of splitting the wood, drill 1/8-inch pilot holes first. Space the deck boards evenly over the deck supports, making sure that each is set flush against the inside surface of the lower safety rail **(I)**. Attach each board with five 3-inch deck screws in the pattern shown below, predrilling pilot holes.

2 Install the second lower side safety rail **(I)**.

Deck

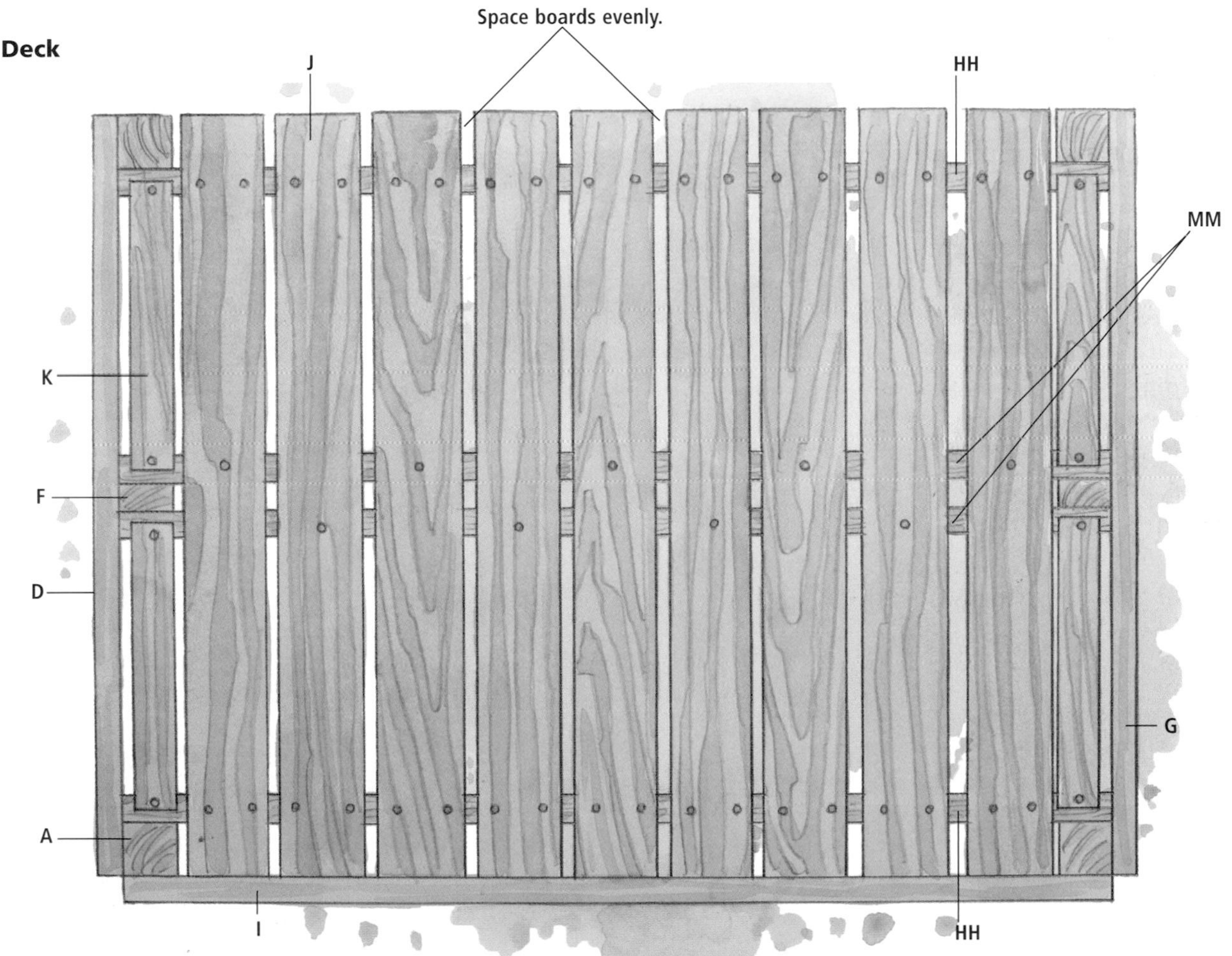

Anchor the fort

1 The fort is anchored to the ground with the help of four 18-inch stakes **(L)**, cut from the leftover ends of three boards; see the Shopping List on page 109. Cut the stakes to width, then make 45-degree cuts to create a pointed lower end.

2 With the fort in position, drive a stake into the ground flush against an inside face of each corner post. Leave 6 inches above the ground, then drill pilot holes through the stake and drive two 3-inch deck screws to attach it to the post, as shown right.

Anchor stake

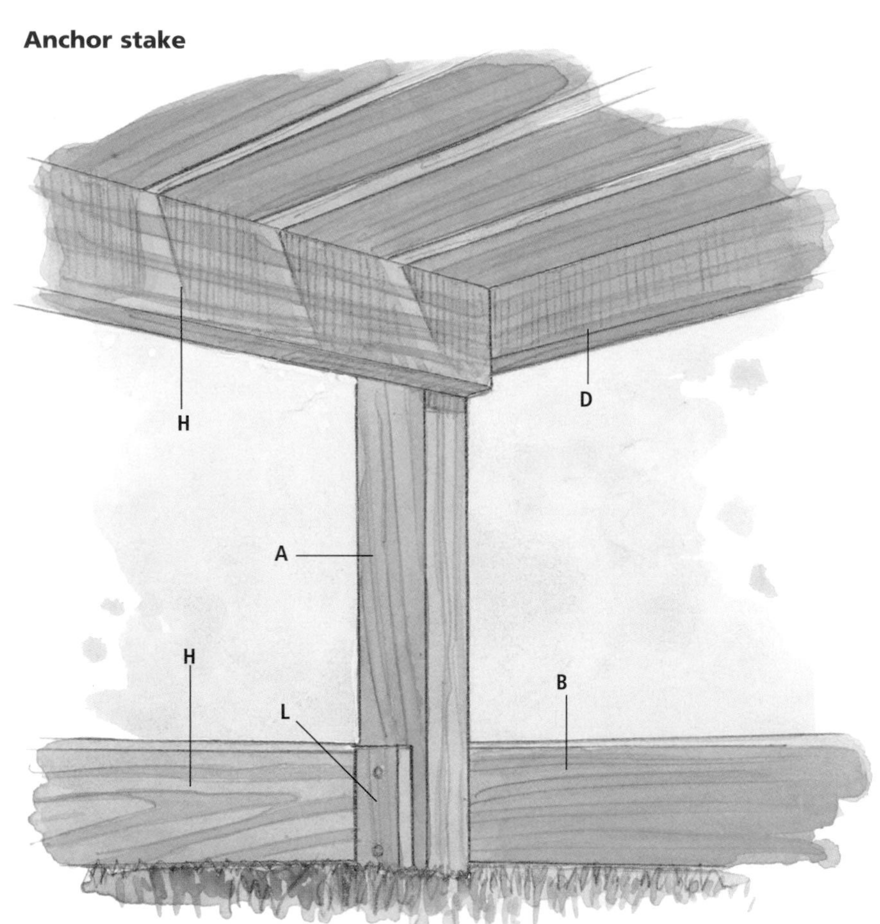

Build the second story

1 Position the top edge of the top side rail supports **(I)** 78¾ inches from the bottom of the corner posts and even with the safety rails **(E)** on the front and back panels. Attach the rail supports to the corner posts as described for the side fascias.

2 Position the lower tarp boards **(M)** at the outside top of the corner posts and attach them with three 3-inch deck screws at each end, as shown in the Side View drawing on page 115. The ends of the boards should meet square and tight against the 1½-inch overhang of the top fascias **(C)**.

3 Arrange six rail pickets **(N)** along the inside of the rail supports on both sides of the fort. Starting at the back panel, allow a 3-inch space between the first picket and the corner post; from there, allow an even space between each picket. (This space will vary slightly because of construction details, but it must be less than 3 inches to prevent children from becoming caught.) Attach each picket with two 2-inch deck screws at the top and bottom; for now, do not attach the two pickets adjacent to the front corner post where the swing beam **(W)** will be.

4 Position the top tarp board **(M)** at the top of the center posts **(F)** and attach it with three 3-inch deck screws at each end.

5 To complete the back panel, position two pickets between the back center post and each of the back corner posts; the pickets should rest on the deck and be 3 inches from both posts. Attach each picket with two 2-inch deck screws at the top and bottom.

6 Drape the tarp over the top tarp board and center it. Attach one edge to the outside of one of the lower tarp boards, using four 1-inch snap screws; these are screws with broad heads that help prevent rips. After setting each snap screw onto the board, give the tarp a stretch before setting the next. Complete one side of the tarp, then go on to the other.

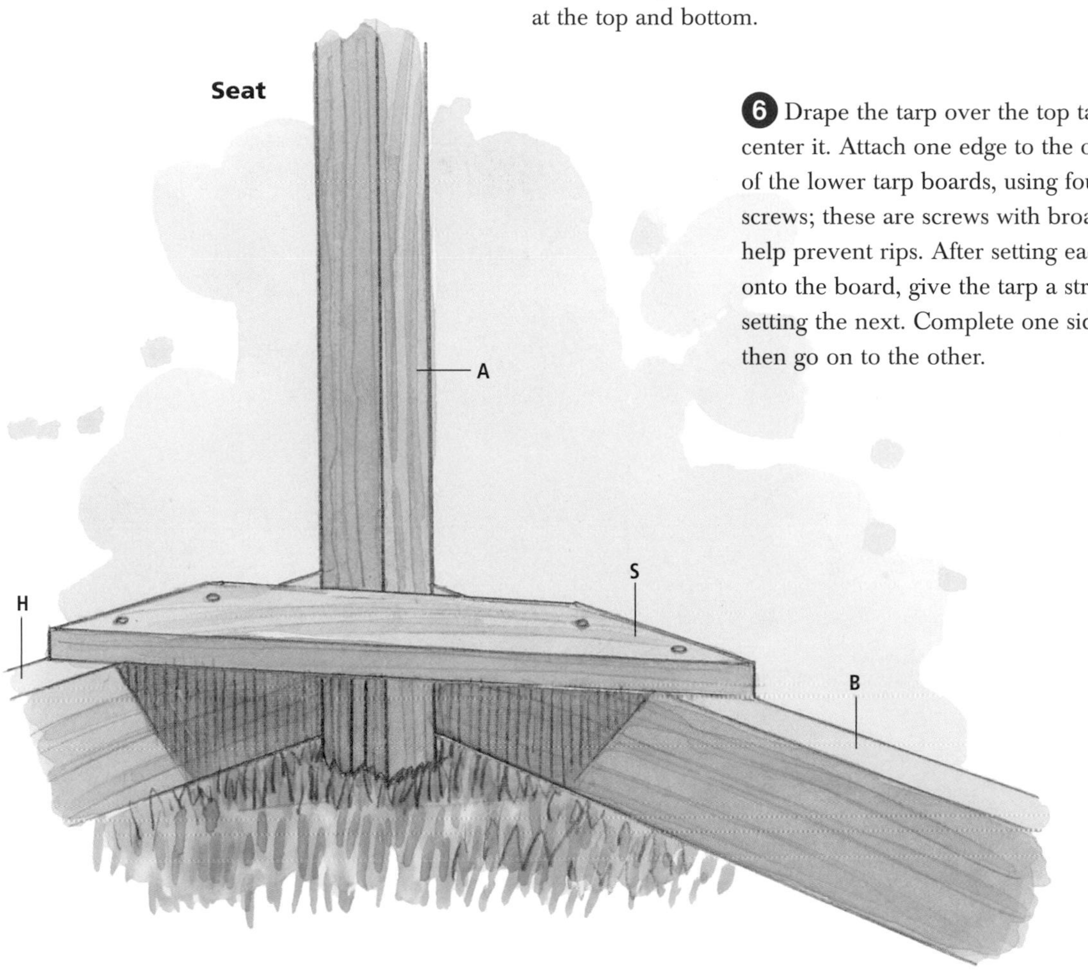

Add the sandbox seats, lower safety rail, and slide

1 Position boards for the sandbox seats **(S)** across the corners of your choice and trace each on the underside along the outside of parts **B** and **H** to lay out the cuts. Cut the ends of the seats and attach them as shown above with two 3-inch deck screws at each end.

2 Position the swing-side safety rail **(Z)** about 18 inches above the top of the sandbox fascia on the long side facing the swings; the rail helps prevent a child in the sandbox from walking into the path of a swing. The ends of the rail are attached to the front and back panels by $\frac{3}{8}$x$3\frac{1}{2}$-inch lag bolts with $\frac{3}{8}$-inch flat washers.

3 Buy an 8-foot slide of any style. (The length of a slide is generally twice the height of the platform it attaches to.) Attach the slide to one side of the ladder, following the manufacturer's directions.

FORT FROLIC (CONTINUED)

Make the swing set legs

1 The two legs **(T)** meet at angled edges. Cut the legs to length, if you haven't already done so, then lay out the angle. Start by finding the centerline along one end of each leg. Then mark a spot along one edge 3½ inches from the top, as shown below right. Use a straightedge to draw a line that connects the points. Depending on the exact finished dimensions of the boards, the resulting triangle will be about 1¾ inch by 3½ inches.

2 Cut along the line. If you are using a circular saw, lay out the line on the opposite side of the 4×4 leg as well, cut as deep as the saw will cut on one face, then repeat on the other face.

3 Measuring down 16¼ inches from what will be the top end, draw a line across each leg. Find the center point of the leg on this line and drill a ½-inch hole. Use a ship auger or electrician's bit to drill through the 4×4.

Drilling guideline

Leg top

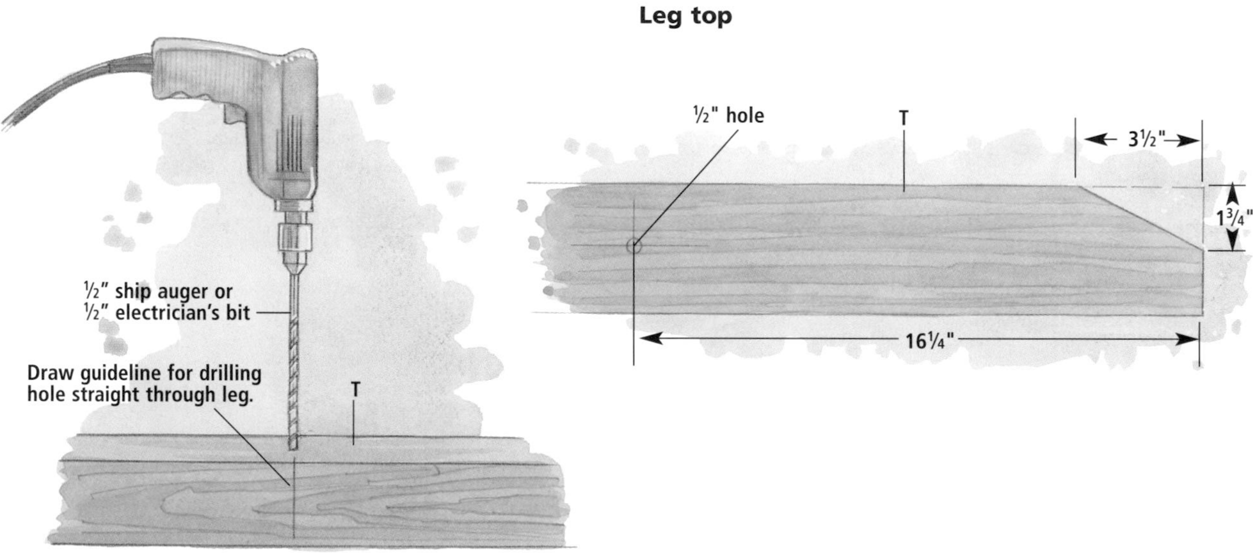

Make the swing supports

1 Cut the cross member **(V)** to length. This is the horizontal part that completes the A-frame. To mark the angles at the ends, mark the top edge at the point shown in the drawing below and draw a straight line from that point to the end on the opposite side. (You could instead lay out this cut as a 25-degree angle as shown on the opposite page. This cut will also remove about 1⅝ inches from the ends.) Mark the hole centers 2¾ inches from each end at the middle of the board. Drill a 1⅛-inch diameter counterbore at each mark with a ⅜-inch hole through the part.

Cross member

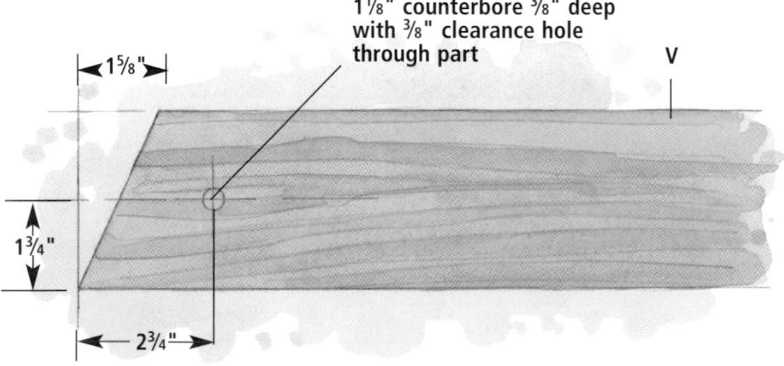

2 The tops of the legs are sandwiched between a pair of leg blocks **(U)** that will secure one end of the swing beam **(W)**. This is one of the few pieces where small inaccuracies will make assembly difficult. Take your time to measure and cut the blocks precisely, and make sure you drill the holes so that they are perpendicular to the surface. While you'll be able to tell if the drill is angled to one side or the other, it can be harder to see if the drill is slanting to the front or back. Draw a line as shown in Drilling Guideline drawing opposite, and use it as a guide.

Cut the leg blocks 19½ inches long. Drill a ½-inch-diameter hole through the center of both blocks as measured from end to end and side to side. Because the blocks are square in cross section, the first hole you drill can be in any face. Turn the blocks over to the exit hole, and drill a 1½-inch diameter counterbore about 1¼ inches deep and centered over the hole as shown in the drawing below.

Note that this technique for drilling the counterbores differs from the other recesses you've drilled. The counterbore bit will wander a little, but drilling the bolt holes first ensures they are accurately located.

Angle layout

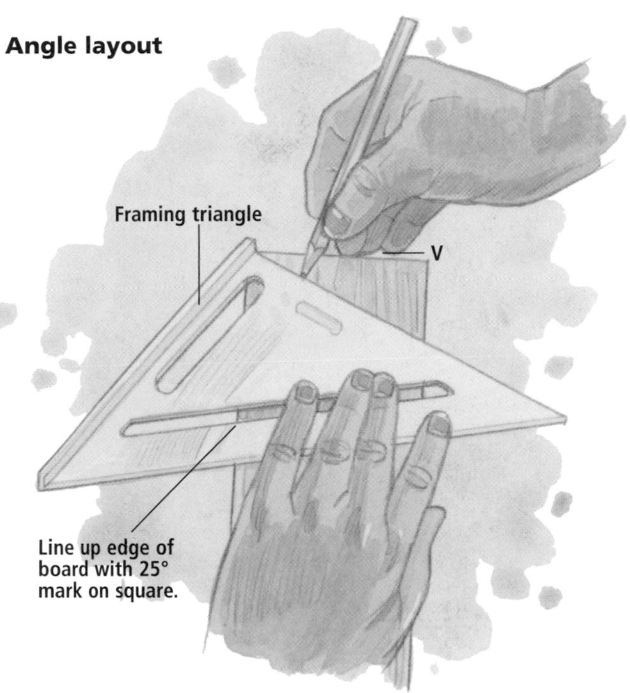

Leg blocks

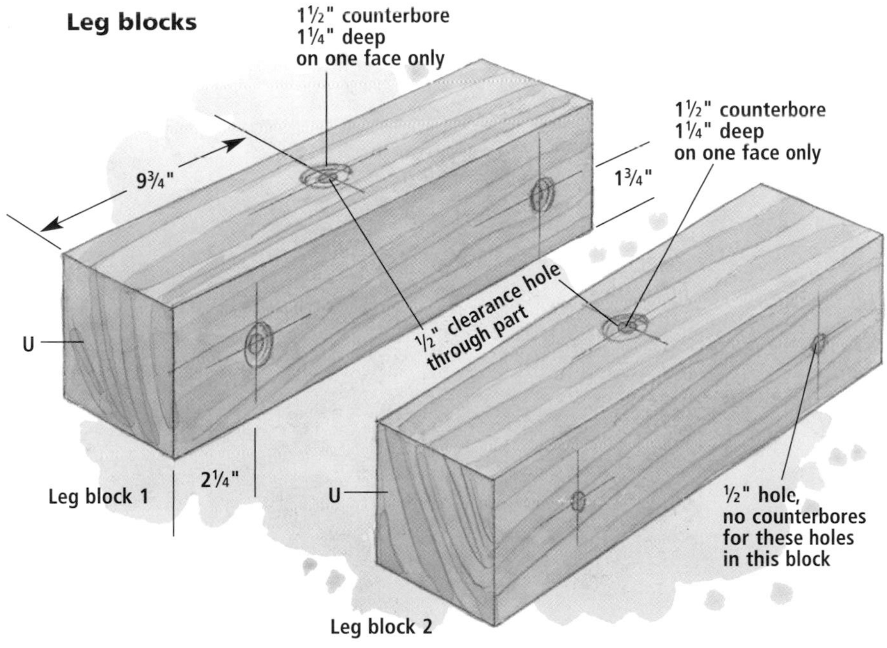

3 Rotate the leg blocks one-quarter turn so that you are looking at a face without a hole. Measure precisely and find a point 2¼ inches from each end and centered from side to side. Drill a ½-inch-diameter hole at each point in the two blocks, making sure the hole is perpendicular to the surface. On one block drill centered 1½-inch-diameter counterbores about 1¼ inches deep on the exit side of these two holes. This is leg block 1; these holes are not counterbored in leg block 2.

Swing beam

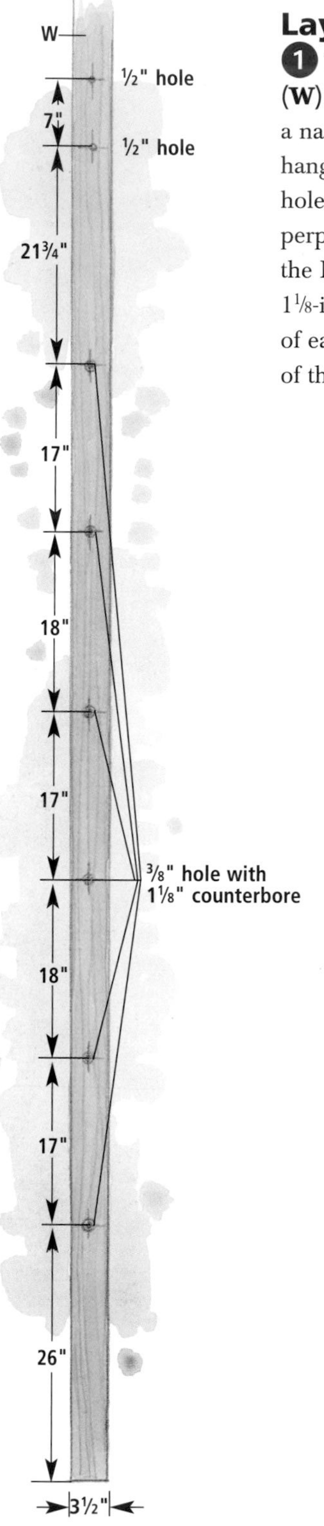

Lay out the swing beam

1 The swings are suspended from a stout 4×6 beam (**W**). Lay out the points shown left along the centerline on a narrow face. Drill six ⅜-inch-diameter holes for swing hangers like those shown right. Drill two ½-inch diameter holes for the legs. The ½-inch-diameter holes must be perpendicular to the face, so apply the technique shown in the Drilling Guideline drawing (see page 120). Drill 1⅛-inch counterbores about 1 inch deep on the exit side of each ⅜-inch hole. The counterbores will be on the top of the beam. The ½-inch holes are not counterbored.

2 Place ⅜-inch flat washers in the six swing counterbores and put a washer on each of the swing hangers. Put the hangers through the ⅜-inch-diameter holes from the bottom of the beam. Secure the hangers with ⅜-inch lock nuts. Tighten the hanger nuts twice a month when the swing set is in frequent use.

Swing hanger

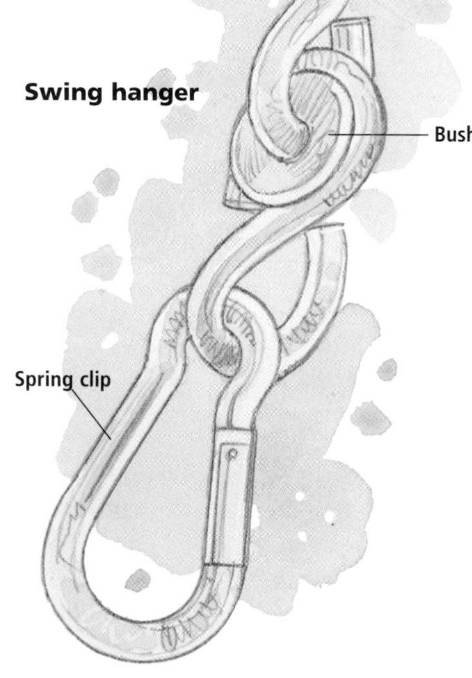

Assemble the legs

1 Place two of the legs on a flat surface with the angled tops together, in the form of an upside-down V. Place two ½×10½-inch carriage bolts with ¾-inch flat washers through the pair of holes in leg block 2 (the one with only one counterbore). Position the counterbore so it will face the ground when the swing is set up, and place this block under the top end of the leg assembly. Pass the bolt threads through the corresponding holes in the legs. Place leg block 1 over the bolt threads with the two counterbores facing up and the single counterbore facing the bottom of the legs. Place a ½-inch flat washer into the counterbore over each bolt followed by a ½-inch lock washer and a ½-inch nut. (You could use locking nuts instead of lock washers.) Tighten the nuts finger tight.

2 The angled tops of the legs are secured by two ⅜×5½-inch lag screws with ⅜-inch flat washers, as shown in the Leg Assembly drawing on page 124. To mark the hole positions, bring the angled faces snugly together. Slide a square along the outer face of one leg to a point where the combined thickness of the legs is 6 inches. Draw a line there, square to the outer face. Transfer the line to the opposite face, and lay out a hole on it ¾ inch from the center of the leg, as shown below. Repeat the process on the opposite leg, positioning that hole ¾ inch on the other side of center. Drill a ¼-inch pilot hole through each leg, going about 1 inch deep into the other leg.

Lag screws

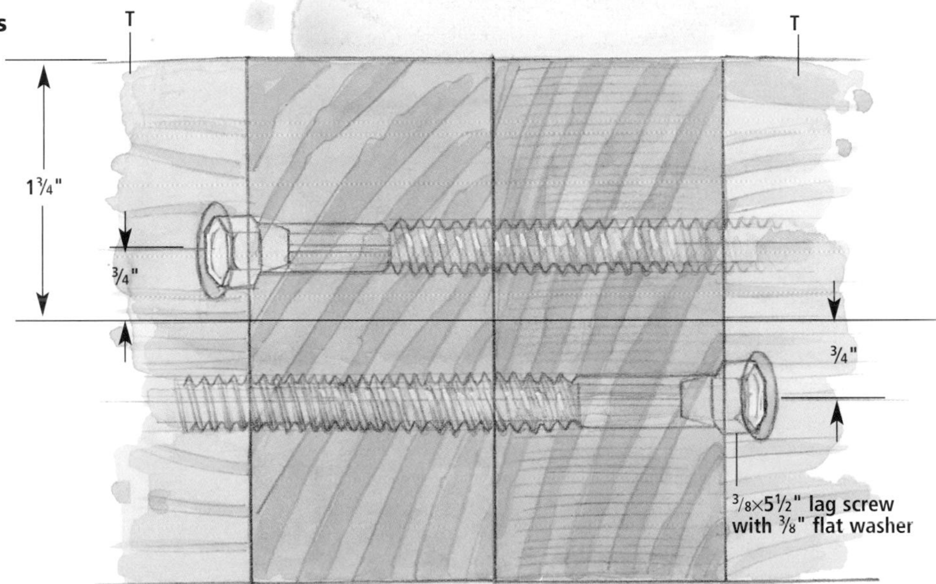

3 Place the cross member **(V)** across the legs, with the ends flush with the outside edge of the legs. Predrill ⅜-inch clearance holes through the counterbores. Drill ¼-inch holes into the legs and attach the cross member with ⅜×3½-inch lag screws with ⅜-inch flat washers.

4 Repeat the process on the second set of legs.

Attach the swing beam to the legs

1 With the aid of a helper, stand the leg assembly with one leg flat on a level surface, as shown opposite. The cross member and leg block counterbores should be on the outside of the assembly. Find the end of the swing beam that has the two ½-inch-diameter holes and place it through the opening made by the blocks at the top of the legs. Make sure to put the swing beam in so that the eye of the hangers will face the ground when the swing set is upright.

2 Attach the swing beam with two ½×9-inch carriage bolts with ¾-inch flat washers. Place the bolts through the top of the swing beam and into the center holes of the leg blocks (**U**). Place ½-inch flat washers over the threads in the counterbores followed by ½-inch lock washers and nuts.

3 Tighten all the nuts and lag screws on the swing set. Use a socket wrench and ratchet handle for those recessed in counterbores.

4 With your helper, turn the swing set right side up and rest the free end of the swing beam on the ground. Install one spring clip on each hanger, as shown on page 122. You may need to tap the spring clips over the eye of the hanger with a hammer. Give a final check to make sure that all hangers and bolts are tight.

Leg assembly

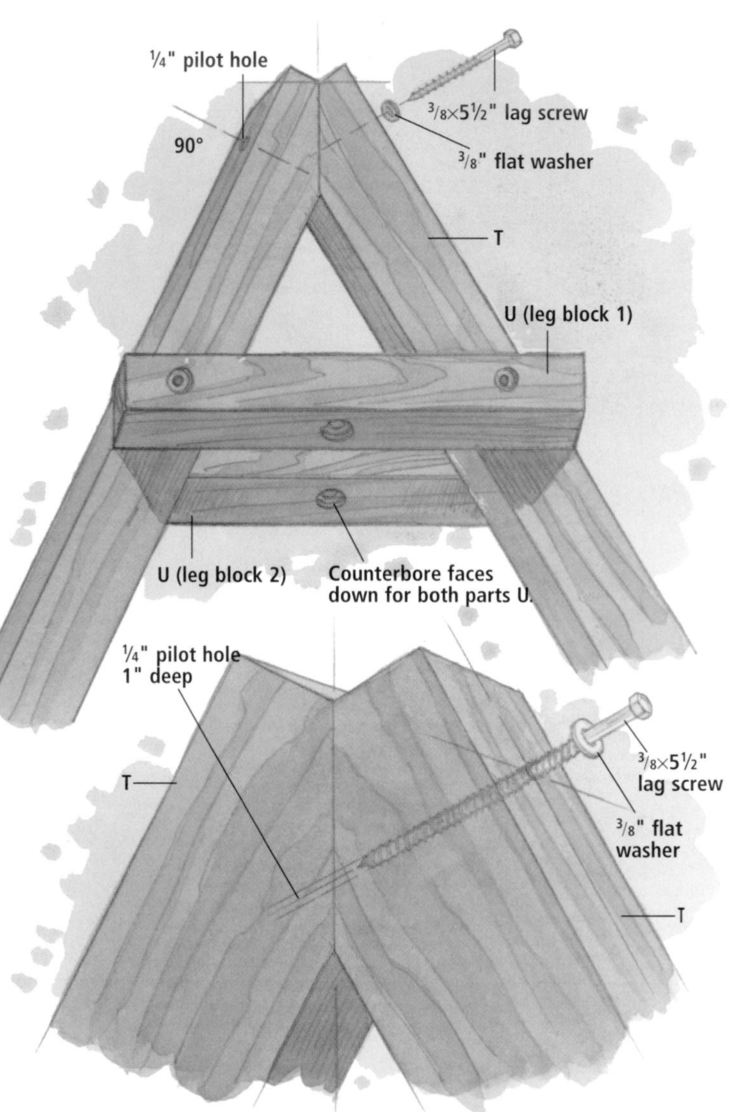

Attach the swing set to the fort

1 With your helper, put the free end of the swing beam against the back face of the front corner post, positioned so the beam is parallel with the front of the fort. If possible, the beam should be slightly higher on the end with the legs to compensate for the gradual settling of the legs into the ground. Use a level to check the beam. (See page 126.)

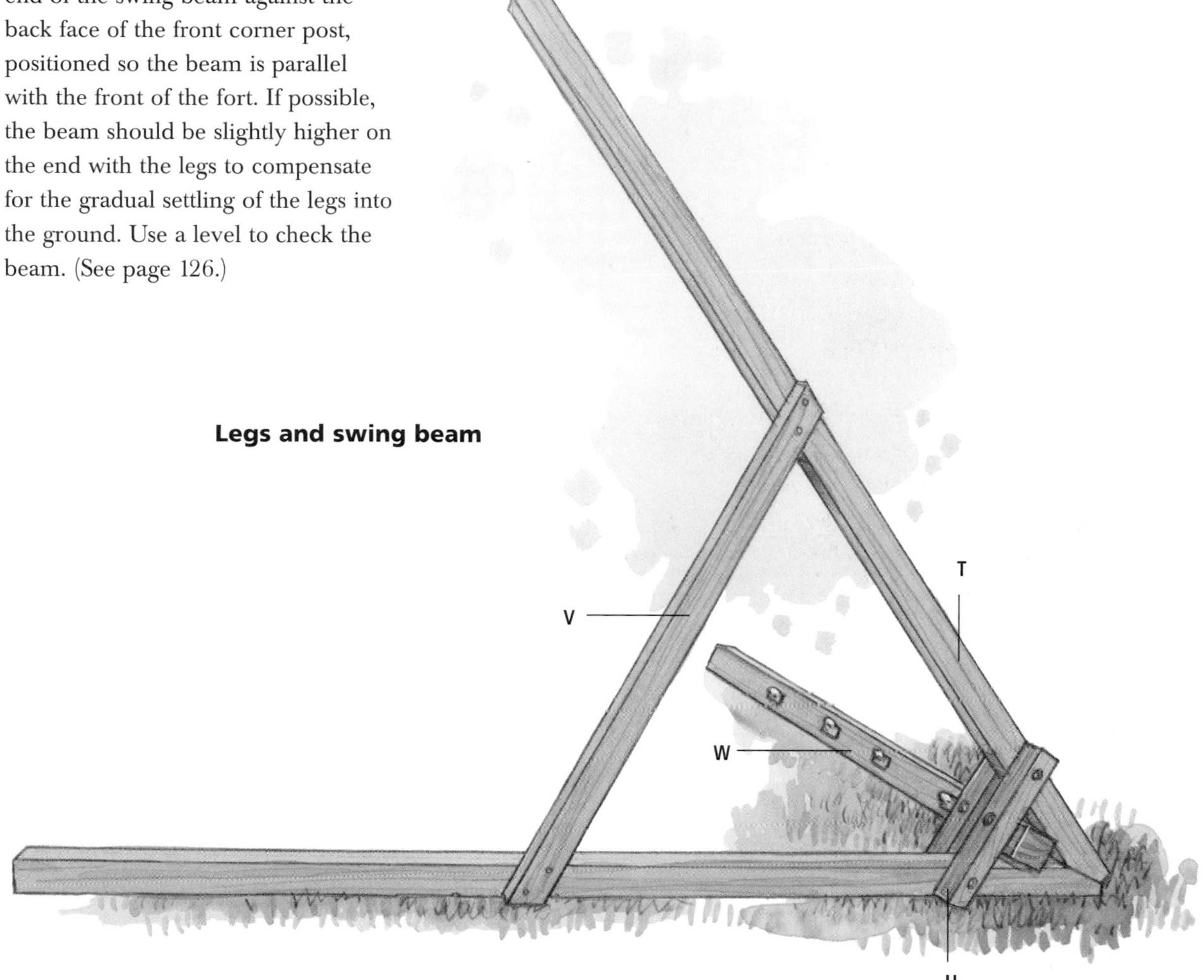

Legs and swing beam

Use the Right Hardware in Pressure-Treated Lumber

The compound used for pressure treatment helps wood resist rot, but it also reacts with iron to cause corrosion. If you're using pressure-treated lumber, use either stainless-steel or steel fasteners that have been double-dipped galvanized. Avoid the ones that are electroplated galvanized. Incorrect fasteners can lose their strength within a year and could break.

Supporting swing beam on fort

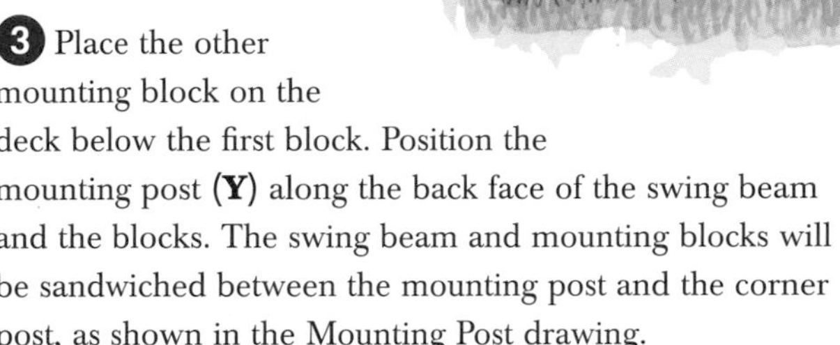

2 While your helper holds the swing beam in place, put a mounting block **(X)** under the beam to place it at the desired height. Temporarily attach the block to the inside of the top rail support with one 3-inch deck screw. Have your helper hold the beam until you have installed all the bolts as described below.

3 Place the other mounting block on the deck below the first block. Position the mounting post **(Y)** along the back face of the swing beam and the blocks. The swing beam and mounting blocks will be sandwiched between the mounting post and the corner post, as shown in the Mounting Post drawing.

4 Use a square to mark a horizontal line across the center of the mounting post, the end of the swing beam, and the corner post. Using the line as a guide to watch the angle of the drill and keep the hole from slanting, drill a $\frac{1}{2}$-inch-diameter hole though the center of all three. Drill a $1\frac{1}{2}$-inch counterbore about 1 inch deep over the center of the hole in the mounting post. Place a $\frac{1}{2}\times10\frac{1}{2}$-inch carriage bolt with a $\frac{3}{4}$-inch flat washer through this hole from the front face of the corner post. Place a $\frac{1}{2}$-inch flat washer in the counterbore, followed by a $\frac{1}{2}$-inch lock washer and $\frac{1}{2}$-inch nut. For now, tighten by hand, rather than with a wrench, so that the bolt doesn't pull the joint back open.

5 Lay out the two pilot holes for the lag bolts that hold the mounting block between the mounting post and the corner post. The upper hole in each should be roughly 2 inches from the top of the block; the lower hole should pass through roughly 2 inches from the bottom. To lay out the holes, use a square to extend horizontal lines across the posts and block as a guide to help you keep the drill level. All the pilot holes are $\frac{5}{16}$-inch diameter. Drill the upper hole in each block from the front face of the corner post, through a block, and into the mounting post; drill the lower hole in each block from the back face of the mounting post, through a block, and into the corner post. Drive a $\frac{3}{8}\times10$-inch lag bolt with a $\frac{3}{8}$-inch washer into each of the four holes. Finally, tighten with a wrench the bolts you had tightened by hand, and check all the other nuts and bolts for tightness.

6 To secure the mounting post, predrill a ¼-inch hole through the bottom of the deck and into the bottom of the post–you may have to drill it at a slight angle. Drive a ⅜×5½-inch lag screw with a ⅜-inch flat washer through the deck board and into the post.

7 Put the remaining two pickets in place, with spacing between them less than 3 inches apart for safety.

Mounting post

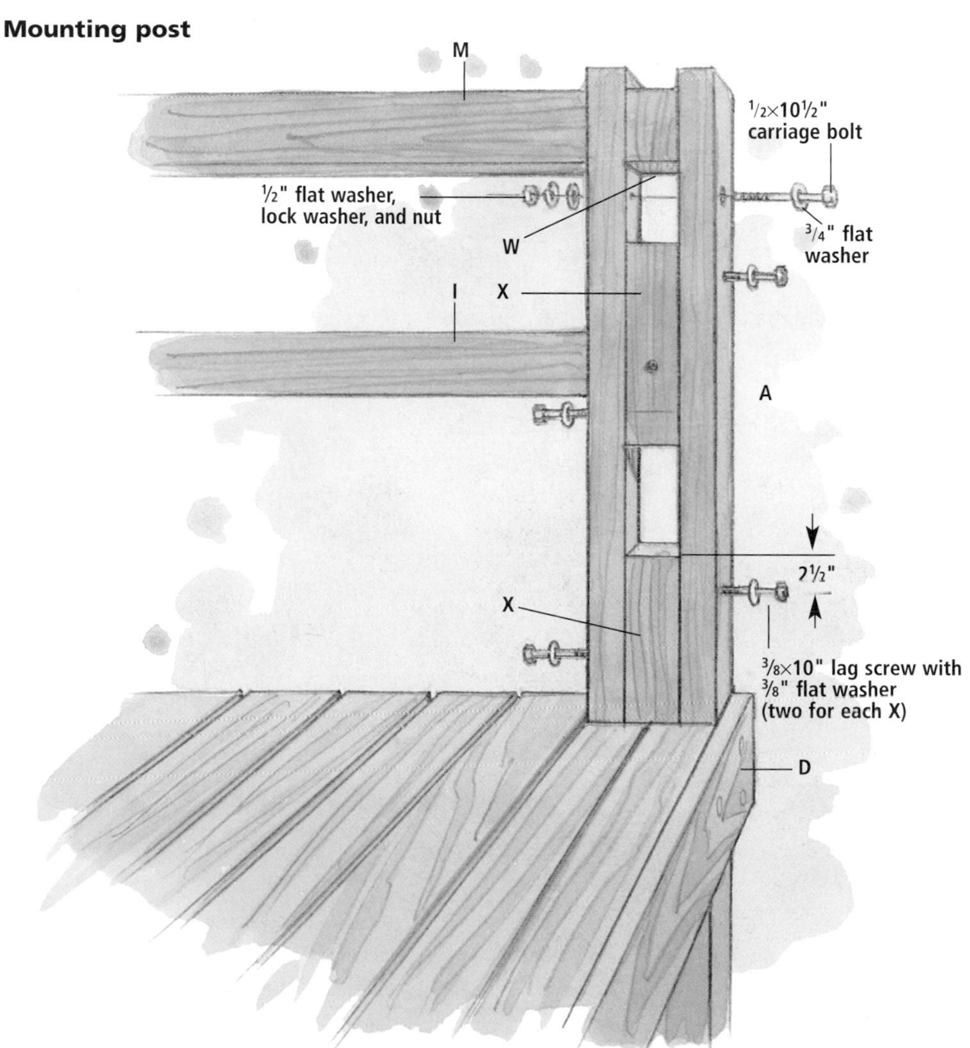

Complete the fort and swing set

1 Place a stake (**L**) flush against each swing set leg, hammering it into the ground until a 6-inch section is showing. Drill pilot holes through the stake and drive two 3-inch deck screws through it and into the leg.

2 Buy swings with coated chains. Hang the swings from the spring clips. Fill the base of the fort with sand. To keep neighborhood cats from mistaking the fort for a huge litter box, cover the sandbox with a tarp when it isn't in use, staking the tarp to the ground.

Cottage Playhouse

Yes, the kids can make a playhouse by tossing a blanket over a card table. But this cozy cottage, with its gable roof, four-pane windows, arch-top door, and scalloped trim, will bring the fantasy to life.

Building the playhouse won't be a summerlong project. The walls and roof are six sheets of ¾-inch plywood. Choose exterior-grade plywood if you plan on installing the playhouse out in the yard; if it will be indoors, you might use birch-veneer plywood with its easily paintable surface. The playhouse is joined along each corner with screws. Disassembly is straightforward too; just back out the screws, and the structure can be stored off season against a wall in the garage. Permanent assemblies are reinforced with water-resistant wood glue suited to outdoor use.

Exploded view

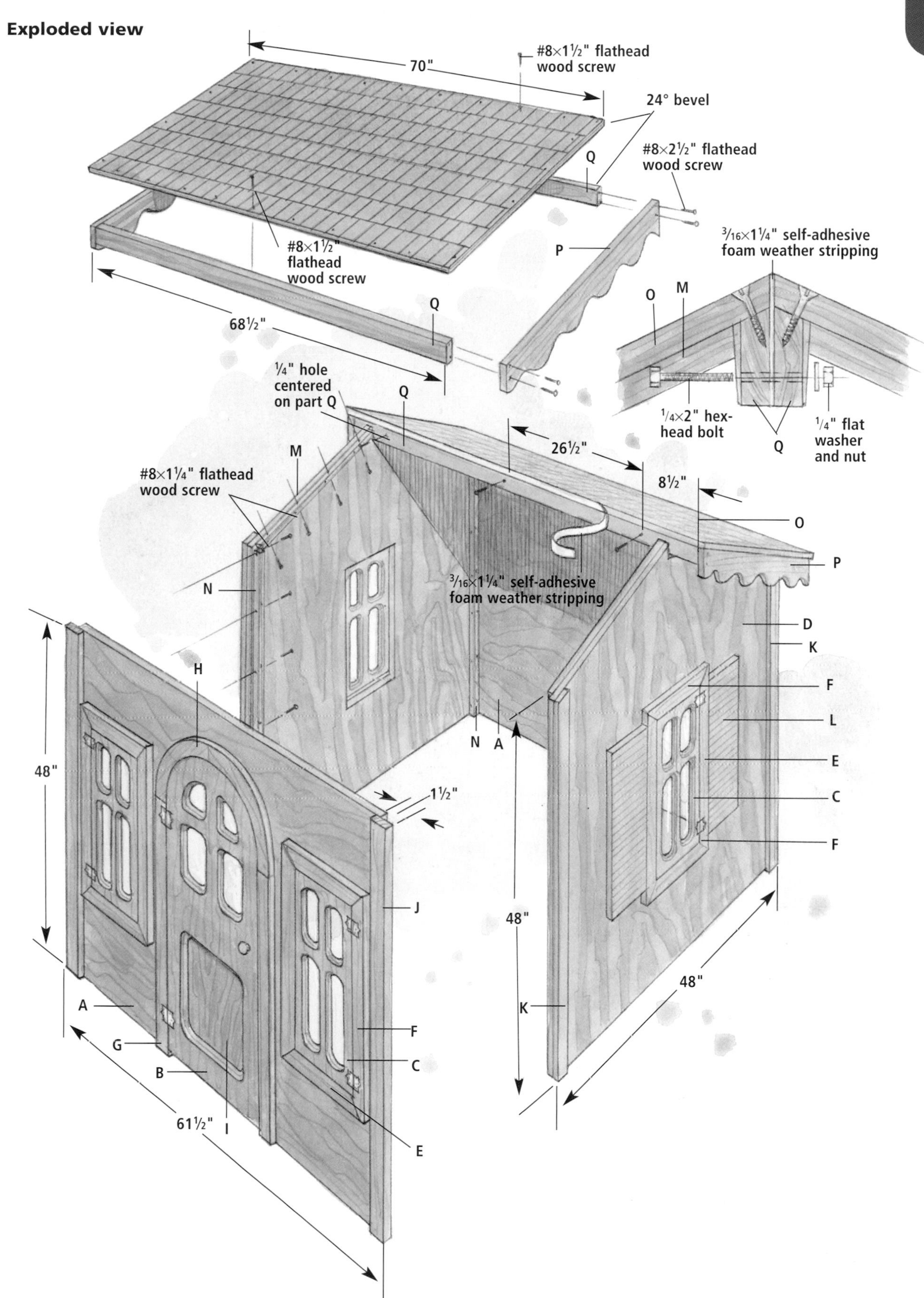
70"
#8×1½" flathead wood screw
24° bevel
#8×2½" flathead wood screw
Q
P
#8×1½" flathead wood screw
68½"
Q
³⁄₁₆×1¼" self-adhesive foam weather stripping
O
M
¼×2" hex-head bolt
Q
¼" flat washer and nut
¼" hole centered on part Q
Q
M
26½"
8½"
#8×1¼" flathead wood screw
O
P
N
³⁄₁₆×1¼" self-adhesive foam weather stripping
D
K
H
F
L
N
A
E
48"
1½"
C
F
J
48"
48"
K
A
F
G
B
C
61½"
I
E

MATERIALS LIST

QUANTITY	PART	DESCRIPTION	FINISHED SIZE	MATERIAL
2	A	FRONT, BACK	$^3/_4$×48×58$^1/_2$"	P
1	B	DOOR	$^3/_4$×17$^7/_8$×41"	P
4	C	WINDOWS	$^3/_4$×9$^7/_8$×21$^7/_8$"	P
2	D	ENDS	$^3/_4$×48×58$^3/_4$"	P
8	E	WINDOW SIDES	$^3/_4$×2×26"	C
8	F	WINDOW TOPS, BOTTOMS	$^3/_4$×2×14"	C
2	G	DOOR SIDES	$^3/_4$×2×33"	C
2	H	ARCHED DOOR TOPS	$^3/_4$×4$^3/_4$×22$^1/_4$"	C
1	I	DOOR PANEL	$^1/_4$×13$^3/_8$×14$^3/_4$"	C
4	J	FRONT BATTENS	$^3/_4$"×2$^1/_4$×48"	C
4	K	END BATTENS	$^3/_4$×1$^1/_2$×48$^{11}/_{16}$"	C
4	L	SHUTTERS	$^3/_4$×7×22"	C
4	M	ROOF CLEATS	$^3/_4$×$^3/_4$×23$^7/_8$"	C
4	N	WALL CLEATS	$^3/_4$×$^3/_4$×48$^3/_8$"	C
2	O	ROOF PANELS	$^3/_4$×30×70"	P
4	P	ROOF END TRIM	$^3/_4$×4×31$^1/_4$"	C
4	Q	EAVES, RIDGE BOARDS	$^3/_4$×2$^1/_2$×68$^1/_2$"	C
10	R	CATCH SUPPORTS	$^3/_4$×$^3/_4$×2"	C

QUANTITY	DESCRIPTION
	CABINET KNOB
10	ORNAMENTAL CABINET HINGES
10	MAGNETIC CATCHES AND STRIKE PLATES
	$^1/_8$" ACRYLIC FOR WINDOWS
	#6×$^1/_2$" FLATHEAD WOOD SCREWS
	#8×1$^1/_4$" FLATHEAD WOOD SCREWS
	#8×1$^1/_2$" FLATHEAD WOOD SCREWS
	#8×2$^1/_2$" FLATHEAD WOOD SCREWS
	2$^1/_4$×2" HEX-HEAD BOLTS WITH WASHERS AND NUTS
	WATER-RESISTANT WOOD GLUE
	$^3/_{16}$×1$^1/_4$" SELF-ADHESIVE FOAM WEATHERSTRIPPING
	WOOD PUTTY
	ACRYLIC CAULK
	PRIMER
	EXTERIOR LATEX PAINTS

*MATERIALS KEY: P—PLYWOOD C—CEDAR

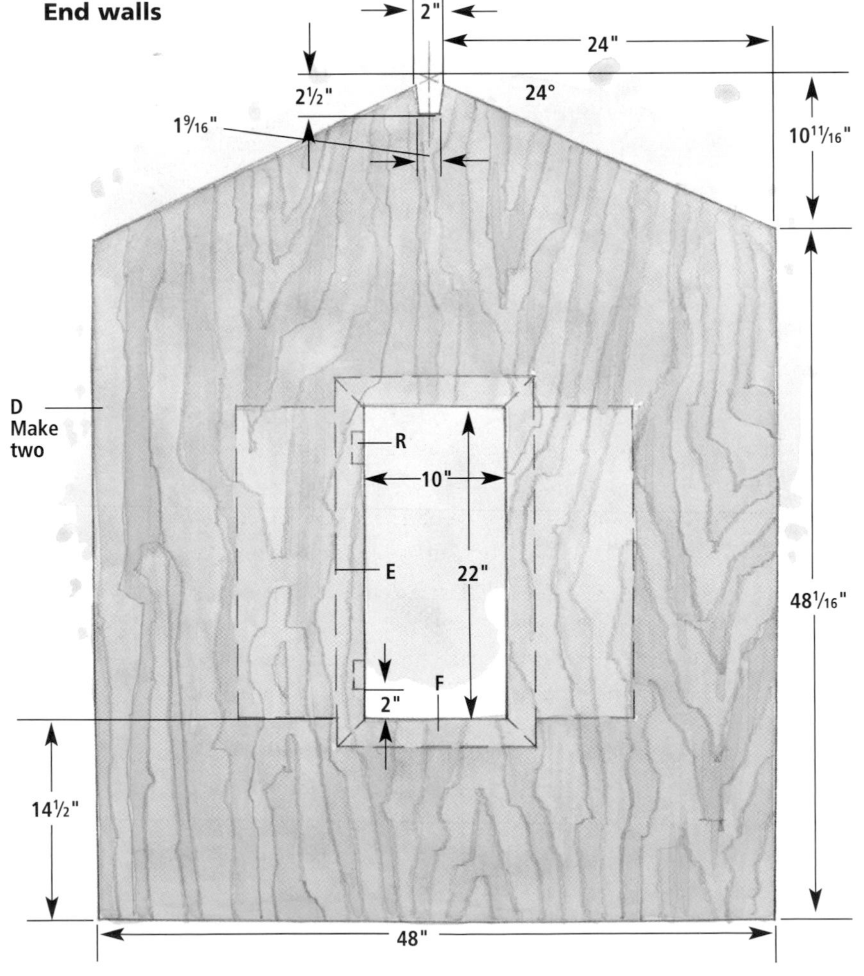

Cut the walls

1 Lay out walls **A** and **D** (two of each) on four 4×8-foot sheets of plywood. See the drawings left and opposite for dimensions and angles. Lay out the overall shapes, then lay out the window and door openings.

Front and back walls

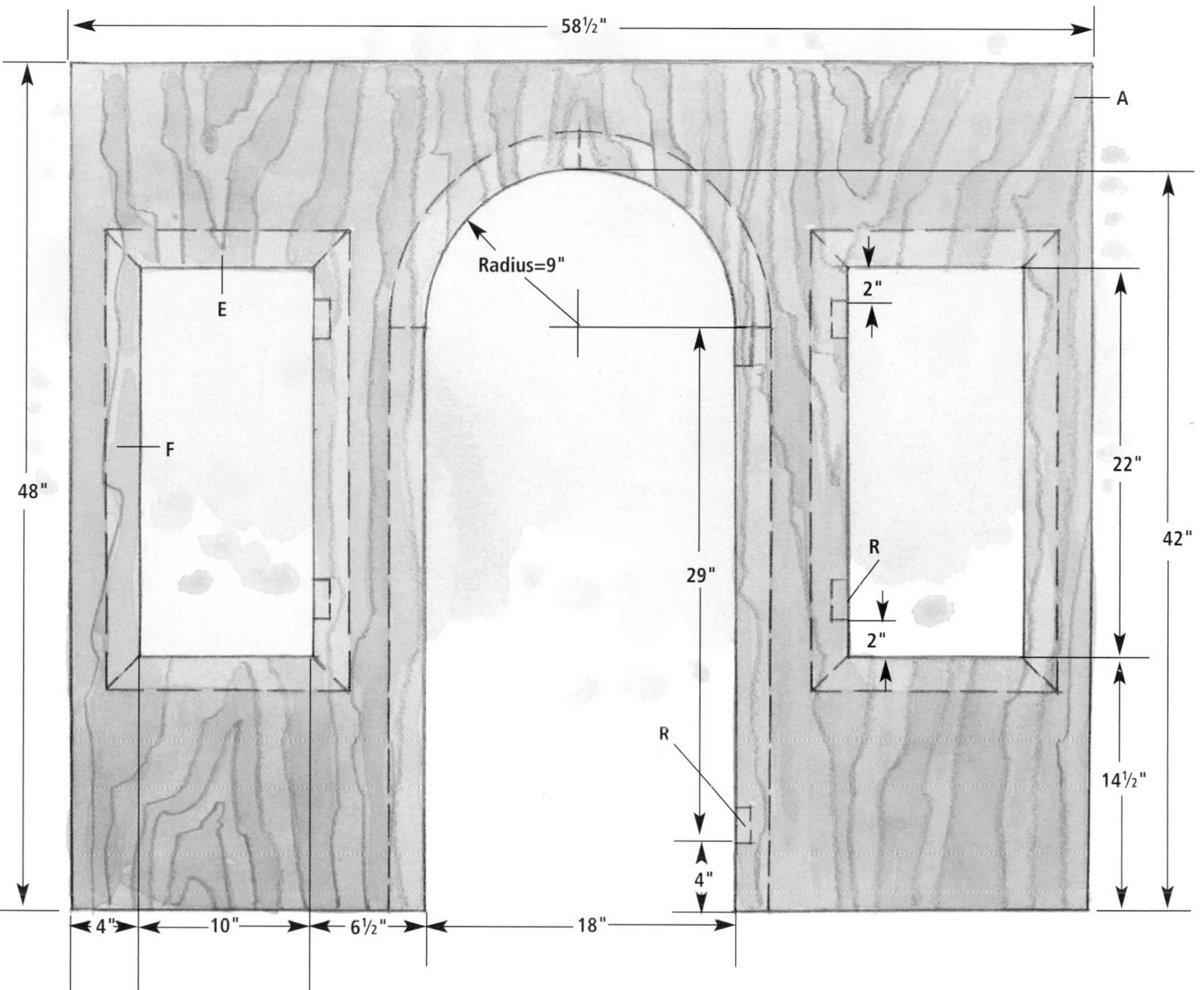

2 Cut out the walls with a circular saw, guiding it by clamping a straightedge to the work piece. Cut out the doorway in the front wall with a jigsaw. To cut the windows in the front and end walls, start with a plunge cut, in which you start the jigsaw with the blade parallel to the work surface over the cutting line, then slowly tilt the moving blade into the cutting line to pierce the wood. (See the illustration on page 133.) When making these cuts, cut along the lines neatly because you will be using the cutouts to make the door and windows in the next step. Cut the tapered notch at the peak of both gable-end walls, using the dimensions shown opposite.

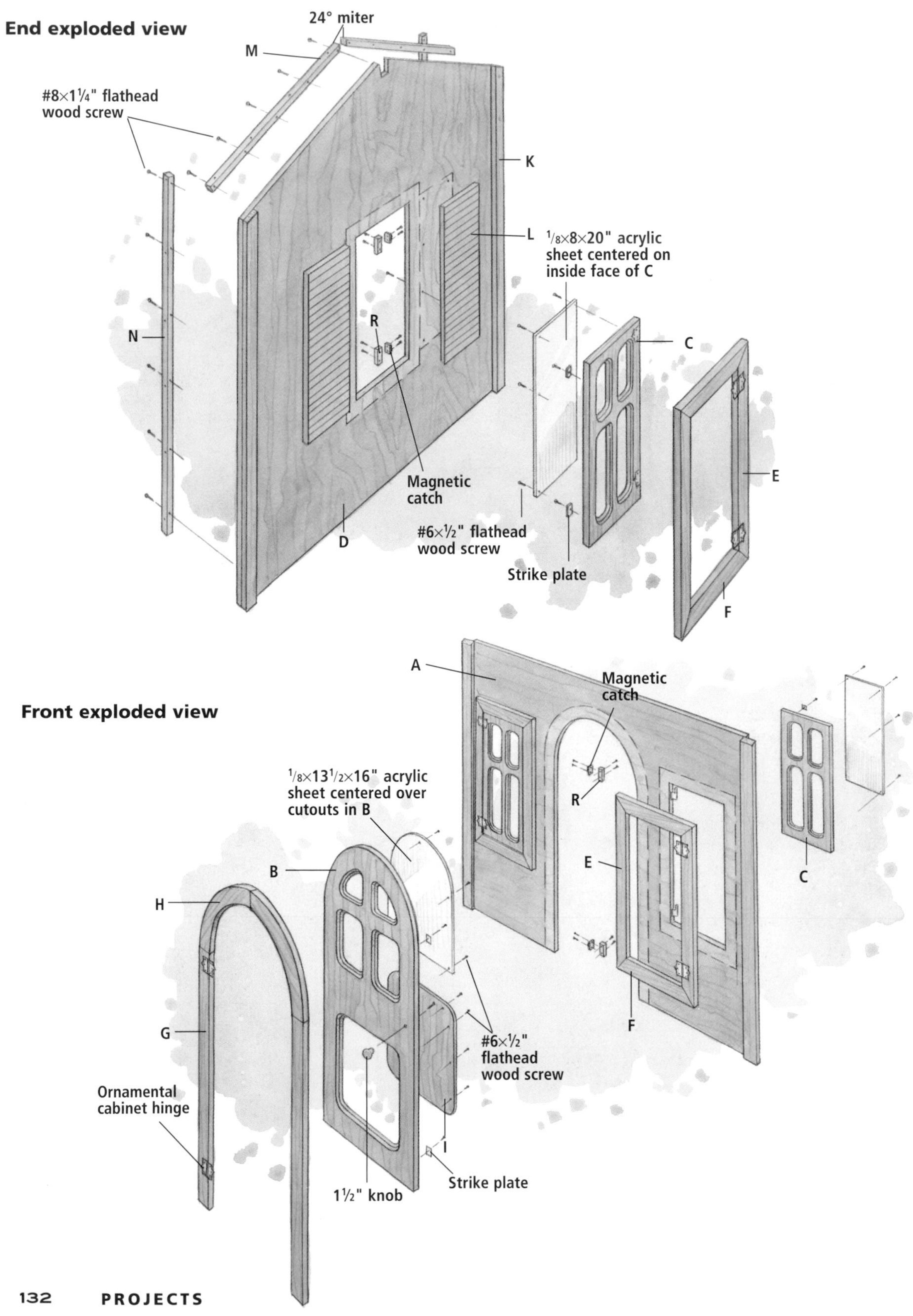
End exploded view
24° miter
M
#8×1¼" flathead
wood screw
K
L
1/8×8×20" acrylic
sheet centered on
inside face of C
R
N
C
E
Magnetic
catch
D
#6×½" flathead
wood screw
Strike plate
F
A
Magnetic
catch
Front exploded view
1/8×13½×16" acrylic
sheet centered over
cutouts in B
R
E
C
B
H
F
G
#6×½"
flathead
wood screw
Ornamental
cabinet hinge
I
Strike plate
1½" knob

Plunge cutting

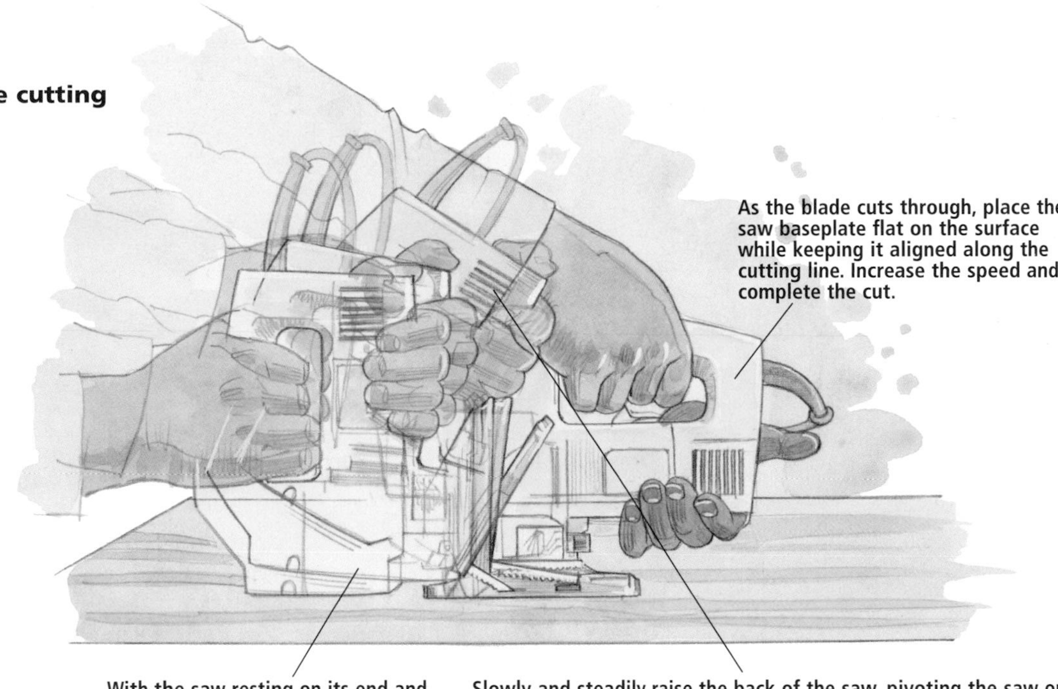

As the blade cuts through, place the saw baseplate flat on the surface while keeping it aligned along the cutting line. Increase the speed and complete the cut.
With the saw resting on its end and the blade parallel to the work surface above the cutting line, start the saw at a slow to medium speed.
Slowly and steadily raise the back of the saw, pivoting the saw on the front end of its baseplate. As the blade contacts the wood, it will start to tear away the surface. Keep the saw on the cutting line and pivot it up until the blade cuts through the wood.

3 Lay out the panes for the door (**B**) and windows (**C**), as shown right. Use a compass to draw the rounded corners and the curved arch-top windows on the door. (Woodworking supply shops carry trammel points that work like a compass for drawing large arcs; one point holds a pencil lead and the other is a metal pivot point. Attach the points to a yardstick.) Smooth out the round corners of the pane openings with a drum sander attachment in an electric drill. For the four windows, place a 1/4-inch round-over bit in a router and rout the edge of the openings. Switch to a 3/8-inch round-over bit and do the same for the pane openings in the door.

4 Drill a hole in the door to mount a wood or porcelain cabinet knob.

Window

Make windows from wall cutouts.

C

9 7/8"

1 1/2"

6 5/8"

1"

21 7/8"

11 1/4"

1 1/2"

2 15/16"

1"

2 15/16"

1 1/2"

1 1/2"

Radius=1" on all inside corners
Make panel I to overlap opening 1" on all sides.

1/4" round over on all inside edges

Door

Make door from front wall cutout

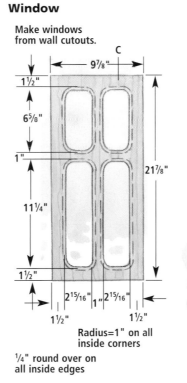

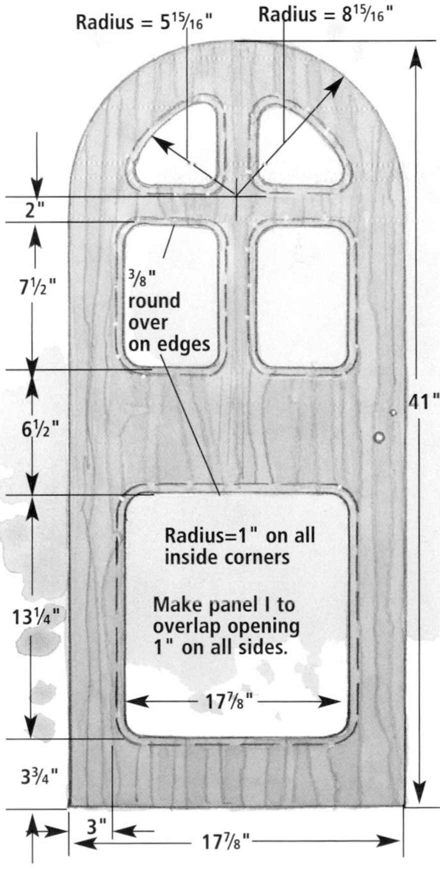

Cut the trim and glazing

1 Lay out and cut the window trim (**E** and **F**) and vertical door trim (**G**), using 3/4-inch solid stock as shown in the drawings below. The pieces of window trim meet at mitered ends. The two curved door trim pieces (**H**) are cut from 4 3/4-inch-wide stock, onto which you draw the outer and inner curves with a compass or trammel point, as shown on the opposite page. Begin with pieces measuring 4 3/4×22 1/4 inches, then make 45-degree cuts at either end to form the pieces indicated by broken lines in the Door Trim drawing.

Place one of the pieces on a work surface and find the midpoint of the longer parallel side. With a square, measure 11 inches toward what will be the inside of the arc (the shorter parallel side). Place a piece of 3/4-inch scrap wood at this spot. Clamp both pieces of wood to keep them stationary. Again measure 11 inches from the midpoint with a square, and mark a center on the scrap wood. Place the center of a compass or trammel point on the mark, and swing arcs at 9 and 11 inches. On a board 4 3/4 inches wide, the shorter arc should intersect the corners of the shorter parallel edge, as shown below left. The longer arc should just touch the middle of the longer parallel edge.

Door trim

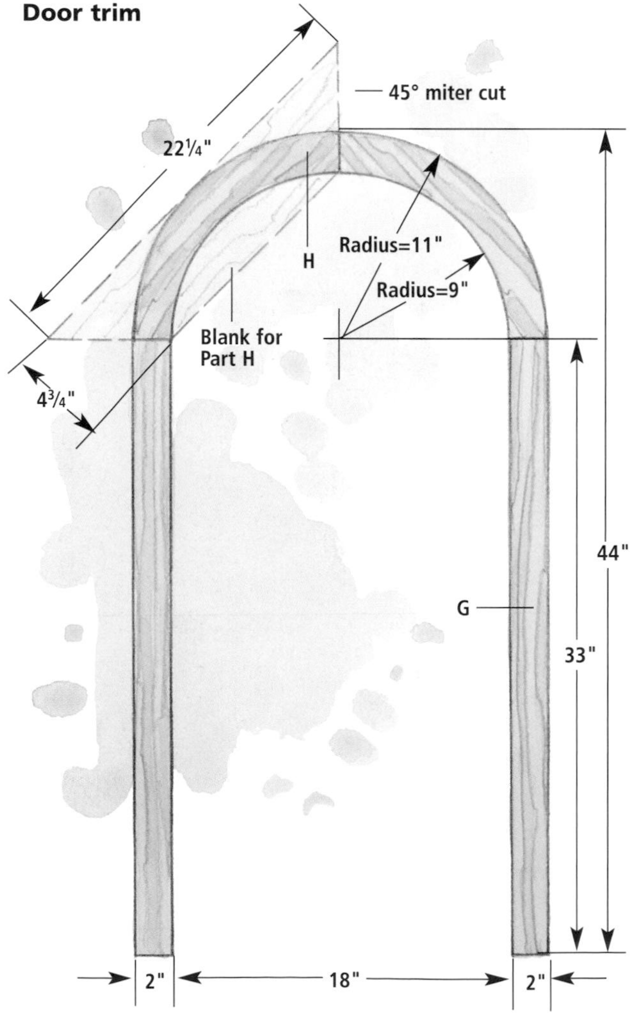

Window trim

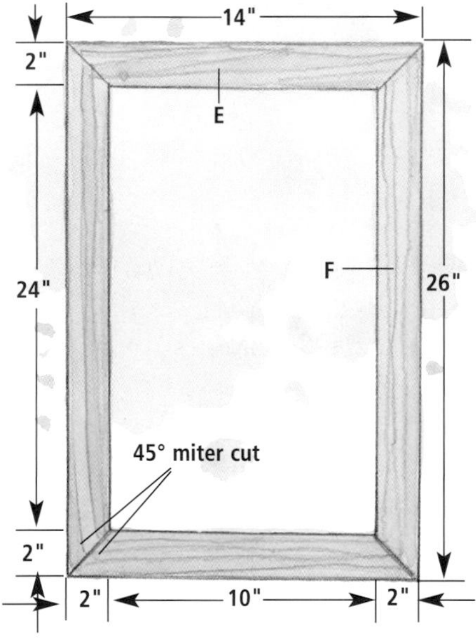

2 Cut out the first curved piece of trim with a jigsaw and hold it up to the arched doorway opening to make sure it fits. If necessary, file and sand the piece to align it with the opening, then use it as a template to make the second piece.

3 Attach the window and door trim around the respective cutouts with water-resistant wood glue and enough clamps to provide consistent pressure.

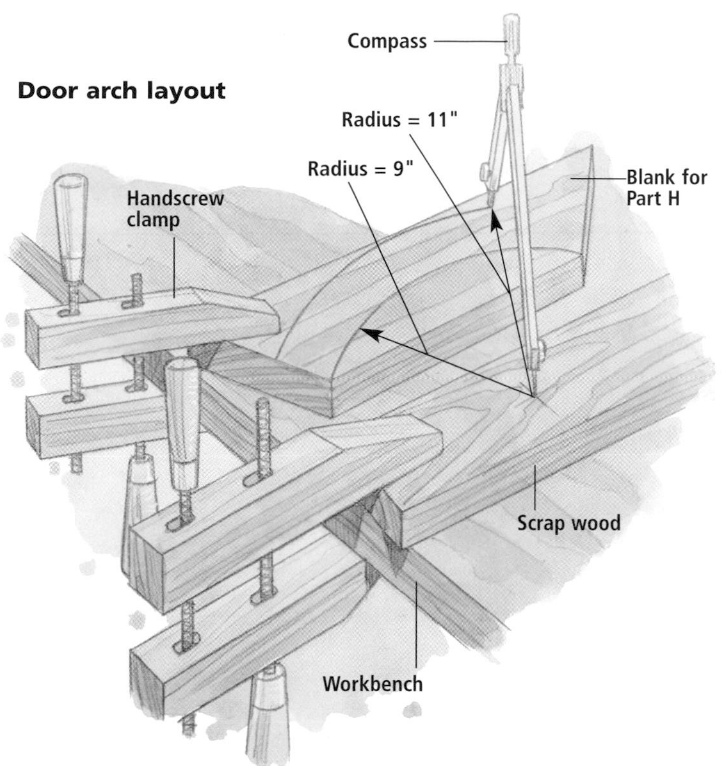

❹ Cut out the door panel (**I**) from 1/4-inch plywood to the dimensions given in the Materials List. Draw and cut the radiused corners as shown in the Front Exploded View and Door drawings. The panel creates the appearance of a traditional frame-and-panel door. Center it carefully over the lower cutout on the back of the door, overlapping it 1 inch on all sides. Drill mounting holes and attach the panel with #6×1/2-inch flathead wood screws.

Add the battens and cleats

❶ The wall panels lock together with wood strips called cleats and battens. See the Corner Assembly drawing on page 136 for a top view of how the pieces fit together. Cut the corner battens (**J** and **K**). Make 24-degree miter cuts at the top ends so that they will align with the pitch of the roof, as shown right.

❷ Glue and clamp the corner battens to the front and back walls. One batten at each corner overhangs the edge of the plywood by the thickness of the plywood plus the thickness of the batten. Hold a scrap of each together and use them to check if the overhang is right. Align the beveled ends of the battens with the top edge of the walls.

❸ Glue and clamp the corner battens (**K**) to the end walls (**D**). Make the battens flush with the vertical edge of the walls and align their beveled edges with the pitch of the walls.

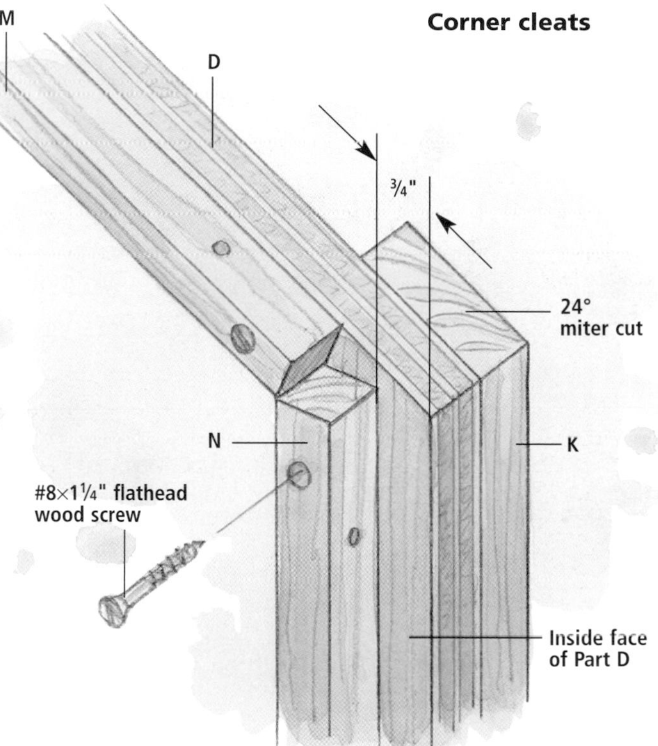

Make the shutters

1 Make the four shutters **(L)** from a single 22×30-inch panel of plywood. Rout ⅛-inch-deep grooves 1 inch apart center to center with a ¼-inch round-nose bit. Guide the router by clamping a straightedge to the panel as shown right. First, draw lines 1 inch apart across the 30-inch dimension of the plywood. To accurately run the bit along each line, measure from the edge of the router base to the center of the bit and rip a piece of wood to this width. Use this piece as the straightedge, aligning it initially with your layout lines. (After you've routed a few grooves, you'll align it with the center of a groove.) Once the straightedge is in place, clamp it, and guide the router against it to rout a groove. (You can use the same bit and a similar procedure if you choose to rout a shingle pattern on the roof panels, as shown on the opposite page.) After routing, cut the panel into four 7-inch-wide shutters.

Routing the shutters

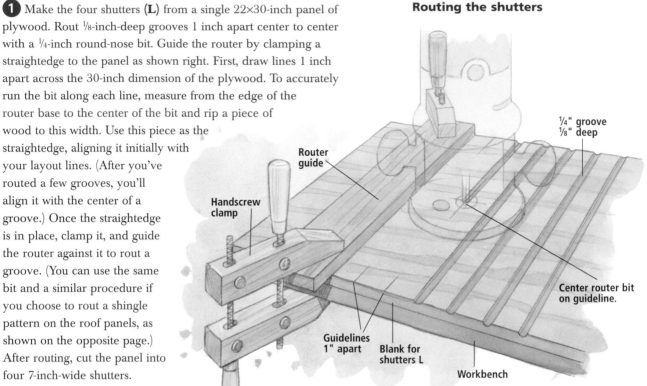

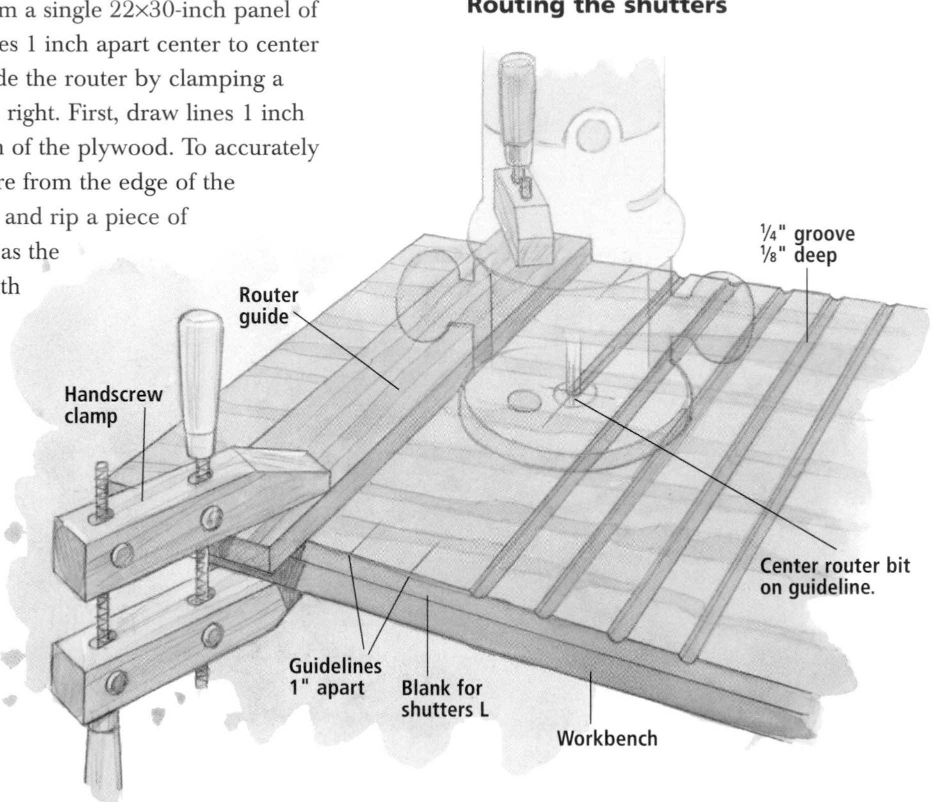

2 Rip the roof cleats **(M)** and corner cleats **(N)** from solid stock, as specified in the Materials List. Cut 24-degree miters on the top end of the roof cleats so they align with the edges of the notch you'll cut at the top of the gable-end walls.

3 Identify the inside corner of each roof and corner cleat as shown on page 129 and right. Rout a ⅛-inch round-over along the edge.

4 Attach the cleats at the edges of the wall and roof panels. Drill countersunk holes, apply waterproof construction glue, and drive #8×1¼-inch flathead wood screws. (See pages 132 and 135.)

Corner assembly

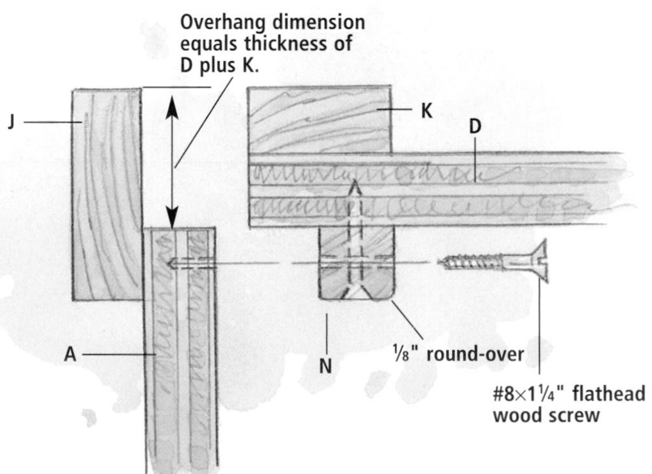

Raise the roof

1 Cut the two roof panels (O) to the dimensions given in the Materials List.

2 If you decide to rout a shingle pattern on the roof, lay out the long lines that suggest the horizontal courses, then the shorter verticals that define the individual shingles, as shown below. You'll have a much easier time making the stopped grooves for the verticals if you use a plunge router. Use a straightedge as explained for cutting grooves in the shutters. (You could paint the lines instead, or paint the roof a solid color.)

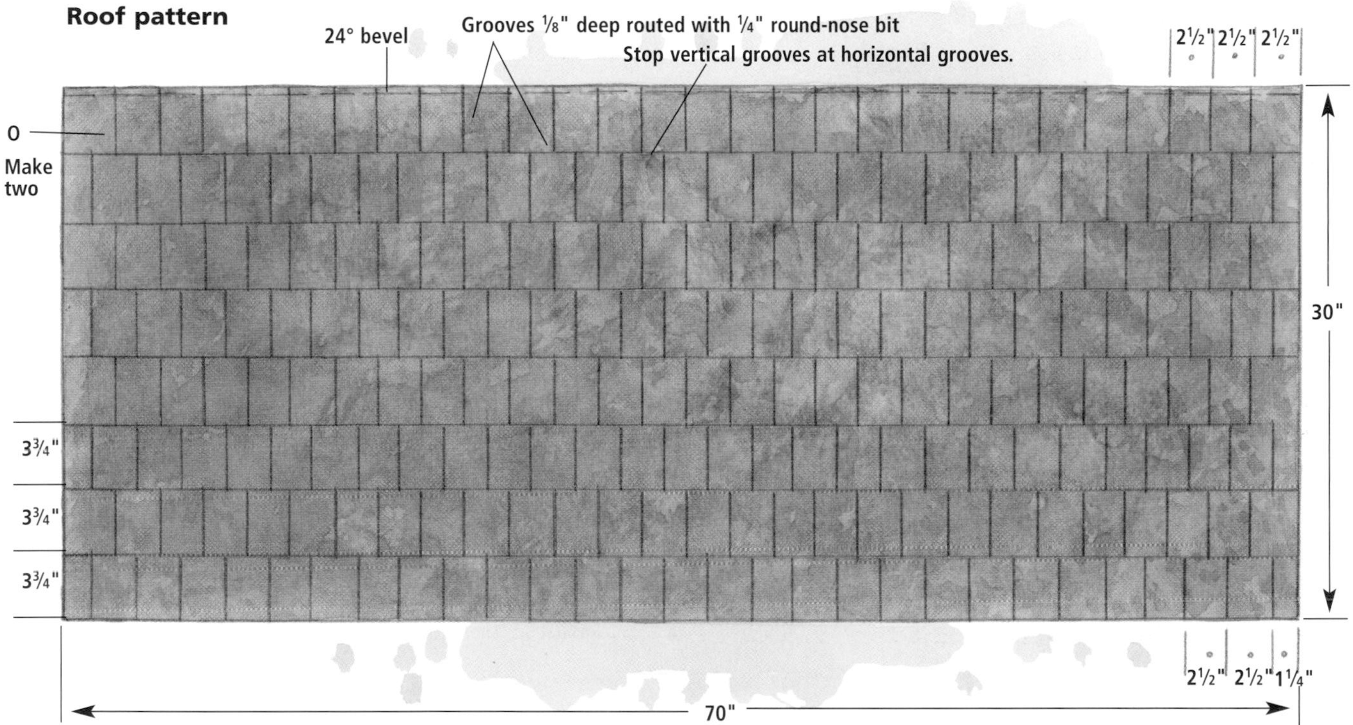

3 Bevel-cut the top edge of both roof panels–where they will meet along the ridge–to 24 degrees.

4 Cut four boards for the roof end trim (P) to the dimensions given in the Materials List. Using the drawings on page 138, create a full-size pattern. Draw the outline on one piece of trim, including the 24-degree bevels at each end. Cut out the piece with a jigsaw and use it as a template to lay out the other three.

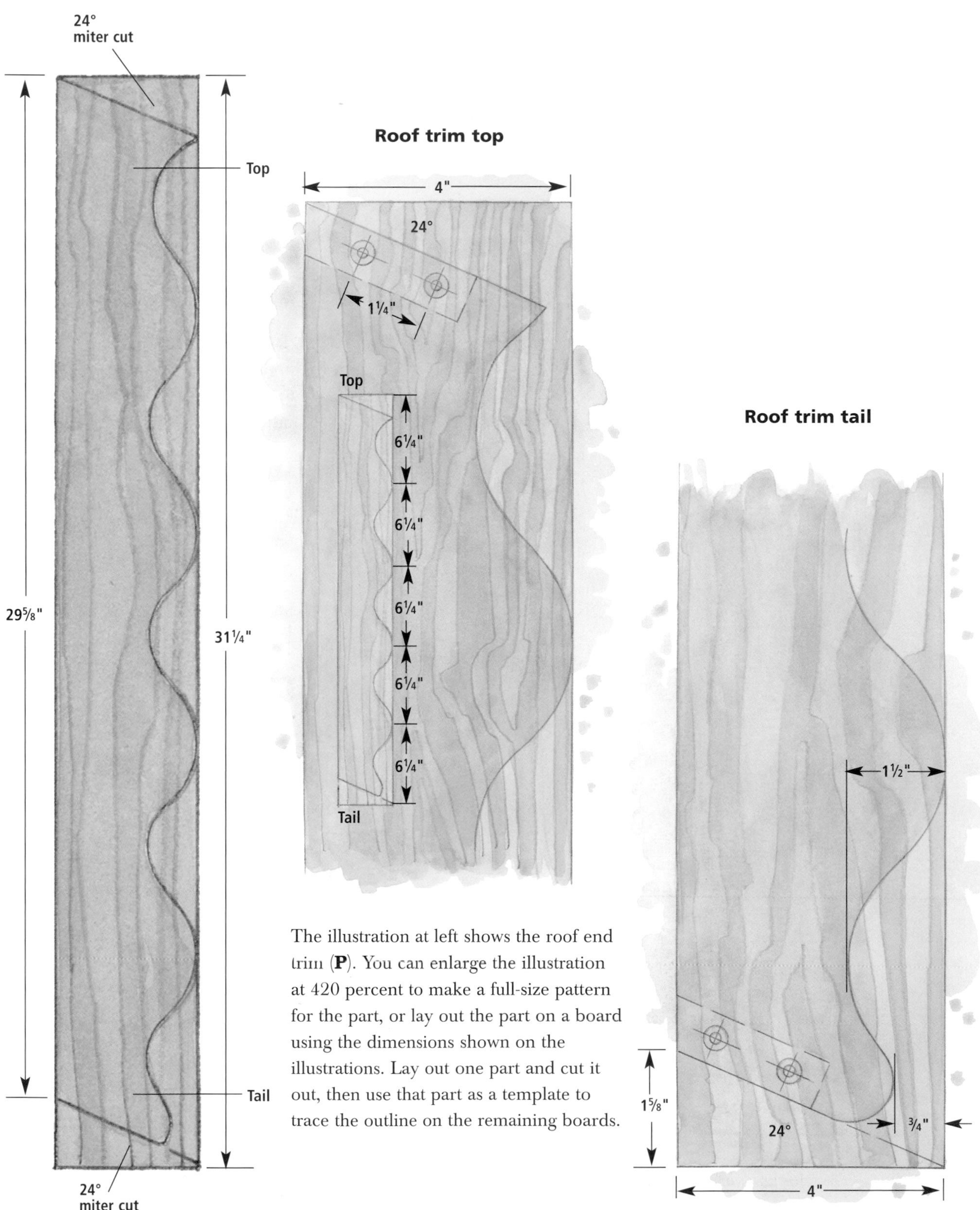

The illustration at left shows the roof end trim (**P**). You can enlarge the illustration at 420 percent to make a full-size pattern for the part, or lay out the part on a board using the dimensions shown on the illustrations. Lay out one part and cut it out, then use that part as a template to trace the outline on the remaining boards.

5 Cut the two eaves and the two ridge boards **(Q)** to the sizes given in the Materials List. Cut a 24-degree bevel along the top edge of each piece, matching the roof pitch.

6 Clamp the two ridge boards together, face to face, and drill three ¼-inch holes through them as shown on page 129. These holes are for the bolts that will tie the two roof panels together and help create a weathertight seam.

7 Clamp the roof trim boards, the ridge board, and the eave on the underside of the perimeter of each roof panel. Make sure all parts fit well, planing and sanding as necessary. Drill the mounting holes as shown, then attach the boards to the panel with glue and #8×1½-inch flathead wood screws.

Erect the four walls

1 Test-assemble the four walls, with a helper on hand to hold everything together while you drill pilot holes through the holes you drilled earlier in the cleats and battens. Drive only about half of the screws now to make sure the corners pull together securely.

2 Drill mounting holes in the trim piece to the left of the door for the two hinges and install the door. Drill holes for the hinges in one trim piece on each window and install the windows. (See page 132.)

Magnetic catch

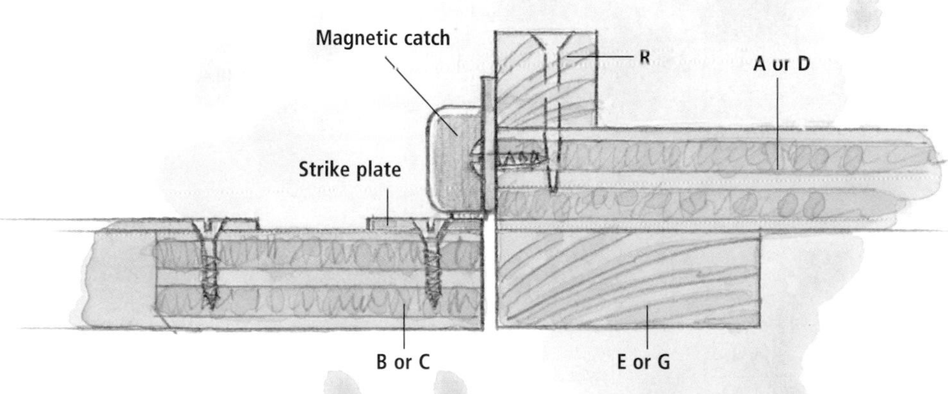

3 Magnetic catches keep the windows and doors closed. To mount them, make 10 catch supports **(R)**, cutting them to the dimensions in the Materials List. The supports are used to back up the catches, which are attached to the edge of the window and door openings. Attach the metal strike plates to the back of the windows and door. See page 131 for the locations of the catches, and the drawing above for an overhead view of a catch.

4 Temporarily put the roof in place to make sure that the two panels sit properly on the walls and meet at the ridge. The three pairs of bolt holes should be aligned with one another. The drawing on page 129 shows how the ridge connects together.

5 Remove the roof, disassemble the walls, and remove the hinges, strike plates, and catches. Fill in plywood voids and recessed screw heads with exterior wood putty. Larger voids in the wood can be filled with a paintable exterior caulk. Sand any sharp edges that will be exposed once the playhouse is completed; do not sand along the interior edges of the corner assemblies, which should meet snugly.

6 Paint all surfaces with an exterior primer. Follow with two coats of a flat or semigloss exterior paint. The roof, trim, windows, shutters, and door can be painted with a semigloss or gloss exterior enamel. Pick any paint scheme that suits you, perhaps using leftover paint to match the colors of your home. Or bring home color samples and let the future residents of the playhouse make their own choices–subject to parental approval, of course.

7 Attach the shutters with #8×1¼-inch flathead wood screws. As shown in the drawing on page 132, drive the screws from inside the playhouse. The windows are cut from ⅛-inch acrylic as shown in drawings right and opposite. (For safety, do not use glass.) You can cut acrylic with a circular saw or a fine-toothed blade that has little or no set. Or you can score the outline of each window by running a utility knife along a straightedge, then placing the acrylic over a scrap of wood with the scored line overhanging about ⅛ inch, and pressing down to snap the sheet. Sand or scrape the edges to smooth them. Drill and counterbore mounting holes. Install the acrylic with #6×½-inch flathead wood screws, driving the screws only until the acrylic is secure to avoid splitting the plastic.

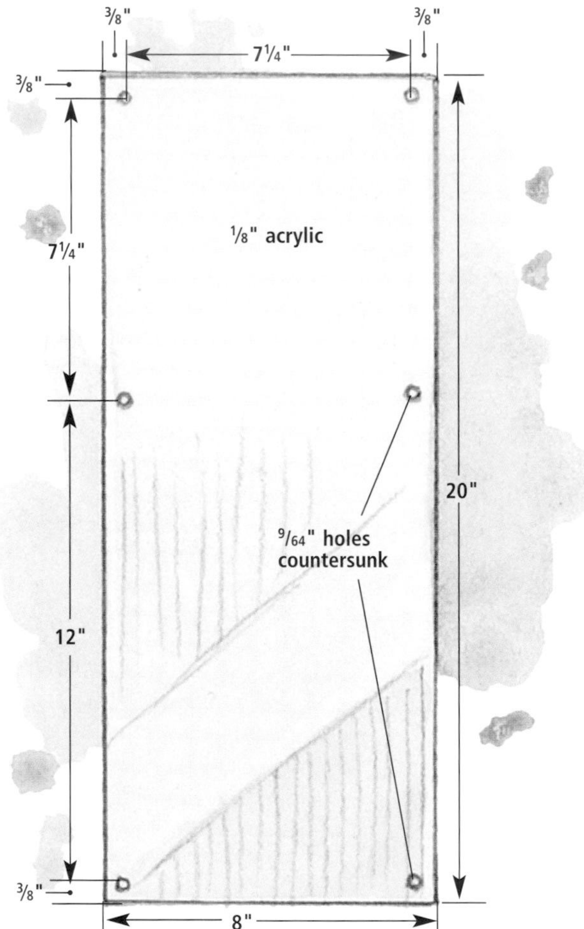

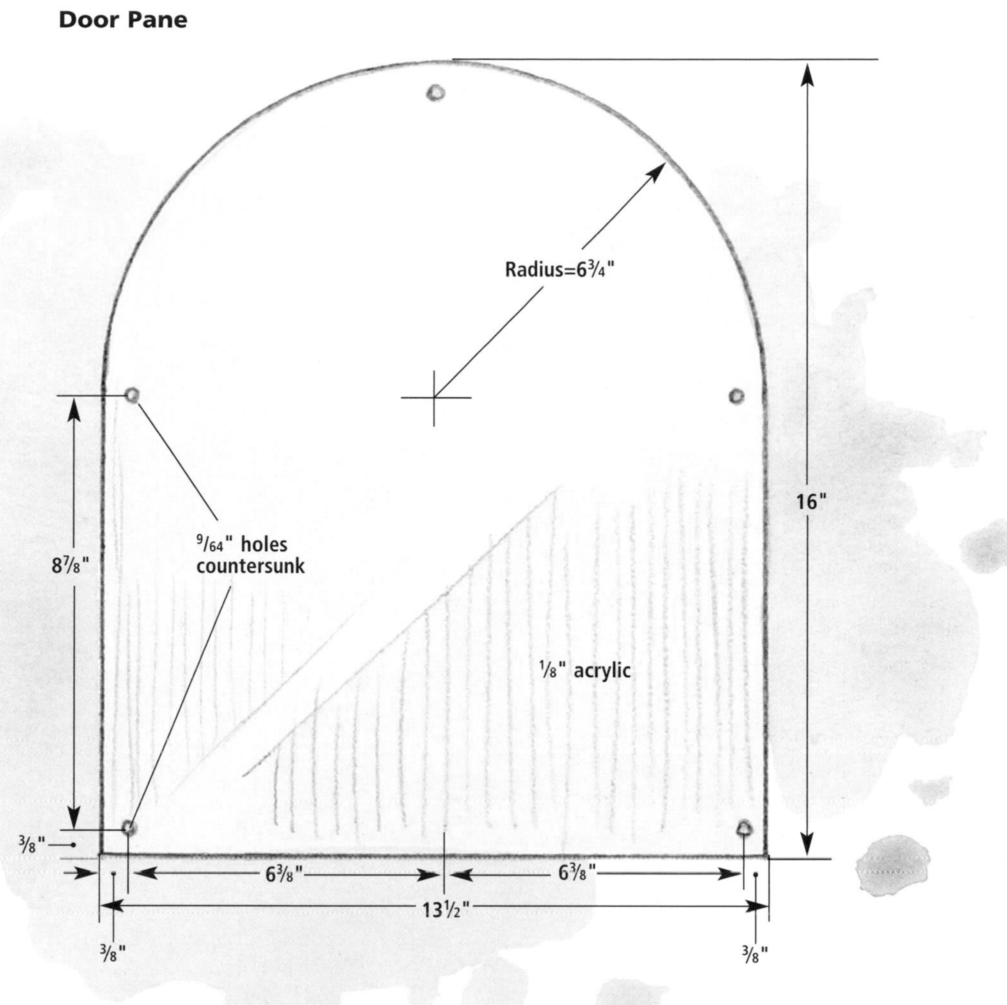

8 Reinstall the windows and door. Run a length of adhesive-backed foam weather stripping along the top edge of one roof panel to make a good seal when the bolts are installed through the ridge. (See the drawing on page 129.)

9 With a helper, assemble the walls and roof with screws (but not with glue), checking for square and plumb as you go. Draw the two roof panels together with the three bolts and attach the roof to the cleats with screws.

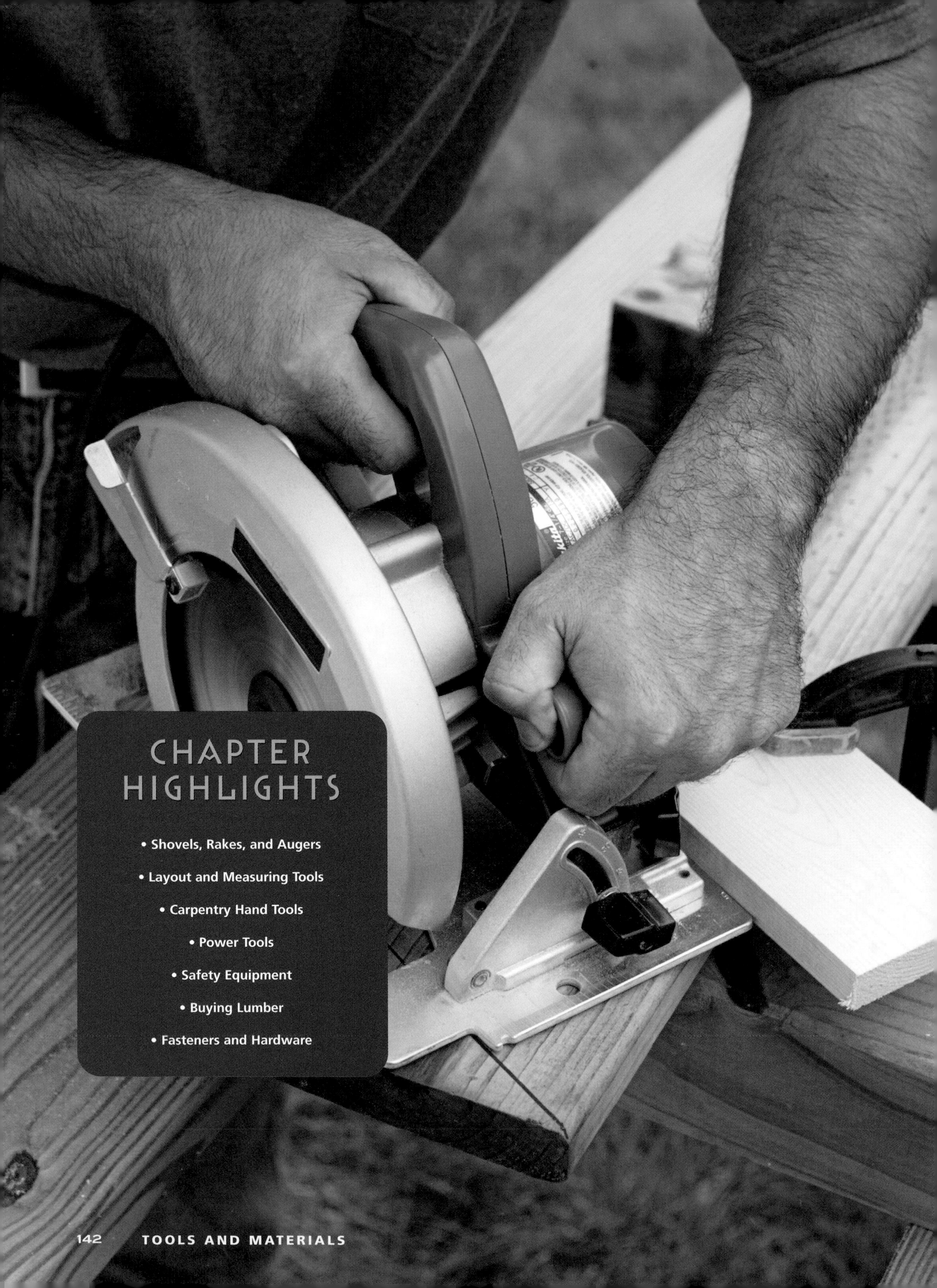

CHAPTER HIGHLIGHTS

- Shovels, Rakes, and Augers
- Layout and Measuring Tools
- Carpentry Hand Tools
- Power Tools
- Safety Equipment
- Buying Lumber
- Fasteners and Hardware

TOOLS AND MATERIALS

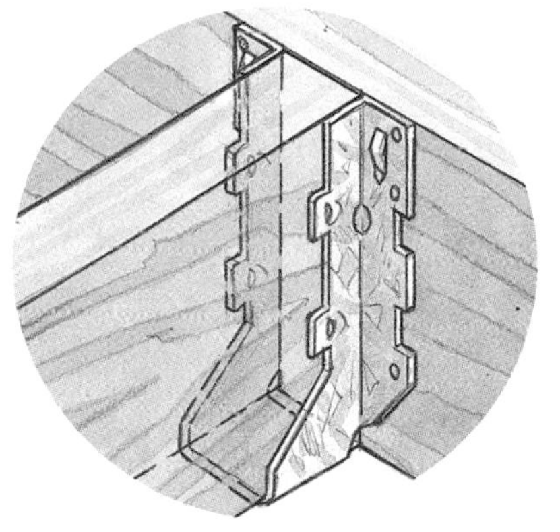

The playset you build will probably see a lot of action. It will not be used gently, so you need to build it well. To ensure safety and durability, start with the best materials for each use and take care in cutting and assembling parts.

Posts set into the ground and parts that rest on the ground are susceptible to rot, so use rot-resistant lumber species or pressure-treated lumber for parts that will be in contact with the ground. Lumber is now treated with compounds that don't contain arsenic. See page 159 for more about pressure-treated lumber.

This section also shows the tools that you will rely on to build the projects in this book. Some of the projects are fairly substantial jobs, on par, perhaps, with a deck or a storage shed. Power tools will make the work easier and usually will result in more accurate joints, which leads to a sturdier structure. If you don't own some of the tools shown, you can probably rent them.

You'll need another adult to help with some of the tasks shown, such as lifting large beams. But there are a lot of places where you can let your kids get involved in the project, which may make it even more fun for them.

Shovels, Rakes, and Augers

The tools you'll need for playset projects depend largely on the project you're taking on, but before you start you should have on hand at least some of the implements shown here. Here's what each of them does:

Drain spade. With its narrow, pointed blade, a drain spade is ideal for digging trenches. It also comes in handy in other tight spots, such as shoveling dirt or concrete around posts that you're setting.

Hand auger. You screw this one into the ground to bore holes for posts. Give it a turn, lift it out of the hole, knock dirt off the blades, and repeat the process until you've reached the depth you want. Or rent a power version like one of those shown opposite.

Clamshell posthole digger. A pair of long-handled shovels hinged together offers another way to dig postholes. You open the shovel blades, jam them into the ground, separate the handles, and lift out a chunk of earth. (You may need to rotate the blades back and forth to cut roots or dislodge small rocks.)

Round-blade shovel. Use this workhorse for all sorts of digging jobs. A long-handled version provides better leverage in excavations more than a foot deep. A square-blade spade (not shown) is best for digging up sod and knifing through tree roots.

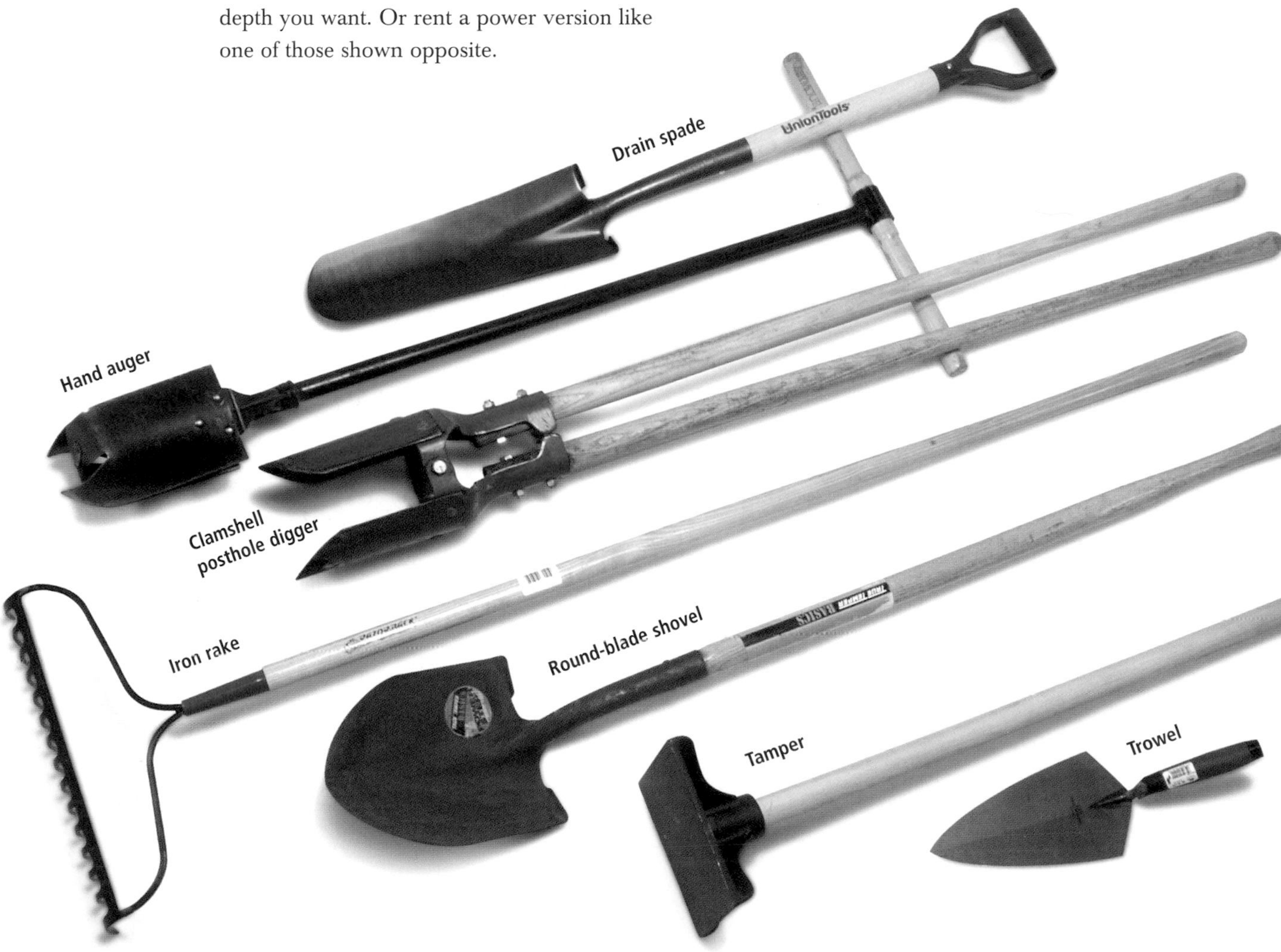

Iron rake. Also known as a bow rake, an iron rake breaks up and levels soil. You can also do these jobs, and mix concrete, with a garden hoe (not shown).

Tamper. Compact soil around posts and in other spots that require firm, dense earth. You can make your own tamper by nailing a 12-inch plywood square to one end of a length of 2×4.

Trowel. Move small amounts of soil in tight spots with this basic gardener's tool. It also comes in handy for mixing concrete and placing it around posts.

Buying tips

Examine tools before you buy. If a handle is too long, short, or heavy for you, try another. Check connections. The best spades, shovels, and rakes have a metal shank extending partway up the handle for additional strength. Trowels are more durable when they have wooden handles driven into a metal shank.

Remember that most manufacturers offer several lines of tools at various price levels. You might decide on an inexpensive version of an item you'll use only a few times but spend more to buy high-quality tools you'll use often.

Caring for landscaping tools

Well-made tools last for years if you don't abuse or neglect them. Here are some maintenance hints:

- Clean tools after each use with a paint stick or steel brush to keep soil from encrusting.
- Wipe wooden handles with linseed oil. Paint them a bright color if you tend to lose tools.
- Sharpen tools for efficiency and safety. Follow instructions that come with each tool. Usually you can do the job with a metal file.
- Check and tighten bolts and screws regularly.
- For safety and to maintain cutting edges, hang tools on the wall of your garage or shed. Protect steel blades against rust by applying oil or petroleum jelly.

Power Posthole Diggers

If you have several postholes to dig, consider renting one of these gasoline-powered machines. Power augers come with interchangeable spiral boring bits for making holes 6, 8, or 10 inches in diameter. They can excavate holes up to 44 inches deep. Some models, like the one above right, can be operated by one person. The larger auger, above left, takes two people to operate but is less likely to kick out of a hole when it hits a rock or tree root.

- To dig with a power auger, mark the depth of the posthole on the bit with tape and set the auger over the spot you've selected. Start the engine, adjust the speed with a handle-mounted throttle, and exert even downward pressure. After digging a few inches, slowly raise the bit to dislodge dirt from the hole.

Layout and Measuring Tools

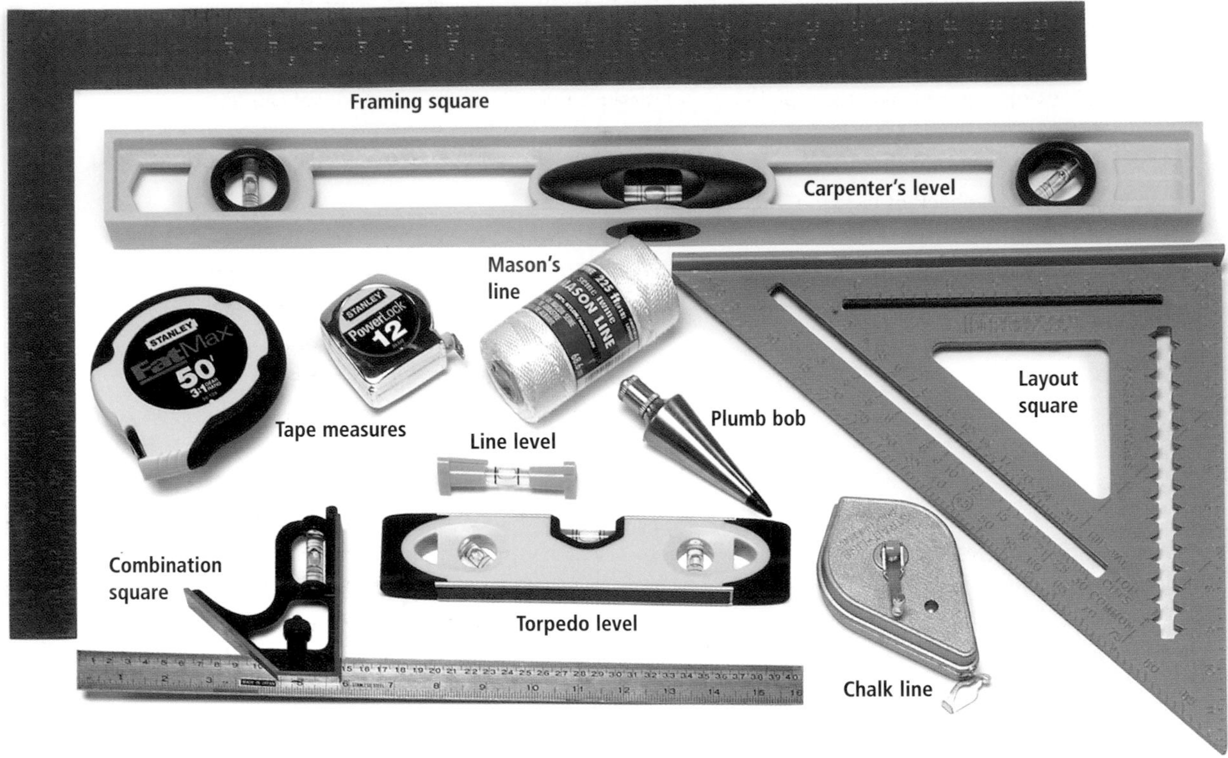

Almost any project requires measurements of some sort, so you might as well get into the habit of clipping a steel tape to your belt as the first step in every job.

Remember, too, that it's surprisingly easy to misread or miscalculate a dimension. Read carefully because mistaken measurements cost time and materials.

Simple linear measurements often aren't enough. In many instances, you also need to know whether something is square, level, or plumb, as explained on page 167.

Making careful, accurate measurements takes time and concentration. Sometimes you have to climb a ladder or stretch into a tight corner. At first, you may find it difficult to make accurate readings, but it's usually even more difficult to correct the results of an inaccurate one later.

The main weapons in the battle against inaccuracy

Framing square. Often called a carpenter's square, a framing square is designed for squaring almost anything. Its large size makes it ideal for squaring large structures and marking sheet material, such as plywood.

Carpenter's level. Usually 24 or 30 inches long, a carpenter's level provides accuracy over broad spans. Bubbles show level, plumb, and often 45-degree angles as well. A similar tool, called a mason's level, is 4 feet long and is useful in leveling long parts, such as the top rail of a fence.

50-foot tape. If you're laying out a large project, a 50-foot or longer cloth or flexible steel tape with a locking device saves time.

12-foot tape. This one has lots of uses. You can measure lumber and other materials for cutting, lay out straight or curved parts, measure depths (as with postholes), and determine positioning. A locking feature holds the tape in position while you make your mark. Many also have decimal equivalents, nail sizes, and other useful information on the back of the tape.

Mason's line. Coupled with the line level shown below it, opposite, a mason's line lets you determine level over a long distance, such as between post tops. The level clips onto the line.

Plumb bob. For determining or marking plumb, use a plumb bob suspended by a cord or mason's line.

Layout square. This small triangular square speeds up layout jobs. A lip along one edge butts up against the square edge of a board so that you can draw 90- or 45-degree lines across it. And its aluminum or plastic body is an effective guide for a circular saw or jigsaw.

Torpedo level. A short torpedo level can fit where a longer level can't. Like a carpenter's level, it has vials that measure level, plumb, and 45-degree angles.

Chalk line. Use this for marking long, straight lines on large materials, such as plywood. Hook the end over a small nail at one end of the line, extend the line taut against the material, lift, and snap it to mark the line. The one shown doubles as a plumb bob.

Combination square. Square and mark boards for crosscuts with a combination square. It also may be used as a marking and depth gauge and for laying out 45-degree miter cuts. Most combination squares include a level in the sliding handle.

Electronic Levels

Classic bubble levels are precision instruments, but they have a few limitations. Because even mason's levels measure 4 feet or less in length, drawing a longer plumb or vertical line—on the side of a building, for example—requires sliding the level. And every time you move it, you risk inaccuracy that will compound as you progress. Electronic levels like the laser models shown here project a light beam that makes a plumb or level line on a surface that's as long or high as the surface itself. A buzzer sounds to indicate level or plumb, a handy feature if you're working in low light or in an awkward position.

Carpentry Hand Tools

Assemble your hand-tool collection a few pieces at a time. Start with the basics, then add specialty items and power equipment as you need them. This way you're more likely to invest in quality, and as you gain proficiency, you'll also develop a clearer sense of what tools you'd like to purchase next. Which are the basics? With the assortment of tools shown here you can handle many projects. Here are descriptions of the hand tools shown:

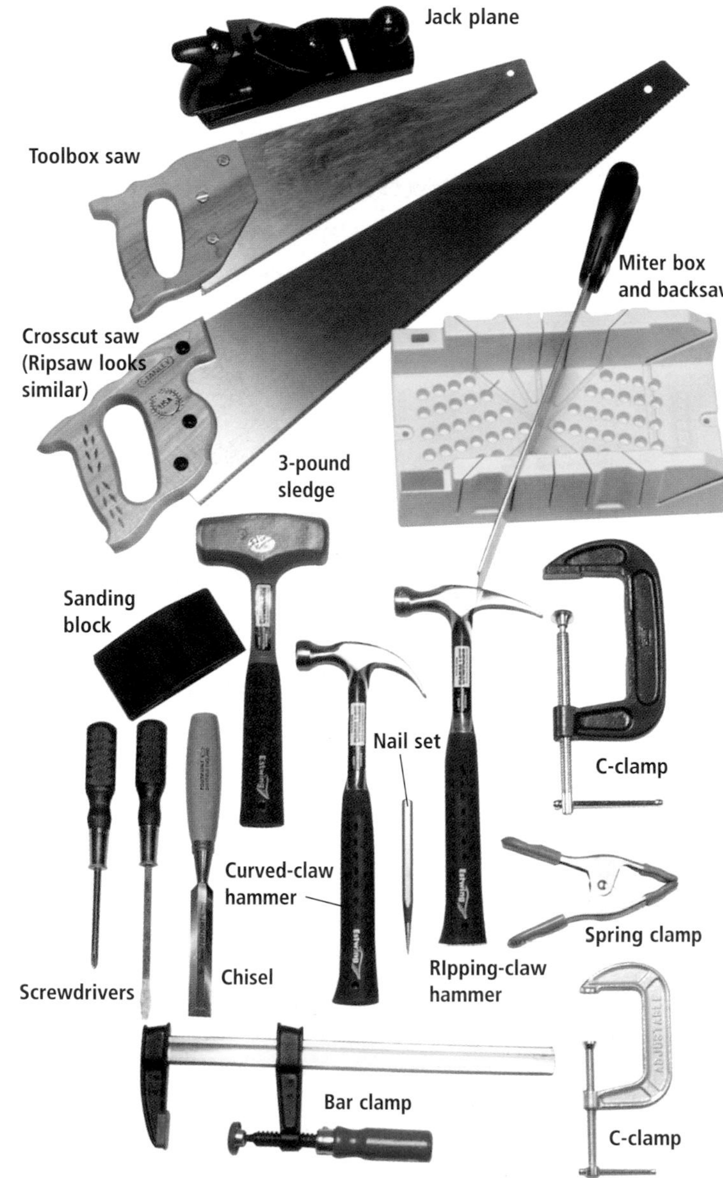

Jack plane. Measuring 12 to 15 inches long, a jack plane makes a good general-use smoothing tool. Later you might want to add a shorter smooth plane and a block plane, which fits in the palm of your hand. A block plane with a low blade angle is good for end-grain planing.

Crosscut saw. A crosscut saw works best across the grain, the most common cutting operation. The short version shown here is called a toolbox saw because it's small enough to fit into a toolbox.

Ripsaw. You can use a crosscut saw to rip a board–saw with the grain–but you'll make slow headway. A ripsaw cuts best with the grain.

Miter box and backsaw. Use these for absolutely square and miter cuts in narrow lumber, such as trim pieces. The box guides the cuts; the saw–a small crosscut saw with a reinforced back–does the work. It's so named because it cuts on the back stroke.

Sanding block. Sandpaper works best when it's held flat against the surface. Buy a wood, plastic, or rubber sanding block or wrap sandpaper around a block of wood.

3-pound sledge. Sometimes called a baby sledge, this hefty hammer easily handles heavy-duty pounding jobs, such as driving stakes.

Curved-claw hammer. Make a 16-ounce curved-claw hammer your first tool purchase. Besides driving many kinds of fasteners, a claw hammer also pulls them.

Ripping-claw hammer. Use a 20-ounce hammer with a ripping claw for driving framing nails and prying boards apart.

Nail set. Countersink or set nails beneath the wood's surface with this inexpensive tool.

Screwdrivers. You'll need both straight and phillips heads for attaching hardware.

Chisels. Use a chisel when you need to cut mortises for hinges, remove excess wood from grooves and joints, shape joints, form inside and outside curves in wood, or trim wood to close tolerances. Chisels with 1/4-, 3/8-, 1/2-, and 3/4-inch-wide blades, often sold in sets, will perform most chiseling chores.

Clamps. An assortment of clamps is essential for most gluing tasks and also can temporarily hold materials together while you drill, saw, screw, or nail them. C-clamps, spring clamps, and bar clamps are handy types to have.

This list of hand tools doesn't include a drill. That's because your first power tool purchase should be a corded or cordless electric drill, which also serves as a screwdriver for outdoor projects. See pages 150–152 for power tools.

Buying tips

Take your time when deciding on any tool, and try to learn what it's made of. With metal tools, you'll encounter several different alloys.

- **Carbon steel**, made of iron and carbon, is fine for screwdrivers and other tools that don't generate heat.
- **Low-alloy steel** includes some tungsten or molybdenum to increase heat resistance.
- **High-alloy steel**, which has a much higher tungsten or molybdenum content, is the best choice for high-speed cutting tools. Power saw blades tipped with tungsten carbide will last the average do-it-yourselfer for years.

Metal tools differ, too, in the way they're made. Casting, the least expensive manufacturing technique, for instance, can result in flaws in the metal that make it liable to chip and break. For striking tools, such as hammers, don't buy the cast type. A broken tool can cause serious injury.

Forged or drop-forged tools are almost indestructible, an important quality for items such as hammers and wrenches. Chisels should be made of high-quality steel with precisely ground bevels and edges.

Japanese Pull Saws

These thin-blade saws cut on the pull stroke, not the push stroke like traditional Western saws. This prevents the blade from buckling and binding, providing more control. The saw can't jump out of its groove and cause damage to the project or the user's hands.

- The thin steel makes the blade flexible, allowing the saw to adapt to specialty tasks, such as cutting dowels flush with the surrounding surface. The unique blade design works equally well for both crosscutting and rip cutting, undercuts, and reverse cuts.

- It's difficult to sharpen these fine-tooth saws, so most have replaceable blades. Some pull saw blades have a single cutting edge; others have teeth for ripping on one side, crosscutting on the other.

Don't overlook tools made partly of plastic. For instance, fiberglass handles on hammers, sledges, and axes are every bit as strong as steel shanks, yet they have even more resilience than old-fashioned wood handles and deliver less shock to your hand and arm.

POWER SAWS

Four types of power saws will accomplish almost everything you'll need to do when you build a backyard play structure.

7¼-inch circular saw. Crosscut and rip lumber and plywood to the right size with this saw, making straight cuts with ease. If you buy only one power saw, this is the one to get. Steel blades dull quickly, so purchase the more durable carbide-tip combination blade.

Jigsaw. This versatile saw crosscuts and rips, though it cuts much more slowly and less smoothly and accurately than a circular saw. A jigsaw's main function is cutting curves, but it is also indispensable for making small cutouts of any shape, as its thin blade can start a cut almost anywhere. Some models feature variable speed control, which is handy if you cut materials other than wood, such as plastic or metal. An orbital-cutting jigsaw cuts faster than a nonorbital model.

Reciprocating saw. Use this saw with a variety of blades that have teeth designed to cut different materials–including wood, nails, screws, and even steel pipe. It's used primarily for demolition and rough cutting.

Power mitersaw. This stationary circular saw is sometimes called a chop saw. It makes quick, clean crosscuts, but its real strength is making extremely accurate miter (angle) cuts. If you have many trim pieces to cut and install, a mitersaw is the tool to use.

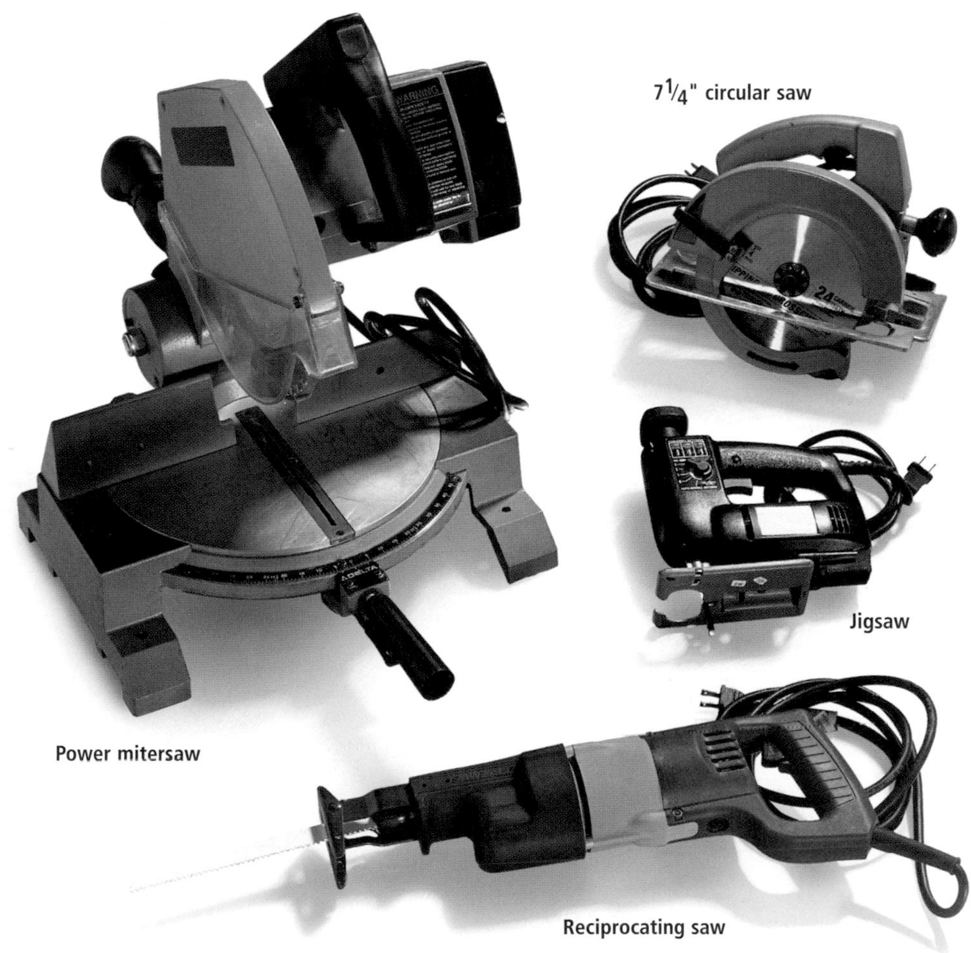

7¼" circular saw

Jigsaw

Power mitersaw

Reciprocating saw

CHAPTER 4

DRILLING AND SHAPING TOOLS

A drill and some bits are all you need for most work. Add a router and you can make your own moldings and decorative edges.

3/8-inch variable-speed, reversible (VSR) drill. This basic tool can handle almost all drilling needs. If you're going to be drilling many holes in concrete, consider getting a hammer drill, which offers an impact action similar to a jackhammer for faster drilling in masonry. Otherwise a high-quality corded drill will do fine. Low-cost, homeowner-grade models and cordless drills less than 12 volts lack the power necessary for hole saws and spade bits. A cordless drill/driver is indispensible if you are building a project with screws.

Twist drills. These bits will drill holes in many materials. Use them for such things as pilot holes for screws. Buy a graduated set of these, from 1/16 to 3/8 or 1/2 inch.

Hole saw. Use a cylindrical hole saw with a power drill to make large holes.

Router. This versatile tool shapes edges and cuts mortises and dadoes, among other things.

Router bits. Many styles of router bits are available. Buy only the profiles you need for your project.

Belt sander. Aggressively smooth and shape wood with this sander. With a coarse belt, it removes wood quickly.

Random-orbit sander. Smooth wood for painting or staining with this finish sander.

Cordless Tools

Cordless tools have revolutionized the market. The most popular is the cordless drill/driver, but you'll also find cordless reciprocating saws, circular saws, jigsaws–even mitersaws.

Cordless tools offer increased portability and convenience. They operate at a specific voltage, ranging from 7.2 to 24 volts. The higher the voltage, the more powerful the tool.

While especially useful if you're working far from an electrical outlet, cordless tools have some disadvantages:

- They usually cost more than corded versions.
- Run time depends on the battery charge and capacity. If you buy a cordless tool, buy it in a kit that includes two batteries and a rapid recharger. This way you can use one battery while the other is recharging.
- Worn-out batteries are expensive to replace.
- Some cordless tools simply aren't powerful enough for some jobs, such as drilling into concrete or boring large holes with a spade bit.
- Cordless drills, for example, are often heavier and larger than their corded counterparts, making them more tiring to hold and difficult to use in tight spots.

Cordless tools are generally sold with a charger designed to recharge that tool's battery. You'll find nickel-cadmium (nicad) batteries in most tools you shop for, but those with nickel metal hydride (NiMH) batteries are generally worth the extra cost. They provide more run time and faster recharging with less weight.

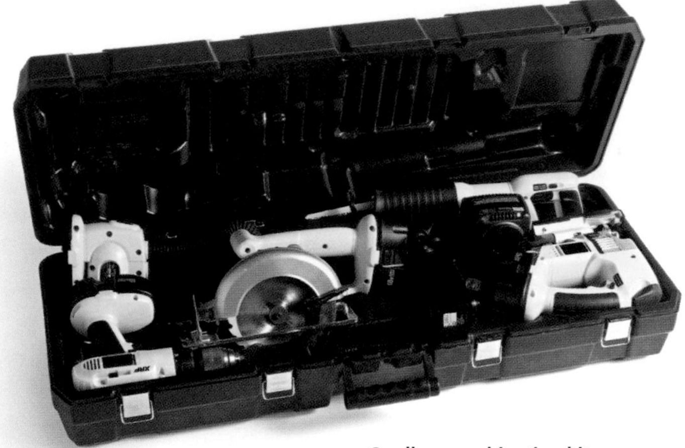

Cordless combination kit

If you own more than one drill, the second one should definitely be a cordless drill/driver, with a battery of 12 volts or more, a ⅜-inch chuck, a two-speed transmission, and an adjustable clutch that releases when it reaches a preset torque level. This keeps you from breaking or burying screws as you drive them.

Buy Quality

The best rule to follow for tool purchases is to buy only the tools that you really need—but buy the highest-quality tool you can afford. That said, a low-price homeowner-grade tool is sometimes a smart buy for something you'll use infrequently or for only one job.

Many of today's medium-priced tools boast features, power, and durability that once could be found only in costly professional-grade tools. When comparing tools, rely on amperage ratings to compare power rather than horsepower ratings, which can be deceiving. Tools that are more durable and long lasting feature ball or needle bearings instead of bushings, and precisely machined gears instead of die-cast or nonmetallic gears. Before you buy a tool, hold it and move it around to make sure it is comfortable to grip, light enough to handle, and well-balanced.

SAFETY EQUIPMENT

Buy these pieces of safety equipment at the same time you buy the tools that require their use.

Industrial-quality safety glasses or goggles. These have side shields to protect your eyes. Glasses or goggles labeled Z87.1 are industrial quality. If you wear prescription glasses, either buy prescription safety glasses or get goggles that fit over your glasses. Try goggles on before you buy them. Find a pair so comfortable that you won't mind wearing them all the time while working.

Earmuffs or earplugs. Protect your hearing when you use noisy power tools. Try them on before you buy to find the most comfortable pair. If they are not comfortable, you will be less likely to wear them.

Dust masks. Particle and dust masks protect your lungs during dusty operations such as sawing, sanding, and drilling holes in concrete. Check the label before you buy and match the mask to the type of work you will be doing.

Work gloves. Wear gloves for dirty work such as unloading materials and cleaning up debris. Do not wear them when you are working with power tools–you are more likely to lose your grip or fumble a tool or piece with gloves on. Gloves can also get caught in a spinning blade or drill bit. Wear rubber gloves to keep your hands clean and prevent irritation when applying paint and finishes.

Leather boots. Boots are a good footwear choice when you are using power tools; they offer more protection against cuts and bruises than does lighter footgear. At the very least, wear sturdy, rubber-soled shoes to prevent slipping when you're working.

First aid kit. It's good to keep a first aid kit nearby during a project, especially if you have youngsters helping you. A handy item to have is a pair of sharp-pointed tweezers with a magnifying lens attached for pulling splinters.

ACCESSORIES

Cou will be working outside without the benefit of a well-organized workshop. Several items will help make your work easier and safer.

Extension cords. When you have to work at a long distance from an outlet, use heavy-duty cords; those with 12-gauge wire are good. Lightweight cords can overheat, posing a fire or shock hazard, and they will rob tools of the power they need. Always use cords with three-prong plugs and plug them into a ground fault circuit interrupter (GFCI) for work outside. Uncoil the cord so it doesn't develop kinks, which can damage the conductors. Protect the cord from sharp edges and, if it crosses a walkway, tape it down with duct tape.

Sawhorses. You should have a pair to hold lumber at a comfortable working height. You can create an impromptu worktable with a sheet of plywood across two horses. Wooden horses are heavier than metal or plastic models, but have advantages. You can nail a couple of 2×4s across them for added stability, for example. Also you might damage your saw blade if you happen to cut into a metal sawhorse.

Work lights. Lights make it easier and safer to work in dim light or deep shade. Halogen models throw a brighter, whiter light than incandescent lights and often come with adjustable stands. Be careful, though–they get very hot.

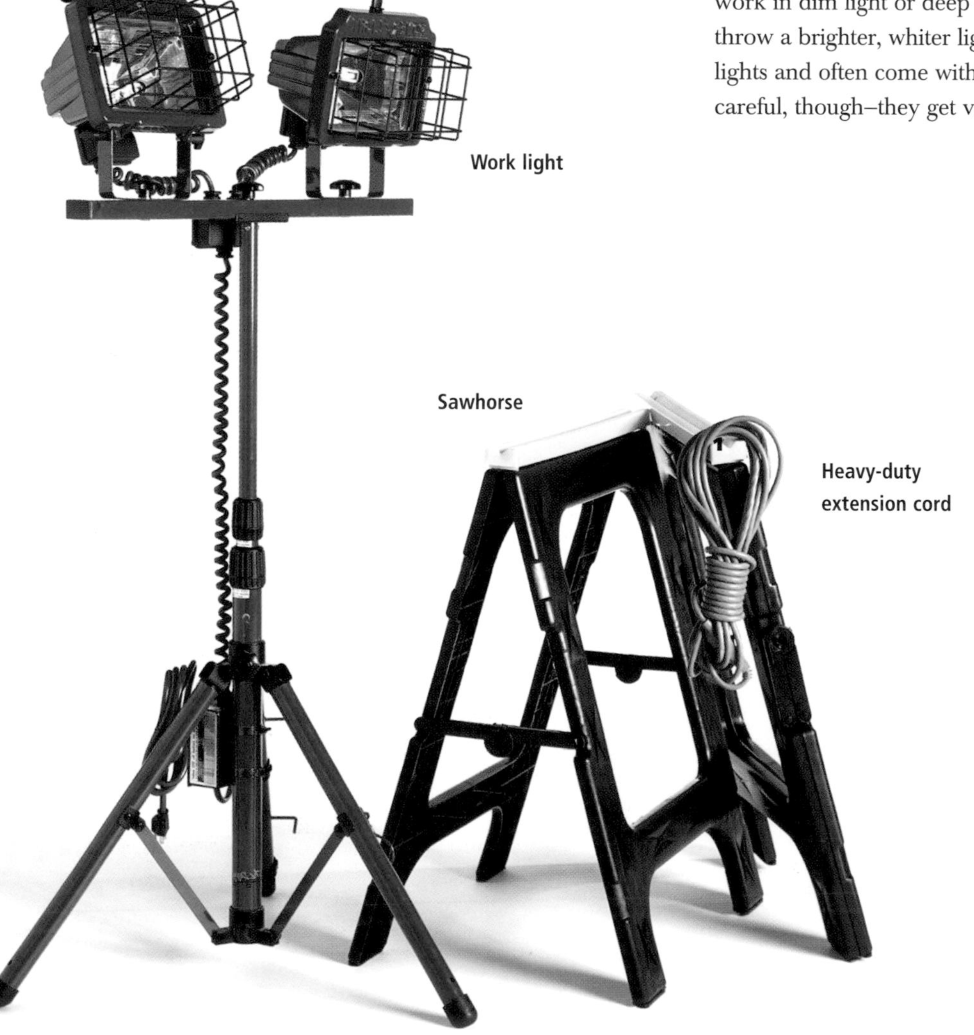

BRUSHES AND ROLLERS

Whether you've built your play structure out of cedar, redwood, or pressure-treated pine, it pays to apply a water-repellent sealer to the wood. The natural chemicals found in cedar and redwood, and the applied chemicals in pressure-treated pine, make them insect and rot resistant, but the wood is still subject to weathering. If you don't apply a sealer, expect surface cracks and splits to appear. Look for a clear or semitransparent (tinted) water-repellent sealer with mildewcide and a UV stabilizer. Avoid solid stains as they sit on the surface and eventually wear off. Unless the wood was kiln dried or (in the case of pressure-treated wood) kiln dried after treatment (KDAT), let it dry for two months before applying a finish.

Brushes. Brushes get the nod for most finishing chores. Get brushes with synthetic bristles (nylon, polyester, or nylon/polyester blend) for water-base finishes and latex paints, and natural bristles (animal hair) for oil-base finishes and paints. The pores of natural bristles absorb water readily, making them puffy and hard to control. Oil-base finishes will attack and break down synthetic bristles, so you'll end up with bristles sticking to the surface. Disposable foam brushes work fine with either type of finish.

Rollers. Rollers make short work of large, flat surfaces, and you can buy smaller trim rollers for tight spots. Mohair and lamb's wool rollers are meant for oil finishes; synthetic fibers, which are much cheaper, will work with oil or latex finishes.

Roller covers vary in nap depths from $\frac{1}{16}$ inch to $1\frac{1}{2}$ inches. Use a long-nap roller for painting rough surfaces such as concrete block. Use a medium nap for applying sealer to play structures.

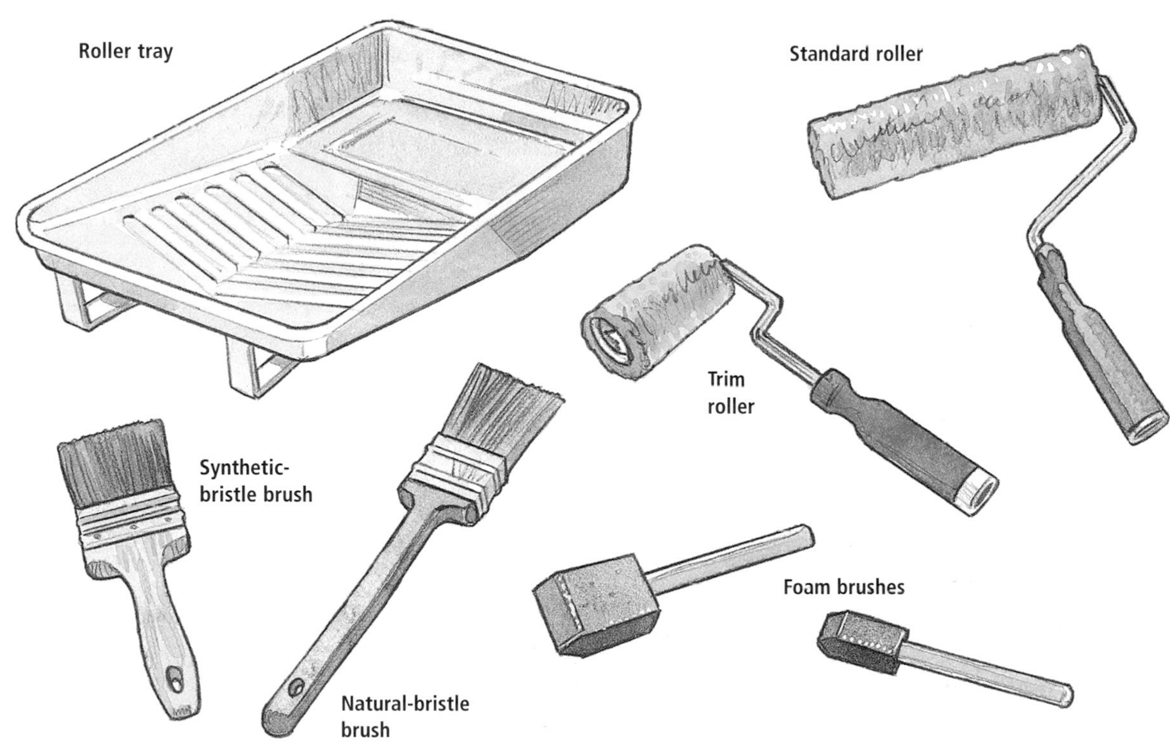

Buying Lumber

Some trees withstand the elements for centuries with nary a complaint. But cut one down and mill it into lumber, and it becomes vulnerable to extreme heat and cold, wind, rain, snow, ice, airborne pollutants, damaging ultraviolet radiation, insects, and more. Fortunately, some species hold up much better than others when they're made into lumber.

The heart of the matter

How well a board resists decay depends largely on what part of the tree it came from.

Heartwood, the tree's mature central core, is the toughest. You can easily identify heartwood in many species by its much deeper color.

Sapwood, which comes from the outer part of the tree, is usually lighter in color and is also a lightweight performer when it comes to strength and decay resistance. Heartwood of any species is preferable for outdoor use.

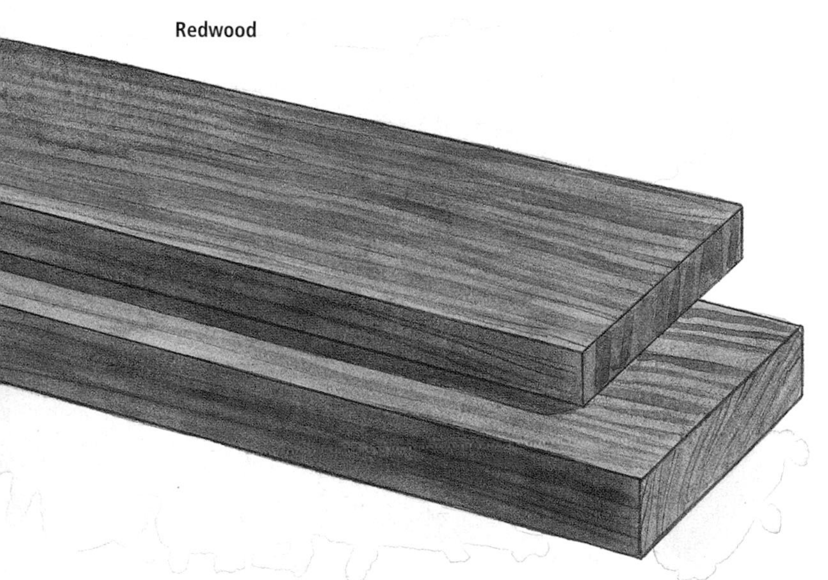

Softwood choices

Once, almost everybody used redwood for outdoor projects. Back then, the stock was widely available at a reasonable price in the higher grades that showcased the wood's warm, rich, reddish-brown heartwood.

High-grade redwood is not as widely available today. If it's available in your area, redwood works well for outdoor use. Cedar costs much less than redwood and is much more widely available. Depending on where you live, you may find your lumberyard stocked with cedar native to your region, such as western red or northern white. All cedar species are moderately soft with generally straight grain and a coarse texture.

Treated lumber

Pressure-treated (PT) lumber, typically southern pine saturated with a chemical preservative, works especially well for outdoor structures. Until recently, about 90 percent of the treated wood sold for residential use was treated with chromated copper arsenate (CCA), but questions about the safety of CCA arose. The result was an agreement between manufacturers and the U.S. Environmental Protection Agency (EPA) to phase out CCA lumber by December 31, 2003. Although it is no longer manufactured, some may still be in the supply lines.

Alternatives to CCA for lumber treatment are rapidly gaining ground. (Find out more about these on page 161.) When you shop for PT lumber, look for material certified by the American Wood Preservers' Bureau. A stamp on each board (see page 159) tells when the wood was treated, with which chemical, and where you can use the wood for best results. Wood rated for ground contact is the best choice for posts, for instance.

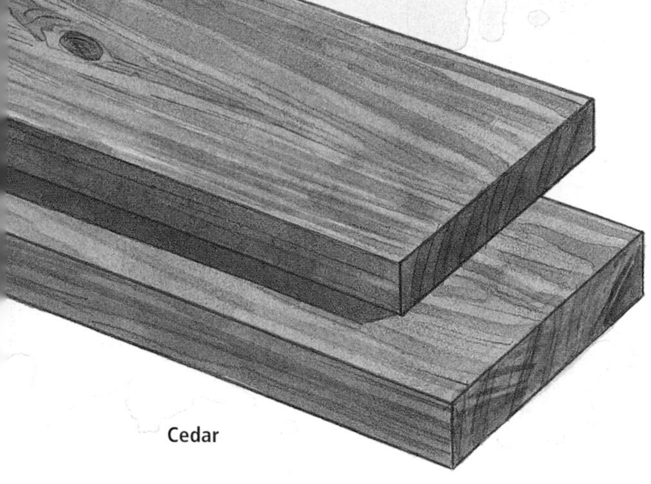
Cedar

Outdoor hardwoods

Hardwoods–domestic and imported–also work well for outdoor projects but are costly. White oak, probably the most widely available exterior-grade domestic hardwood, has closed cells that make it highly resistant to decay. Don't try to substitute red oak; its open cell structure makes it more likely to rot.

The heartwood of white oak is grayish brown, the sapwood nearly white. Other native outdoor-use hardwoods include bald cypress, honey locust, black locust, and sassafras. Most species are regional, and some are difficult to work with.

Exotic hardwoods will give an outdoor playset an exotic look but at a high price. Popular species include teak, various mahogany species, and ipe. Some exotic woods are harvested in environmentally questionable ways. Use exotic lumber from sustainable sources, which is usually identified.

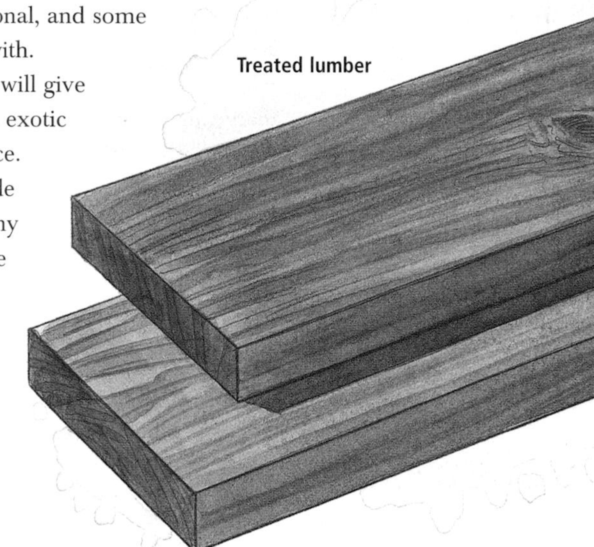
Treated lumber

Reading a Grade Stamp

Grade stamps on boards provide important information about the lumber. Stamps vary depending on the wood, the part of the country the lumber comes from, and which agency grading standards were applied. A typical stamp, shown here, tells you the quality of the wood, the species, whether it has been kiln dried, and which mill cut the board.

In this case, the board came from a tree in a mixed stand of Douglas fir and larch, so it is one or the other. It's green—it hasn't been kiln dried—so it may split and warp with time. It's graded as number 1 and better, the second-highest grade for strength. The highest-grade for dimension lumber is select structural; numbers 2 and 3 are lower. Use at least number 2 lumber for playsets. Use studs rated standard or construction.

Cedar is graded somewhat differently. The best-looking boards are called clear heart, followed by Grade A and Grade B.

Redwood is available in architectural and garden grades. Architectural grades are used for finish work where appearance is paramount. Garden grades may have knots and other imperfections, but they are ideal for outdoor projects, such as playsets. Use a heartwood grade, such as construction heart or deck heart, for parts that will be in ground contact. Grades containing sapwood, such as construction common and deck common, are good choices for aboveground uses.

MAKING A SELECTION

Wood is graded according to how many knots it has and the quality of its surface. Some lumberyards have their own grading systems, but they are usually based on these and other industry-standard grades:

■ **Clear.** Has no knots.

■ **Select.** High-quality wood. Select board grades are B and better, C, and D. Select structural is the top grade in dimension lumber.

■ **No. 2 common.** Boards with tight knots and no major blemishes.

■ **No. 3 common.** Knots in these boards may be loose; board may be blemished or damaged.

■ **Standard.** Middle-grade framing lumber; good strength; used for general framing.

■ **Utility.** Economy grade for rough work.

Inspecting boards

If you order lumber by telephone, you will get someone else's choice of boards, not your own. Lumberyards usually have lots of substandard wood lying around; the only way to be sure you do not get some of it is to pick out the boards yourself. Some lumberyards will not allow you to sort through the stacks because they want to keep wood neatly stacked–the best way to keep lumber from warping. But they should at least let you stand by and approve the selection. If not, confirm that you can return boards you don't like. Here are some lumber flaws to watch for:

■ A board that is heavily twisted, bowed, cupped, or crooked usually is not usable, although some bows will lie down as you nail them in place.

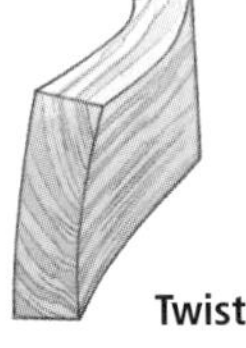
Twist

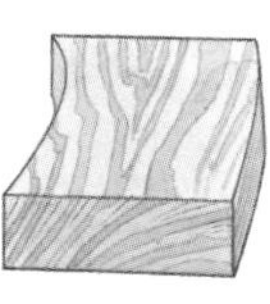
Bow

LUMBER SIZES

■ **Furring.** Rough wood of small dimensions for trim, shims, stakes, light-duty frames, latticework, and edging.

Nominal size	Actual size
1×2	¾×1½"
1×3	¾×2½"

■ **Boards.** Smooth-finished lumber for general construction, trimwork, and decking.

Nominal size	Actual size
1×4	¾×3½"
1×6	¾×5½"
1×8	¾×7¼"
1×10	¾×9¼"
1×12	¾×11¼"

■ **Dimension lumber.** Studs are usually 2×4, sometimes 2×6. Planks are 6 inches wide or wider. Use for structural framing, structural finishing, forming, decking, and fencing.

Nominal size	Actual size
2×2	1½×1½"
2×3	1½×2½"
2×4	1½×3½"
2×6	1½×5½"
2×8	1½×7¼"
2×10	1½×9¼"
2×12	1½×11¼"
4×4	3½×3½"
4×6	3½×5½"
6×6	5½×5½"

Cup

Knots

■ Knots are only a cosmetic problem unless they are loose and likely to pop out.
■ Checking, which is a rift in the surface, also is only cosmetic.
■ Splits cannot be repaired and will widen in time. Cut off split ends.

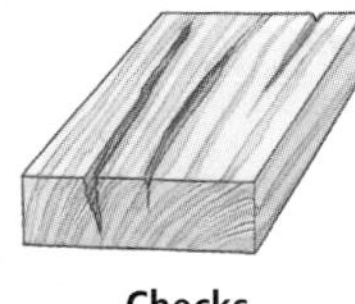
Checks

Splits

Nominal dimensions

Nominal dimensions, such as 2×4 or 1×6, are used when buying lumber. Keep in mind that the actual dimensions of the lumber will be less, as indicated in the table opposite. Lumber prices are often calculated by the board foot–the equivalent of a piece 12 nominal inches square and 1 nominal inch thick. Most lumberyards will not require you to calculate board feet. (To calculate board feet, multiply thickness by width, both in nominal inches, by length in feet, then divide by 12. Example: 2×4, 8 feet long: 2×4×8=64; 64/12=5.33 bd. ft.)

TREATED LUMBER TRUTHS

Pressure-treated lumber has been put under pressure in a sealed vat full of preservatives. The chemicals soak into the wood and bond to it so tightly that they won't leech out into the soil or into the hands of those who use the wood.

Not all pressure-treated wood is the same, however, and the information stamped on the lumber is your best guide to what you're buying. Most important is whether the wood is rated for ground contact or aboveground use. Posts that are buried or that sit on the ground must be rated for ground contact; wood that is above ground can be rated either ground contact or above ground.

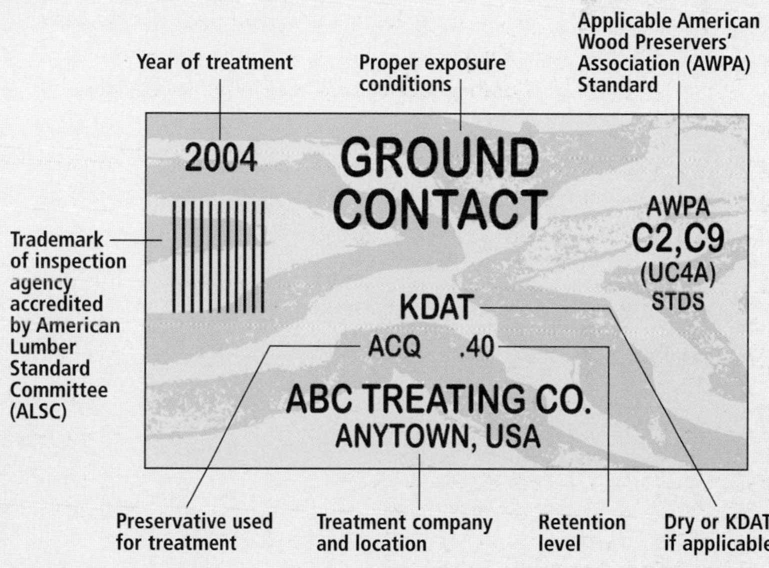

Also check whether the wood was kiln dried after treatment (KDAT). If so, the stamp will have an entry that reads KDAT. KDAT is less likely to warp or split after it's installed, but it isn't a requirement in building outdoor structures.

The stamp will also tell you which of two preservatives was used. There is no practical difference between the two. The chemical for alkaline (or ammoniacal) copper quaternary (ACQ) lumber treatment is made with recycled copper, which replaces the arsenic and chromium used in older pressure-treatment solutions of ammonia. ACQ-treated lumber looks similar to the older pressure-treated lumber, with a slightly browner color.

Copper-azole has been popular for lumber treatment in Japan and Europe for some time and is now also produced in the United States. Like ACQ, copper-azole contains no EPA-listed hazardous chemicals. In fact, azole is used to treat swimming pools and commercially grown fruit. Copper in the mix gives this lumber a greenish tint similar to ACQ, but copper-azole will weather to a brownish tone instead of gray.

FASTENERS AND HARDWARE

Just as important as the boards that go into your play structure are the fasteners and other hardware that will hold them together. Whatever outdoor fasteners and hardware you choose, make sure they are all rustproof; they should be made of galvanized or stainless steel, brass, or other rust-resistant metal. Pressure-treated lumber is especially corrosive.

Nails

Once sold for so many pennies per hundred, nails today are sold by the pound. But nails still are described and sized by this old terminology; for example, a 16-penny or a 4-penny nail. To further complicate things, "penny" is indicated by the letter *d* (probably for *denarius*, Latin for *coin*). The label on the box in the hardware store identifies the size and type of nail that's inside this way: 16d common. (See the chart opposite to translate penny size to inches.)

Just as there are many sizes of nails, there are also many types. If you're installing plastic or metal roofing, specify roofing nails with a rubber washer under the head to seal out water. You can also buy brass, copper, stainless-steel, and bronze nails. To get more holding power, select spiral, threaded, or coated types. Coated nails have a transparent, rosinlike covering that melts from the heat of friction as they are driven in, making them grip wood fibers better.

For small jobs, stay with 1-pound boxes of nails; some stores still sell them in open, bulk quantities by the pound. For most outdoor fastening jobs, you'll need common, box (same as common but thinner), and finishing nails. Also keep an assortment of brads on hand. Brads look like miniature finishing nails; use them for molding and finishing jobs.

Screws

Screws are tough and provide exceptional holding power in wood. They're also easy to remove, making them ideal for projects you may want to disassemble later. For projects where fasteners will show, screws add a quality look that nails can't match.

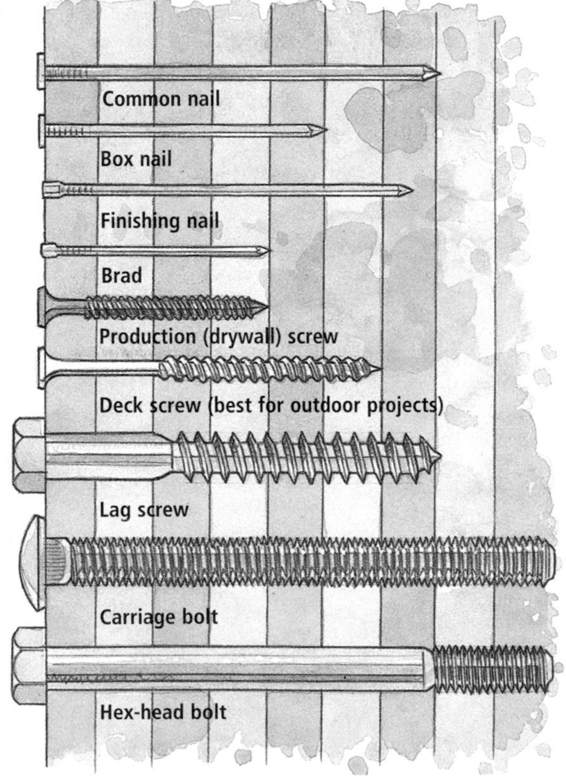

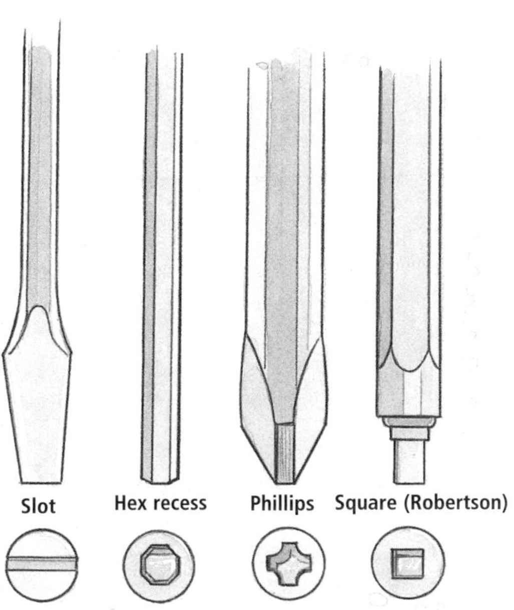

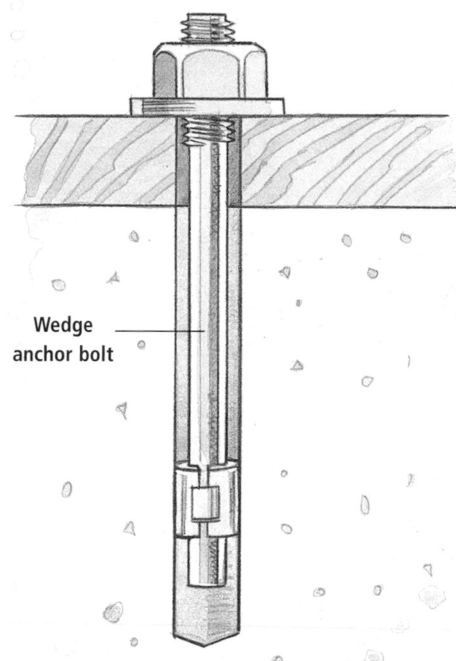

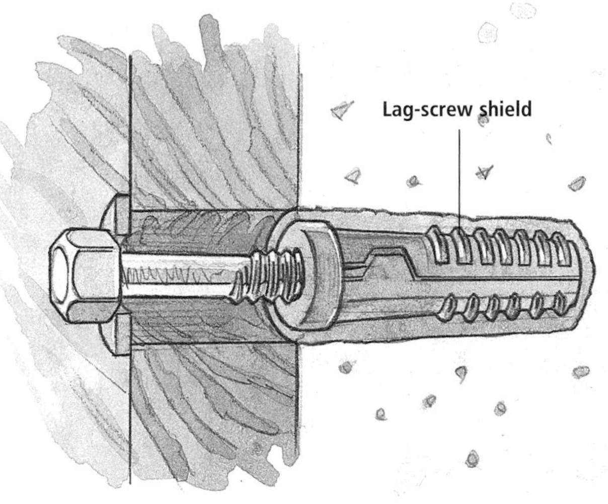

Screw heads vary in style and slot type. Common styles are flathead, ovalhead, roundhead, and panhead. Common head types are slot, hex recess, phillips, and square. Lag screws are heavy-duty fasteners with a screw thread and a hex head like a bolt. They are good for joining large framing members.

Use washers with screws, except flatheads, to prevent the screw head from pulling into or marring the material being fastened. Some washers are decorative.

To attach wood to masonry, use lag screws with lead expansion shields like the one shown above right. You can also use expansion anchor bolts that wedge into the hole under tension and studs that are installed with structural epoxy for many applications.

Bolts

When you need a fastener that can't pull loose yet allows you to disassemble and reassemble a joint, you're literally down to nuts and bolts. If you need to fasten two items together securely and have access to both sides of the material, a two-sided fastener such as a bolt is ideal.

Bolts are sized by length and diameter. They're also classified by the number of threads per inch. For example, a ½-13×3-inch bolt is ½ inch in diameter, has 13 threads per inch, and is 3 inches long.

Sizing Nails and Screws

What size nail or screw will you need for the job? A fastener that's too small won't hold; one that's too big risks splitting the material or poking through the material to which you are fastening.

- Use this table to convert nail pennies (d) into inches:

3d = 1¼"	4d = 1½"	6d = 2"
7d = 2¼"	8d = 2½"	10d = 3"
12d = 3¼"	16d = 3½"	20d = 4"

- Select nails three times as long as the thickness of the material you are fastening. For instance, to attach a 1×4 (¾ inch thick), a 6d nail (2 inches long) will be a bit short. An 8d nail (2½ inches), a little more than three times the thickness of the 1×4, will do better. If that's so long it would go through the base material, use a screw.
- Screws are sized by their length and gauge (diameter). The length of the screw, in inches, should be shorter than the thickness of the materials into which it will be driven. The smooth shank of a screw should go through the top material being fastened.
- The gauges of screws you will need for a given project depends on the fastening strength required. Designated by number, gauges range from No. 0, which has a diameter of 1⁄16 inch, to No. 20, which is nearly ½ inch in diameter.

FRAMING CONNECTORS

Framing connectors–16- or 18-gauge galvanized metal brackets sized to accommodate standard dimension lumber–simplify the joining of major structural members in a play structure. The connectors include predrilled holes through which you can drive common nails (usually 12d) or, for extra strength at critical junctures, wood screws. Some connectors come with nails or include metal prongs that you drive into the wood.

Framing connectors can be bought singly, in small packages, and in bulk–25 to 50 pieces per carton. Buying in bulk can cost half as much as buying singly or in small packages. The illustrations on these pages show some of the many types you'll find. The connectors available from your local dealer may not look exactly like the ones shown, but they make the same connections.

Post beam caps mount on top of posts and include a channel that holds beams of varying dimensions. Manufacturers offer versions for both round and square posts in a variety of sizes, usually 4×4 or 6×6.

Joist hangers attach joists to beams or headers in floor framing platforms and can reinforce almost any right-angle connection. Of course you usually can attach a joist by nailing through the beam or header into the end of the joist or toenailing through the joist into the other framing member.

Multipurpose joist hangers further strengthen joist connections with angled straps that can be nailed to the tops of boards. Here again you can save money by simply nailing or toenailing the joist in place.

Angle brackets, which come in a variety of different styles for different applications, offer yet another way to reinforce perpendicular joints. Some angle brackets attach with screws. As with joist hangers, nailing or toenailing works just as well.

Hurricane ties attach notched rafters to top plates. These expensive ties are basically designed for framing that will withstand more than usual stress, such as where hurricanes, tornadoes, and earthquakes occur and where building codes often require them.

Post beam cap

Joist hanger

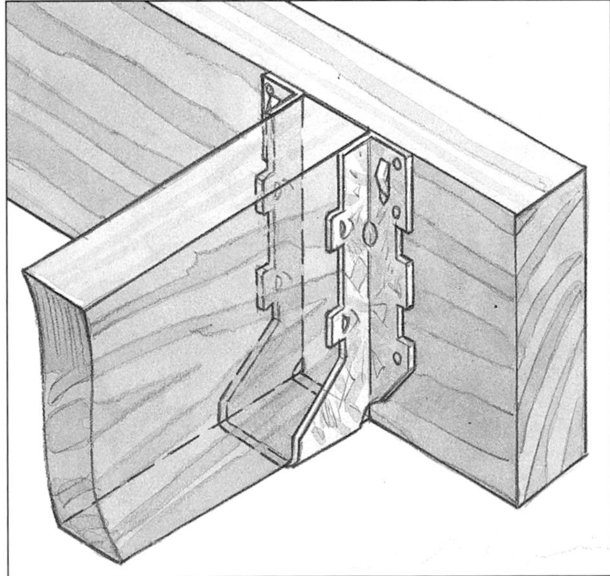

Multipurpose joist hanger

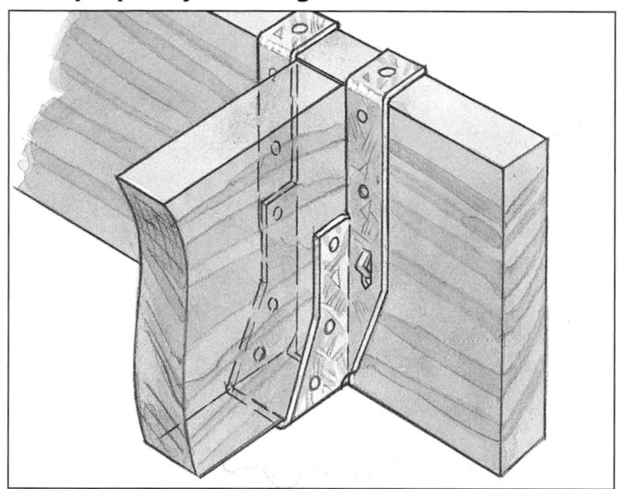

Angle bracket

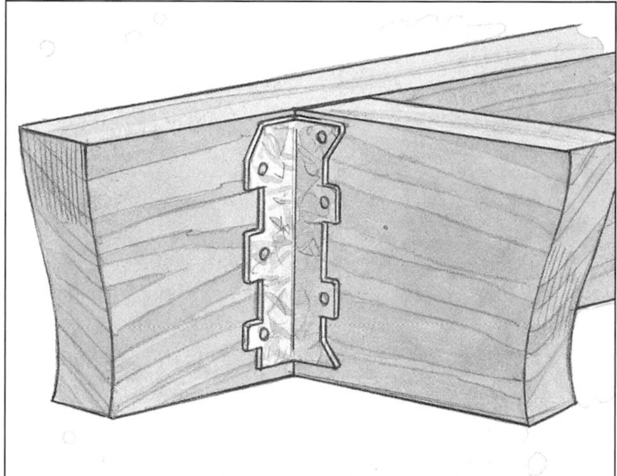

Rafter hurricane tie

Rafter hurricane tie

Do you really need framing connectors?

Connectors make stronger joints, which can be a plus for a playset that will get constant rough use. Connectors can speed a project along by making strong joints quickly too, so they may be worth the cost–especially if their utilitarian appearance isn't noticeable or objectionable. If you are using framing connectors with pressure-treated lumber, look for connectors rated to withstand corrosive effects of the lumber.

Rafter hurricane tie

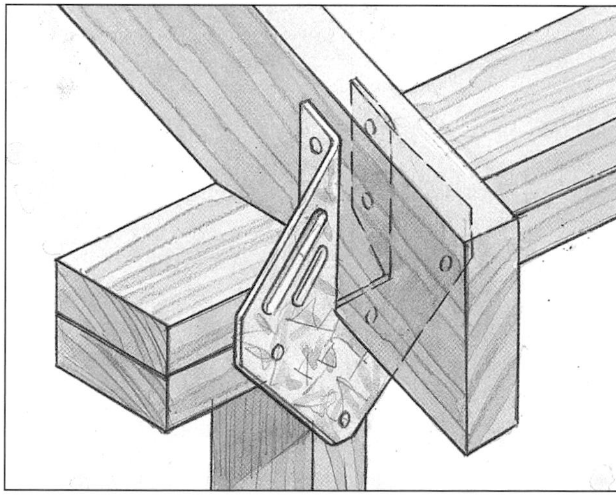

CHAPTER HIGHLIGHTS

- Measuring and Marking
- Using a Hammer and Saw
- Nailing
- Driving Screws
- Fastening with Bolts
- Gluing and Clamping
- Joinery and Carpentry
- Basic Woodworking Joints
- Laying Out Posts
- Applying Finish

TECHNIQUES

If you're new to home improvement projects and it has been a while since you took wood shop, this chapter will help you brush up on the basics of building with wood. And even if you have built many projects before, you'll probably find tips and hints in these pages that will help you work more efficiently and achieve professional-looking results.

From crosscutting with a handsaw to driving screws, the skills and techniques shown in this chapter will serve you in other home projects after you complete the playset. And as you gain an understanding of cutting lumber for project parts and making basic woodworking joints (pages 169 and 178–179), you'll be able to create home improvement projects of your own design.

When you build any of the projects in this book, take time to read the instructions carefully before you start. Questions you come up with or procedures you don't quite understand at first may become clear as you read farther into the project. Identifying the parts in drawings and studying how they go together will resolve a lot of questions. And in many cases, the answers will come to you immediately when you are working with the real parts rather than a mental image.

Take care when you measure and lay out parts. Always double-check measurements before you cut or drill. It is possible–if you happen to read the blade of a tape measure looking at it from the top edge instead of the bottom–to mark a piece 18½ inches long when you want to make it 19½ inches, for instance.

Your reward for taking the time to carefully lay out, cut, and assemble parts will be a safe, sturdy, and durable playset your children will enjoy for years to come.

MEASURING AND MARKING

Precise measurements are important in every project. Learning that there is no such measurement as "about" will save you time, money, and frustration.

But be aware that not all materials are square, especially the ends of boards, dimension lumber, and timbers. Almost all materials–wood, concrete, metal, plastic–have a factory edge. A factory edge is carpenters' vernacular for the milled edge of the material, such as the planed edge of a board or the edges of a sheet of plywood. This edge usually is true, or straight, so use it as a reference point for squaring the rest of the material.

You'll need a sharp-pointed pencil to make accurate marks on your material. Carpenter's pencils, which have flat rather than round leads, work well for marking wood. For even more accuracy, use an awl, which looks like a short ice pick, or a scriber, which resembles a long steel toothpick. (Combination squares often have a scriber that stows in the square's body.)

Squaring up stock

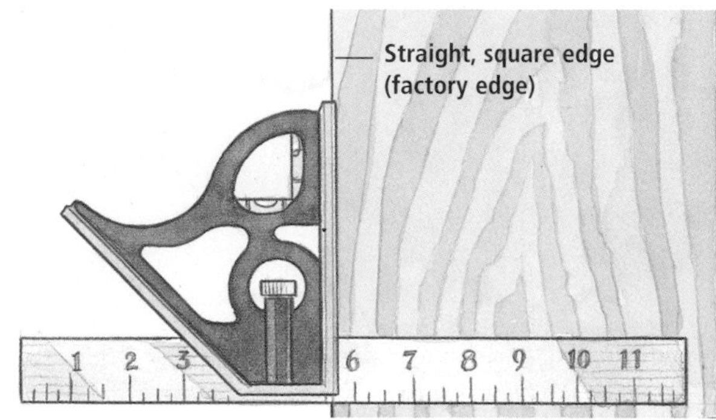

Before you measure, make sure the end or edge of the board you're measuring from is square. Check it with a try square or combination square, as shown. Square it up, if necessary. Measuring from an edge that isn't square leads to problems.

Marking cutoff points

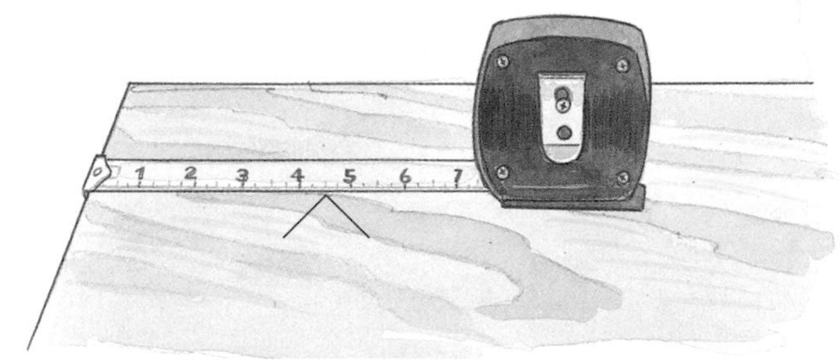

For precision, indicate your cutoff-point mark with the tip of a V-shape mark. A dot is too difficult to see; a short line might veer one way or the other. Always double-check your measurement before cutting.

Marking crosscuts

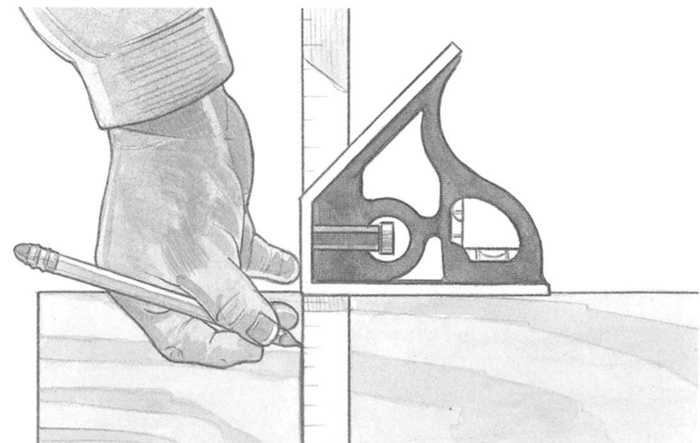

For narrow boards, use a combination square as shown to draw a fine line at the cutoff point. For wider materials, align a framing or carpenter's square to draw the cutoff line.

Saw on scrap side

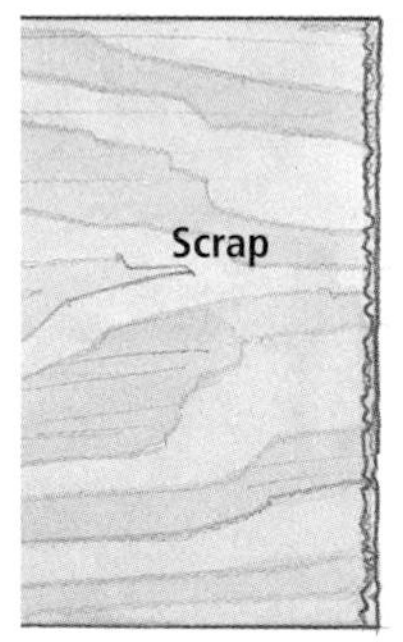

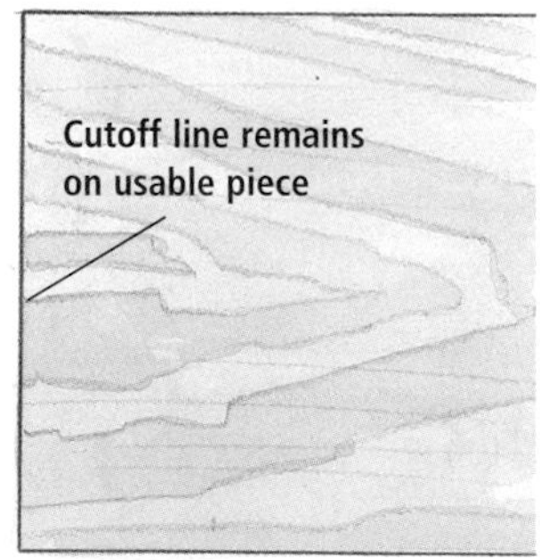

Saw on the scrap side of the cutoff line, not straight down the middle of it. Otherwise material will be cut half a saw kerf shorter than the measurement you intended. Even this small discrepancy—typically 1⁄16 inch—can make a big difference.

Marking angles

A combination square can mark 90- and 45-degree angles and measure depths. The blade slides through the handle to accommodate different widths. Many combination squares have plumb and level vials too.

Using a framing square

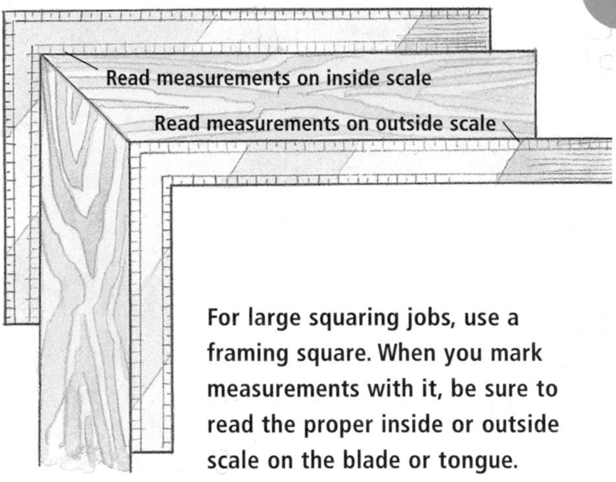

For large squaring jobs, use a framing square. When you mark measurements with it, be sure to read the proper inside or outside scale on the blade or tongue.

Using a post level

A post level comes in handy for many playset projects. It includes three vials that check for plumb on three different planes. Adjust the post until each bubble is centered in its vial.

Using a carpenter's level

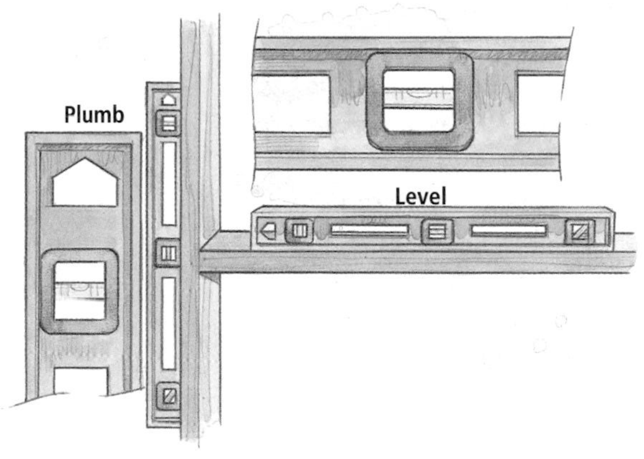

Three vials make a carpenter's level handy. You can check a vial at each end to determine if a post or other vertical element is plumb. The center vial shows whether a horizontal element is level.

Using squares and levels

Square refers to an exact 90-degree angle between two surfaces. When a material is level, it's perfectly horizontal; when it's plumb, it's perfectly vertical.

Never assume that existing construction is square, level, or plumb. It probably isn't. To prove this to yourself, lay a level horizontally along any floor in your home, hold a level vertically against a wall section in a corner, or place a square on a door or window frame. Don't be alarmed at the results. Variation is normal because houses and other structures settle slightly on their foundations, throwing off square, level, and plumb.

How can you check a level's accuracy? Lay it on a horizontal surface and shim it, if necessary, to get a level reading. Then turn the level end for end. If you don't get the same reading, the level needs to be adjusted or replaced. Some models allow you to calibrate the level by rotating the glass vials. Electronic levels (see page 147) come with instructions that tell how to calibrate them.

Using a Hammer and Saw

There's a knack to using most hand tools, but it doesn't take long to acquire these basic skills. Here's what you need to know.

Using a hammer

For maximum leverage and control, hold on to the hammer near the end of the handle, not up around the neck. If you do this and concentrate on the job at hand, you'll find yourself driving nails without straining (or hitting) your arm, wrist, or hand. Always use a hammer with a face slightly larger than the nail you're striking. Before using an unfamiliar hammer, check it for a loose, bent, or split handle. Any of these can cause injury or damage when you swing it.

Using a crosscut saw

There's a special rhythm in using any saw. It's a sort of rocking stroke that starts from the shoulder and works down through the arm and hand. Hold the saw at about 45 degrees to the work. You need to apply very little pressure in this cutting motion. In fact, your main task is to steer the blade. If you apply pressure, the saw will wander off the cutting line or cut at an angle and the edge won't be square.

Driving nails

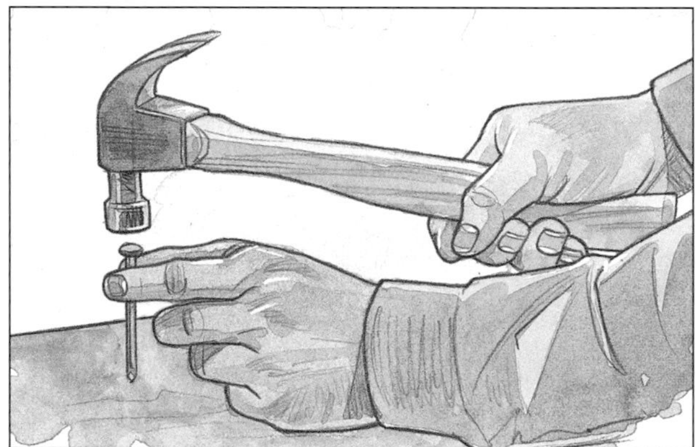

Hold the nail near its head. That way, if you miss, the hammer will glance off your fingers rather than crush them. Ask skilled carpenters how to use a hammer, and they'll show you their hands and tell you, "Carefully."

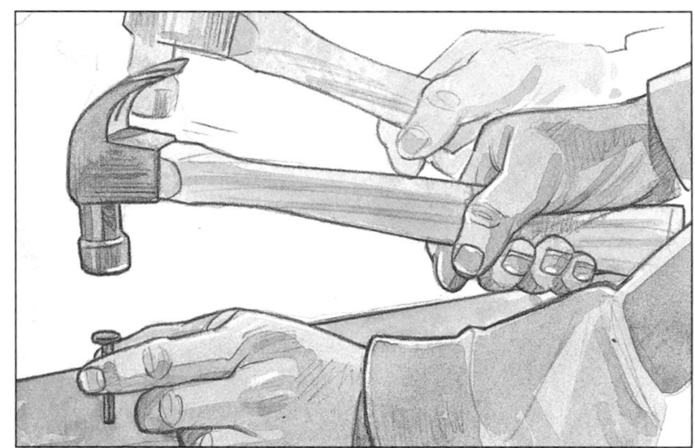

To hit a nail dead-on, keep your eye on the nail, not the hammer. Let the weight of the hammer do the work. You don't need to apply a lot of muscle to it. After a while, you'll find you can sink a nail in just three or four blows.

The last blow from the hammer should leave the head flush with the surface. If you want to drive it deeper, don't dimple the wood's surface. Countersink the nailhead with a nail set.

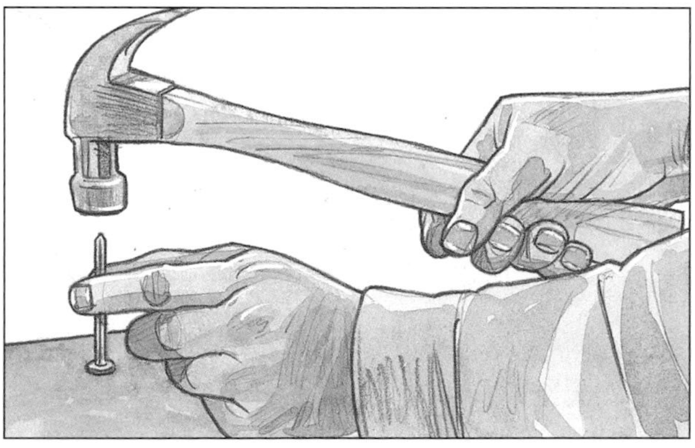

Nailing near the end of a board tends to split the wood. To avoid this problem, blunt the tip of the nail as shown or drill a pilot hole first.

Sawing basics

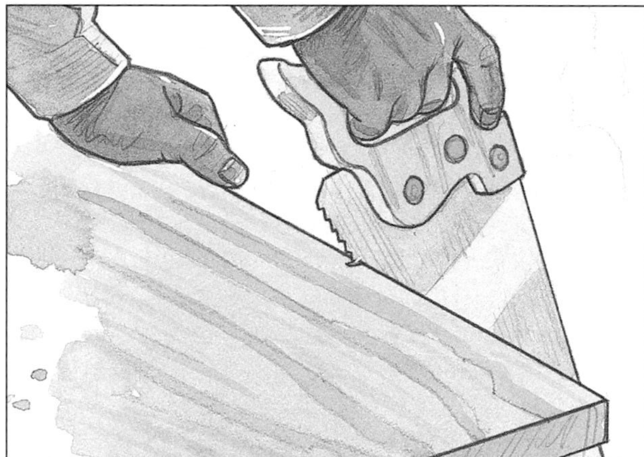

Start a handsaw in a piece of wood at the heel of the saw. The first stroke should be a gentle upstroke. This helps the saw "find" the cutoff line.

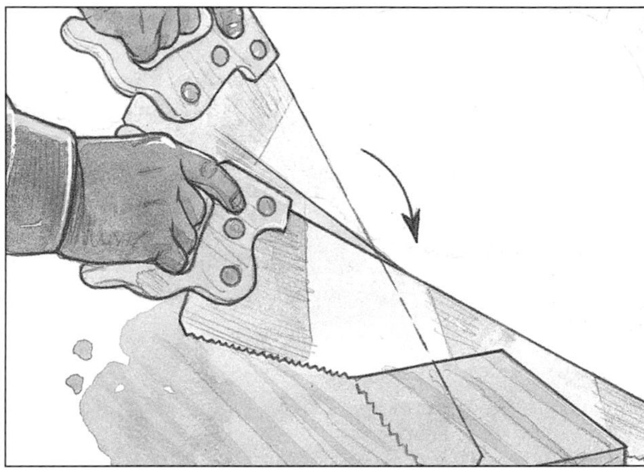

The saw stroke should rock slightly, following an arc as your arm swings from your shoulder. Let the weight of the saw do the work. Pressure won't speed up the cut.

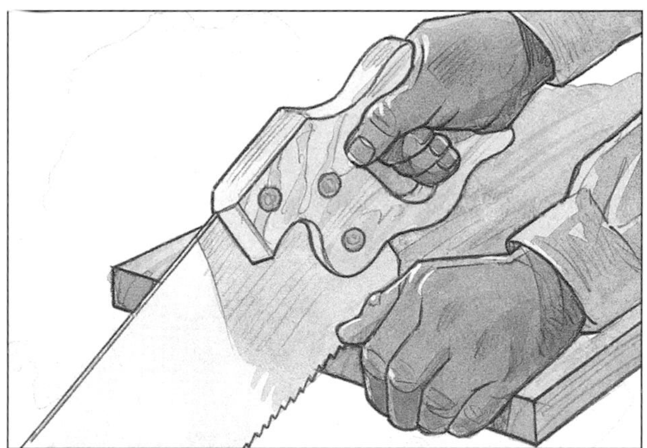

Start a ripsaw at the heel of the saw with a small upstroke, just as you would with a crosscut saw. Remember, a ripsaw cuts on the forward stroke, so relax on the pull stroke.

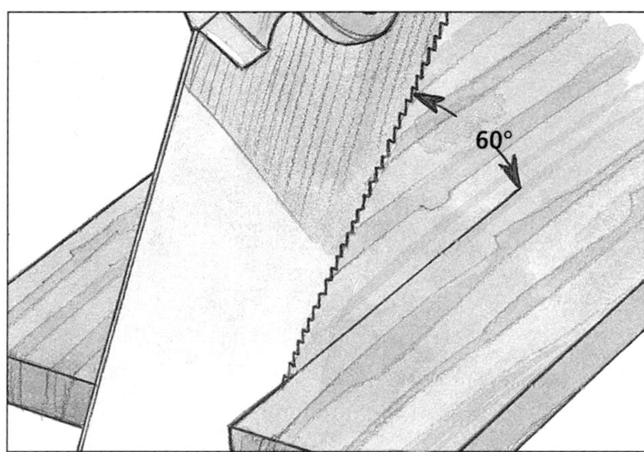

Keep the saw at a 60-degree angle to the work. You'll do this automatically with more experience. If the saw veers away from the cutting line, twist the blade slightly to steer it back.

Using a ripsaw

A ripsaw cuts wood along the length of its grain. This workhorse usually has 5½ teeth per inch set about one-third wider than the blade thickness, so it slides easily. Ripsaws cut only on the forward stroke. Use the same techniques with a ripsaw as you would with a crosscut saw, but hold a ripsaw at about a 60-degree angle to the work instead of the 45-degree angle for a crosscut saw.

With any saw, cut on the scrap side of the cutting line. You can always remove wood with a plane or rasp if your piece is a bit too long, but you can't add it if the piece is too short.

NAILING

Nailing mistakes that mar the wood make a job look amateurish and shoddy. All your careful measuring and cutting will be wasted if the wood ends up with a bent-over nail or "smiles" and "frowns" made by a hammer that missed the nail entirely.

Professional carpenters make nailing look easy because, when properly done, driving a nail home is not a struggle; it's done with a smooth, fluid motion. You may never be as fast at nailing as a professional because the pro gets plenty of practice, but you can learn to drive in nails accurately without damaging the material or yourself. Here's how to do it.

Set the nail

Practice on scrap pieces before you pound nails into finished work. To ensure that the hammer strikes the nail and not your fingers and that the nail will be driven into the board squarely, grasp the nail near its head and the hammer near the end of the handle. Lightly tap the nail until it stands by itself.

Facenailing

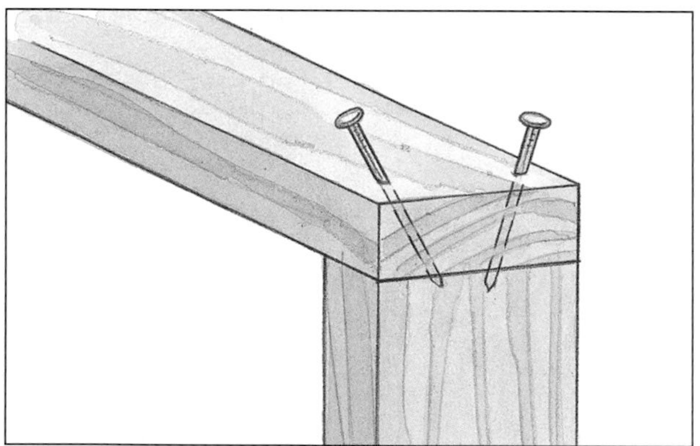

Skewed nails have more holding power, especially in end grain. Drive in one nail at a 60-degree angle in one direction, then drive in another nail at the same angle in the opposite direction. Skewed nails make it difficult for the board to pull loose.

When two framing members meet atop another, like the two 2×4s and the 4×4 post shown, cut the two members to meet at the middle of the third. Drive two nails into each end. Miter-cut ends add visual interest for exposed framing.

Stagger nails to avoid splits. The idea is to avoid driving neighboring nails into the same grain line; two nails will stress the grain twice as much as one nail. Three nails are in different grain lines here.

Drive two nails to attach one framing member to another, as shown. Using more nails than you need won't make the joint stronger and could split the wood.

Toenailing

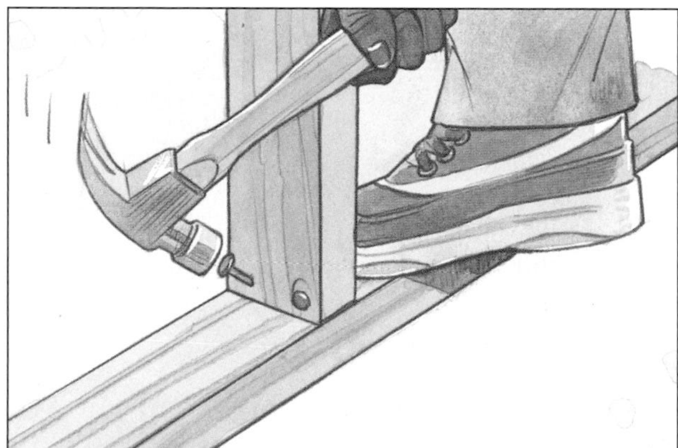

Toenailing, driving nails at an angle through one piece into another, takes some practice. Brace the part you're nailing through with your foot and drive nails at a 45-degree angle into the other part.

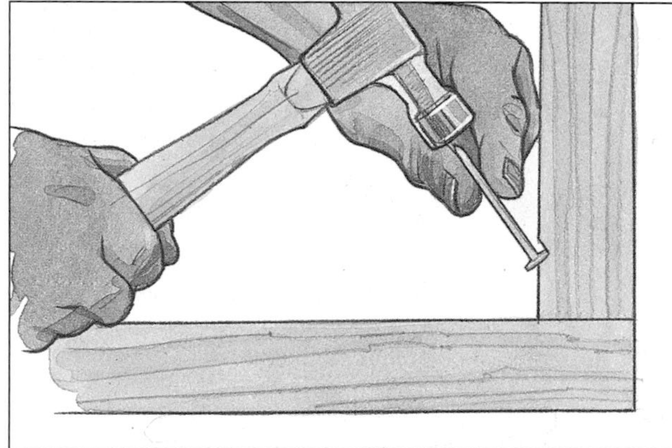

Tap the nail until its point bites into the wood. If you have difficulty toenailing, drill pilot holes for the nails or make a depression for the nail by tapping the head into the wood.

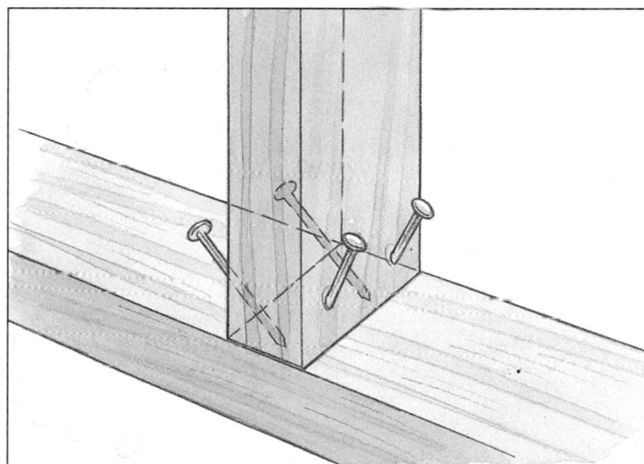

Drive four nails into each joint, two on each side. The first nail may move the vertical piece, but the second nail, driven from the other side, will move it back into position.

To toenail into vertical members, hold the nail at a steep angle, tap it once or twice, then reduce the angle to 45 degrees as you drive the nail home.

Drive the nail home

Once the nail is set in place, remove your hand from it. Keep your eye on the nail as you swing the hammer, letting the weight of the hammerhead do the driving.

Beginners tend to hold a hammer stiffly and keep their shoulders stiff, swinging from the elbow. This leads to a tired, sore arm and to mistakes. Loosen up. Your whole arm should move as you swing from the shoulder. Keep your wrist loose so the hammer can give a final snap at the end of each blow. The entire motion should be relaxed and smooth.

With the last hammer blow, push the head of the nail flush or nearly flush with the surface of the wood. The convex shape of the hammer face allows you to do this without marring the surface of the wood around the head. Let the head of a finishing nail or brad sit slightly above the surface, then drive it home with a nail set.

DRIVING SCREWS

Screw threads grip wood fibers in a way that a smooth nail cannot. When a screw is driven home, the threads exert tremendous pressure against the screw head to hold the fastener firmly in place. With the right tools, driving screws can be almost as quick as nailing. If you make a mistake, it's easy to remove a screw without damaging your work. Screws must be driven with care, however. Start straight; there is no way to correct a crooked start as you drive the screw. Drill a pilot hole or the screw may split the wood and not hold. If the pilot hole is too large, the screw will not grip well.

Make pilot holes for No. 8 or smaller screws with an awl. For larger sizes, drill holes with a power or hand drill.

When do you need a pilot hole?

If there is a danger of cracking the wood, you should always drill a pilot hole, no matter how small the screw. For instance, if the wood is brittle or if you are driving a screw near the end of a board, almost any screw can split the wood. But if you are screwing into a sound board at a spot 2 inches or more from its end, you can probably drive a No. 6 or thinner screw without a pilot hole. If you are screwing into plywood or framing lumber, you should be able to drive No. 8 screws without pilot holes. When you drive brass or aluminum screws for latches and decorative hardware, always drill a pilot hole. To further ensure against breaking soft-metal screws, drive a steel screw of the same size into the hole first.

Drilling pilot holes

To see if a drill bit is the correct size to make your pilot hole, grip both bit and screw together with your fingers. The bit should be slightly smaller than the diameter of the screw threads. The diameter of a pilot hole varies depending on the wood. You can drill a smaller hole in softwood than you would in hardwood. Drill a test hole and make sure the screw will hold tight before you drill holes in the finished material.

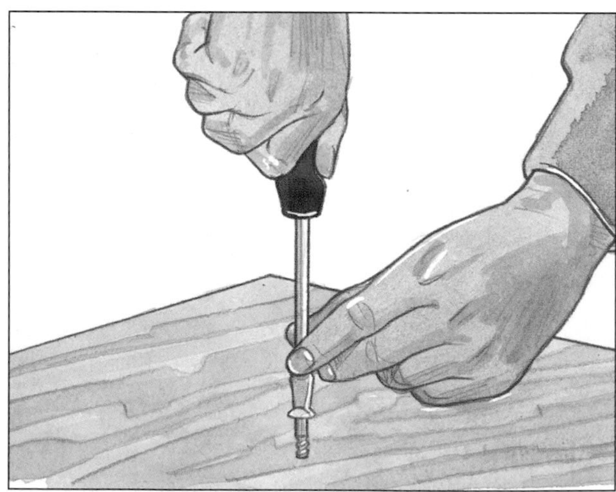

Start a screw by holding the screwdriver handle and blade. Don't hold the screw.

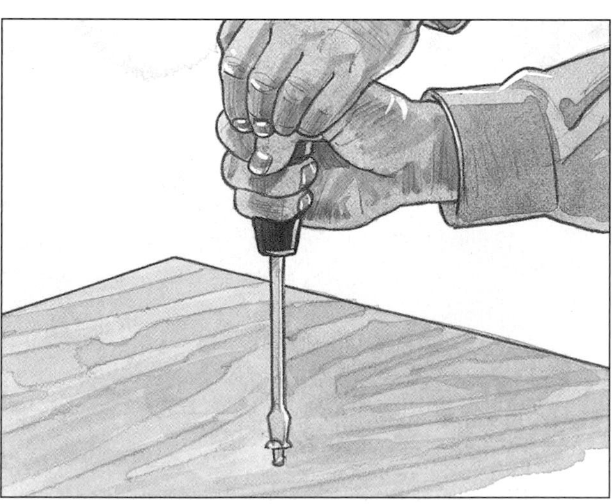

Put more drive on the screwdriver by turning it with one hand and applying top pressure with the other.

When a screw won't turn

If a screw is very hard to drive, make sure the tip of the blade fully fills the screw slot. Try using a longer screwdriver or one with a larger-diameter handle. Another trick to try is to rub wax on the threads of the screw as a lubricant.

Have a collection of screwdriver tips ready, particularly #1 and #2 phillips bits and some slotted bits as well. Consider buying square-head screws and bits. These bits fit into and grab the screw slot better than phillips-head and slotted screws and bits.

Power-driving screws

Even a few screws can take a long time to drive by hand, so consider using a variable-speed drill/driver with a screwdriver bit. If the drill is reversible, so much the better because you can also use it to remove screws.

When driving slotted screws, make sure the bit does not wander partway out of the slot or you could damage the surface into which you are screwing. Don't drive screws too quickly or the bit may slip out of the slot. Maintain firm, even pressure as you work.

A popular screwdriver accessory for a drill/driver accepts interchangeable bits in a magnetic holder. The magnetized bit holds steel screws, making it easy to drive them in hard-to-reach places. A sliding sleeve on the tool also helps hold the screw in place for easier starting. To change bits for different kinds of screws, just pull one out and slip another into the holder.

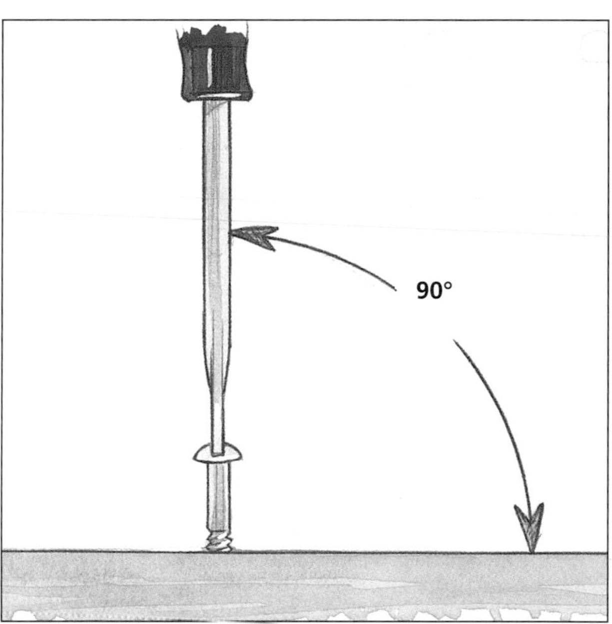

Keep the screwdriver square in the slot. If it's off-center or at an angle, it may slip out and badly strip the slot.

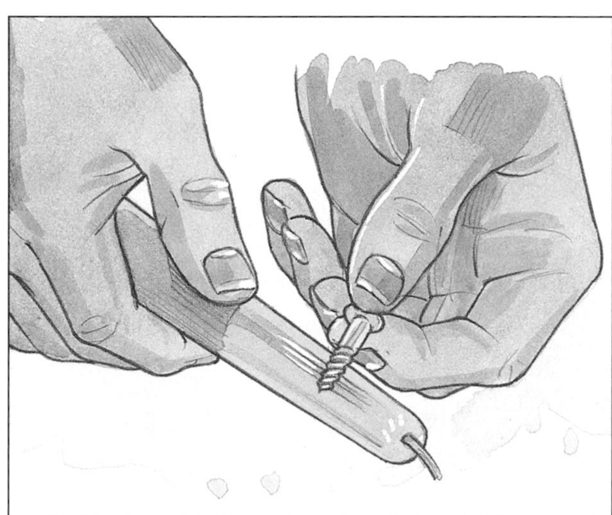

Screws drive easier when threads are lubricated with candle wax. Rotate the screw as you rub it against the candle.

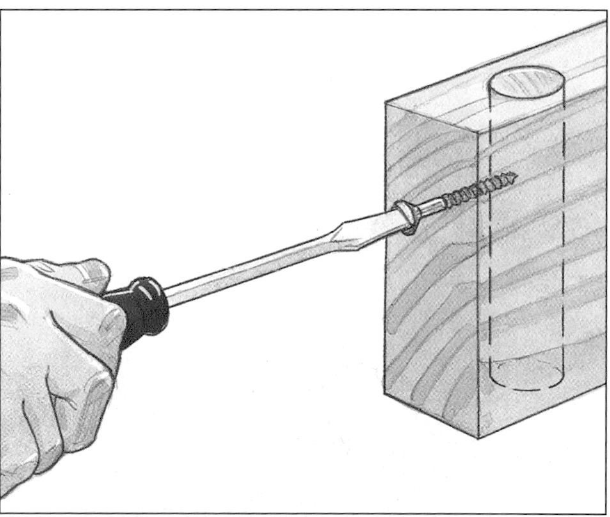

Screws hold better in end grain if you drill a hole and insert a dowel into the board. Use screws long enough to penetrate the dowel.

FASTENING WITH BOLTS

Friction between the fastener and the wood makes nails and screws work. When you tighten a nut on a bolt, however, you're actually clamping adjoining members together, producing the sturdiest of all joints. All types of bolts require a hole to be bored through both pieces being joined.

Be careful: Overtightening bolts can strip threads and damage wood, reducing the holding power of a bolt. Tighten the nut and bolt firmly against the wood, give the nut another half turn, then stop.

Machine bolts

Machine bolts have hexagonal heads and threads running partway or all the way along the shank. When fastening two pieces of wood together, slip a flat washer onto the bolt and slide the bolt through the holes in both pieces of material. Add another flat washer, then a lock washer. The flat washer keeps the nut and the bolt head from digging into the wood. The lock washer prevents the nut from coming loose. Use two wrenches, one to hold the bolt and the other to draw the nut down onto the bolt.

Countersunk bolts

Use a socket wrench to install a machine bolt in a place that's hard to get at or when the bolt head is countersunk into a hole in the wood.

Carriage bolts

A carriage bolt has a plain, round head. Insert it into the hole and tap the head flush with the surface. Slip a flat washer, a lock washer, and a nut onto the bolt. Tighten the nut. The square or hexagonal shoulder under the bolt head keeps the bolt from spinning as the nut is tightened. No washer is needed under the head. The lock washer should keep the bolt from working loose. As added protection, you can thread another nut onto the bolt, snug it against the first, then jam the two together by turning them in opposite directions.

Machine bolt

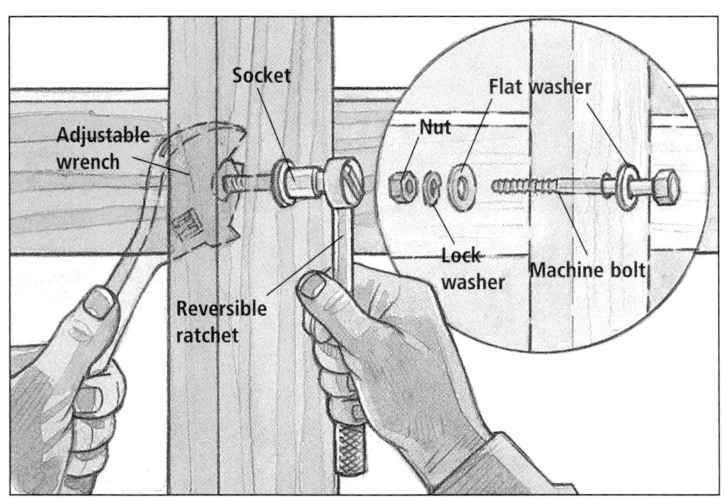

Countersunk bolt

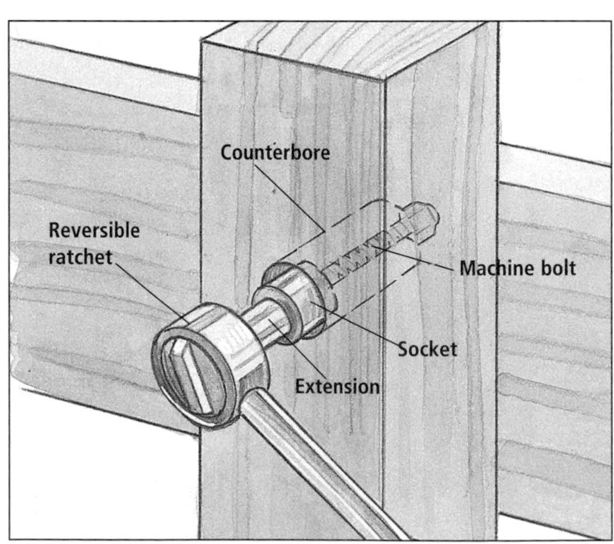

Carriage bolt

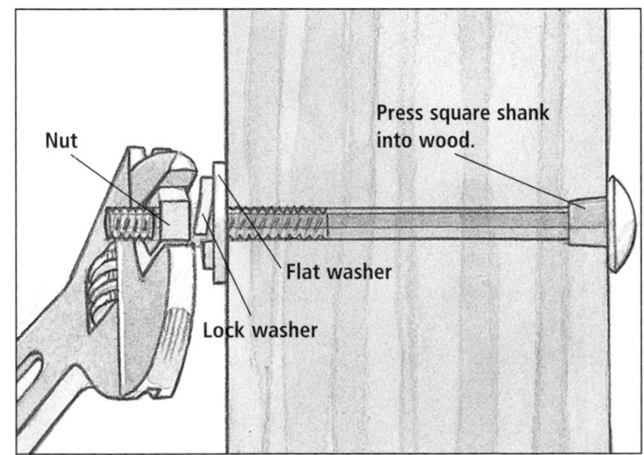

Gluing And Clamping

A joint will be stronger if you use glue in addition to nails or screws. Glue alone will be enough for joints that will not be subjected to great stress. Use exterior woodworking glue or construction adhesive for outdoor projects. Many adhesives set up quickly, but you still need an assortment of clamps for gluing.

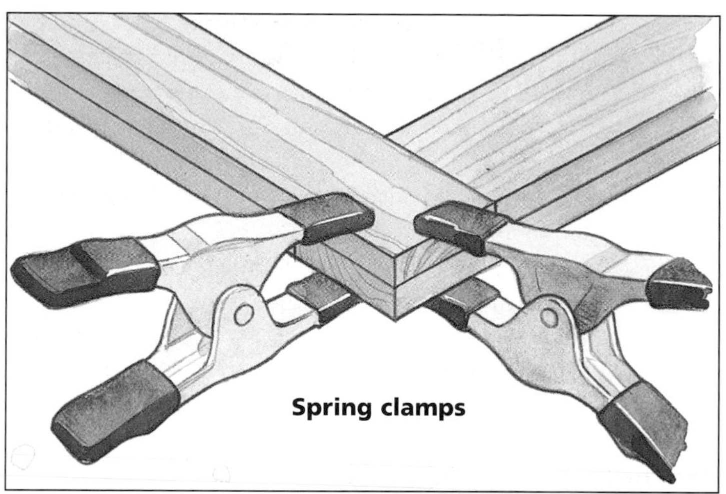

Spring clamps

For light work, these are the easiest clamps to use. Apply glue to both pieces and place them in correct alignment. Squeeze the clamp handles to spread the jaws. When you release the handles, the springs will clamp the work together. You may want to have several sizes of these inexpensive clamps on hand. Thickness capacities range from 1 to 3 inches, and lengths from 4 to 9 inches.

C-clamps

C-clamps are inexpensive and work well when the pieces are not too wide. Use scraps of wood to keep the clamps from marring the boards. C-clamps range in size from 1 to 8 inches with throat depths ranging from 1 to 3½ inches. You can also buy special deep-throat clamps.

Miter clamps

For miter joints, use miter clamps that hold boards at a 90-degree angle. Miter clamps are sometimes called picture-frame clamps. They have smooth jaws that won't mar wood.

Pipe clamps

For large projects, use pipe clamps. Alternate them as shown at right to prevent bowing. They're sold without pipe, so you'll need to buy galvanized steel pipe in the lengths you want. The clamp parts fit ½- or ¾-inch pipe.

Strap clamps

A strap, or band, clamp wraps around objects to be joined and is especially handy for holding together irregular parts. It can clamp several joints at once and will not mar the wood.

Clamps

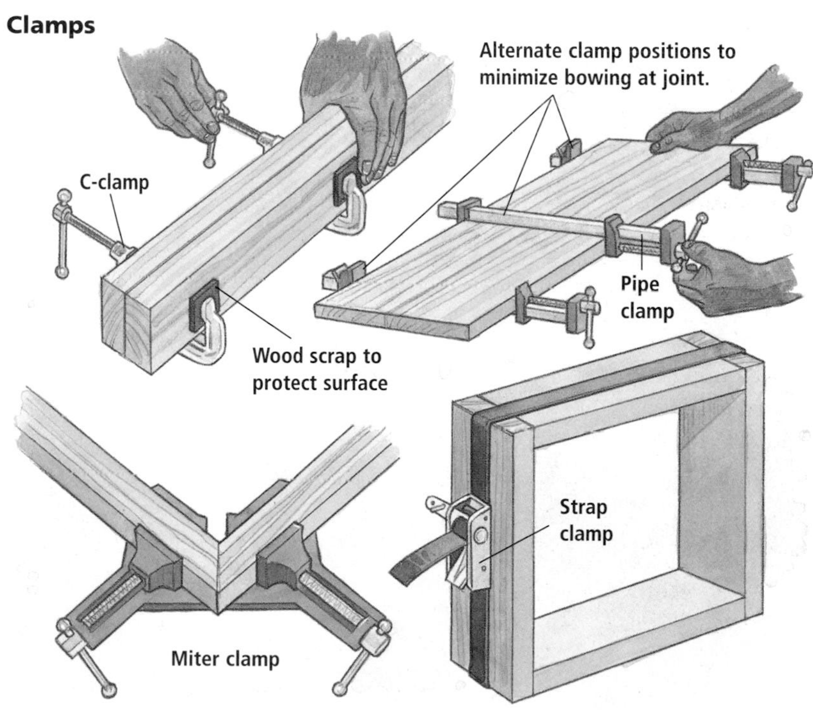

Joinery and Carpentry

There's more than one way to saw a board. The illustrations here show eight common cuts but don't include several others that you probably won't need for a play structure. The first few cuts shown are basic ones you can make with a handsaw. Others shown usually call for power tools.

Crosscuts move across the grain. Since few boards come from the lumberyard in exactly the length you need, just about every project requires at least a few crosscuts, and some need dozens. You can easily crosscut with a handsaw (see page 169). For more speed and precision, use a handheld circular saw, a power mitersaw, a stationary tablesaw, or a radial-arm saw.

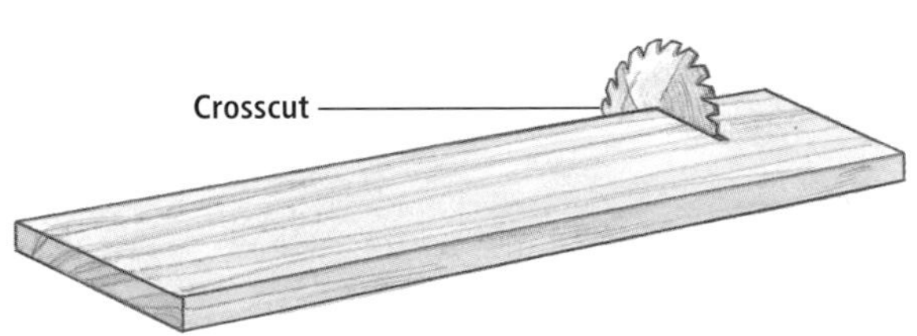

Rip cuts go with the grain. You'll need to rip cut if you want a board that's narrower than standard lumber sizes. Here again, a handsaw works fine (page 169); power saws–handheld or stationary–make faster, more accurate cuts. Most projects require at least a few rip cuts.

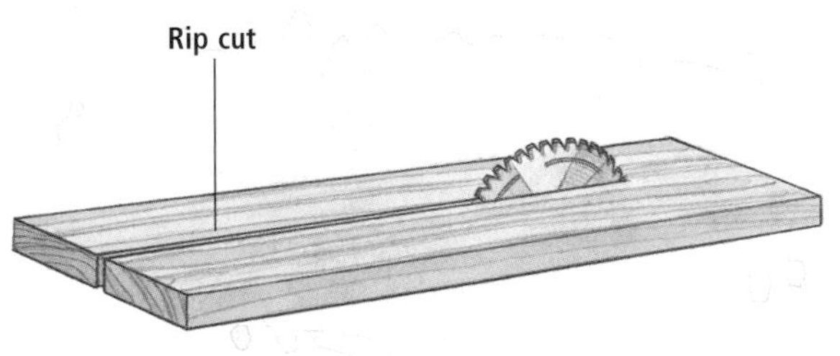

Miter cuts run at an angle, usually 45 degrees, across the grain. Miter cuts are angled crosscuts, and you can make many of them with a crosscut saw. A miter box (page 148) improves accuracy, as will any power saw. To make a right-angle miter joint, you'll need two boards with 45-degree miter cuts.

Bevel cuts, often at a 45-degree angle, can run with or across the grain. You can make bevels with a handsaw, but you'll need a good eye and a steady hand to cut one true from end to end. A tablesaw or power mitersaw (for narrow stock) works better. As with miter cuts, a corner joint requires two bevel cuts.

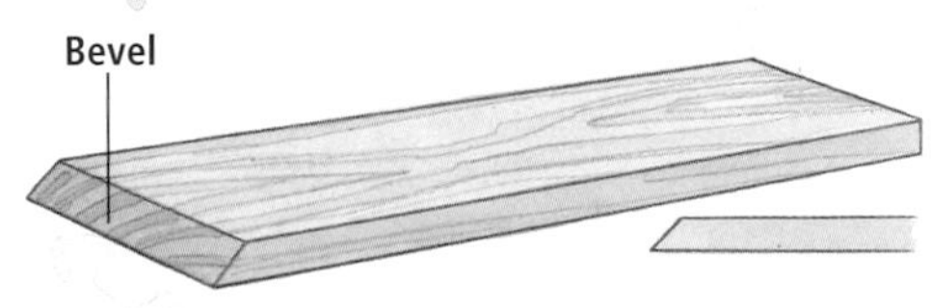

Chamfers can run with or across the grain. A chamfer amounts to a partial bevel and is most often used to give a project a decorative edge. A power saw, plane, and router are the best tools for making a chamfer.

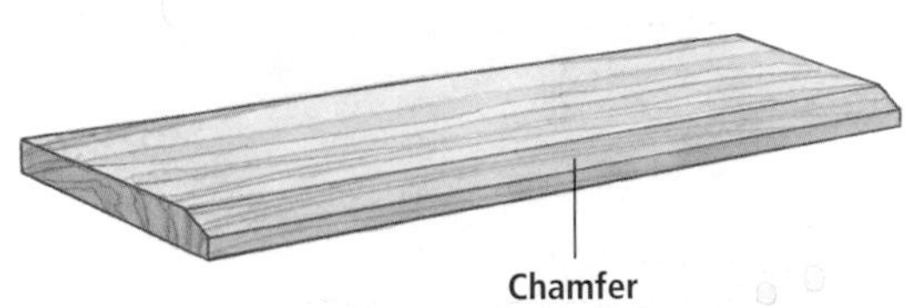

Rabbet cuts can run along an edge or across the end of a board. With care, you can crosscut a rabbet with a handsaw, but you'll need a power saw or router to make one accurately that runs lengthwise along a board. Use wide rabbet cuts to create half-lap joints, shown on page 179.

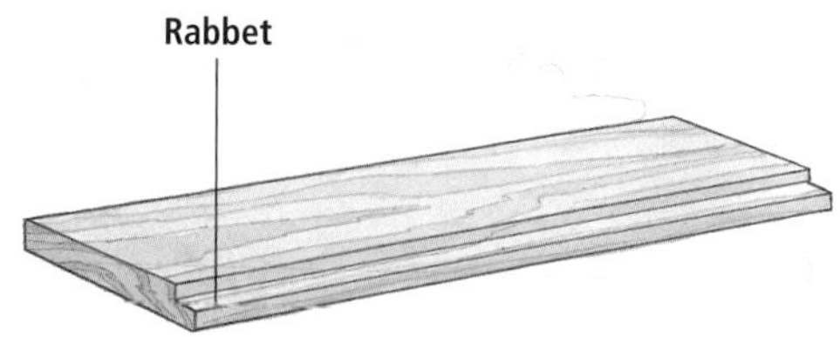

Dado cuts run across the grain. The traditional way to cut a dado is to cut the sides with a handsaw and chisel out the center. A power saw and chisel (or a tablesaw with a dado cutter) or router will do a better job much more quickly. Dado cuts require precision because they usually need to snugly accommodate the end or edge of another project part.

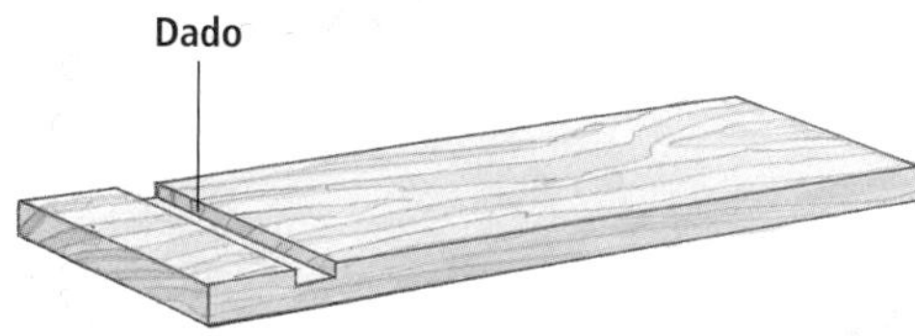

Plow or groove cuts amount to dadoes that run with the grain. You'll need a portable or stationary power saw or a router for this one. As with dado cuts, precision is the key to successful joinery.

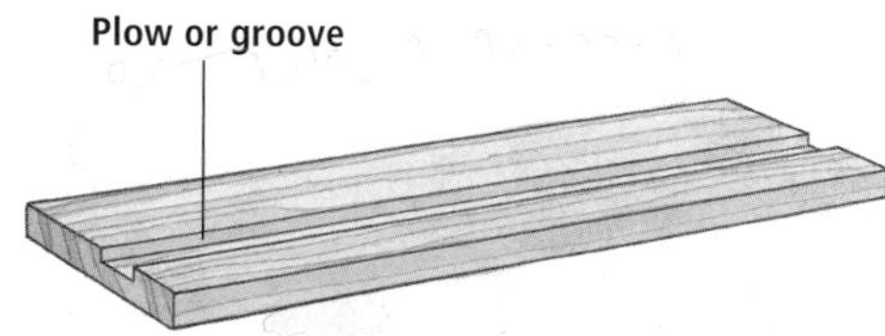

Making Curved Cuts

When you want to add a curve to your play structure, use a coping saw or a handheld power jigsaw.

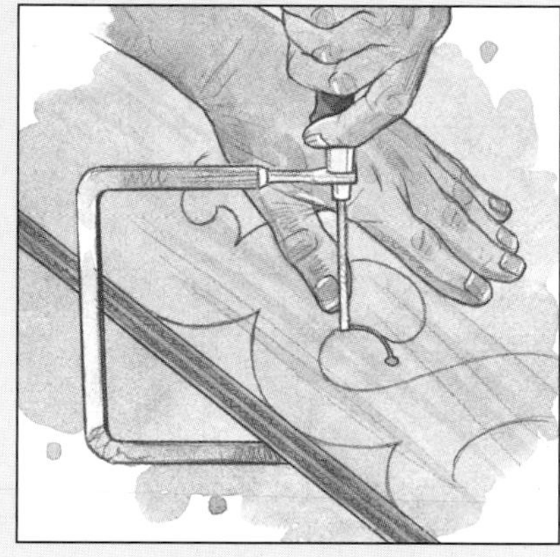

■ Use the coping saw for intricate cutting or scrollwork in thin materials. This hand tool allows you to set the blade in any direction in relation to its frame. To begin a cut from the inside of a board, remove the blade from the saw frame and reinstall it through a starter hole. For delicate cuts, install the blade with the teeth angled toward the handle so that the saw cuts on the back stroke.

■ Most contour cuts require a jigsaw. When you get the knack of using this tool, you can cut curves that are as smooth as any line you can draw. Turn the saw on, then begin the cut. Guide the saw slowly, without forcing the blade. If you wander from the line, don't try to make a correction with a sharp turn. Instead guide the blade gently back to the line, or back up and start again.

Basic Woodworking Joints

Strong wood joints are essential to all carpentry and woodworking projects. It helps if the joints look good too. Here are some of the simplest and strongest joinery methods. Each of these joints can be made with hand tools, but if you have shop tools such as a tablesaw, router, or power mitersaw, the job will go faster and the joint will be tighter. None of the joints requires cabinetmaking expertise.

Butt joints

All of the joints shown on this page are butt joints: two square-cut pieces joined together by placing the end of one member against the face or edge of another member. Of all wood joinery techniques, the butt joint is the easiest to make. Unfortunately, it's also one of the weakest. If a butt joint will be subjected to lateral stress or tension, be sure to reinforce it in some way. Reinforcement devices include corner braces, T-plates, dowels, plywood gussets, and wood cleats, all shown below.

However, you don't have to reinforce butt joints that bear only vertical loads, such as posts supporting a beam.

When making a butt joint, make sure the surfaces you're joining are square. Trim lumber ends with a saw, if necessary. For a strong joint, apply glue to both surfaces and nail or screw the materials together. Then add the reinforcement.

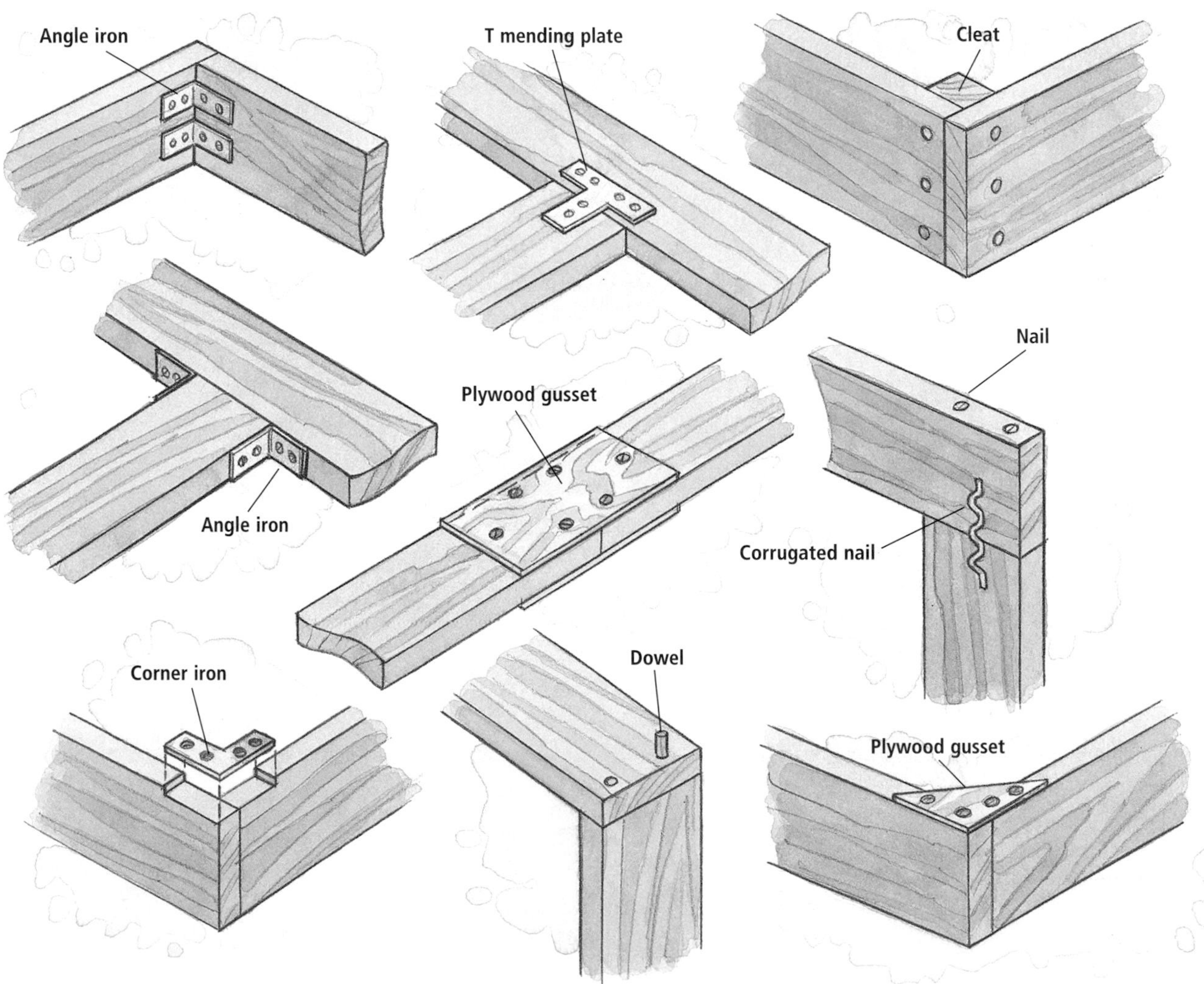

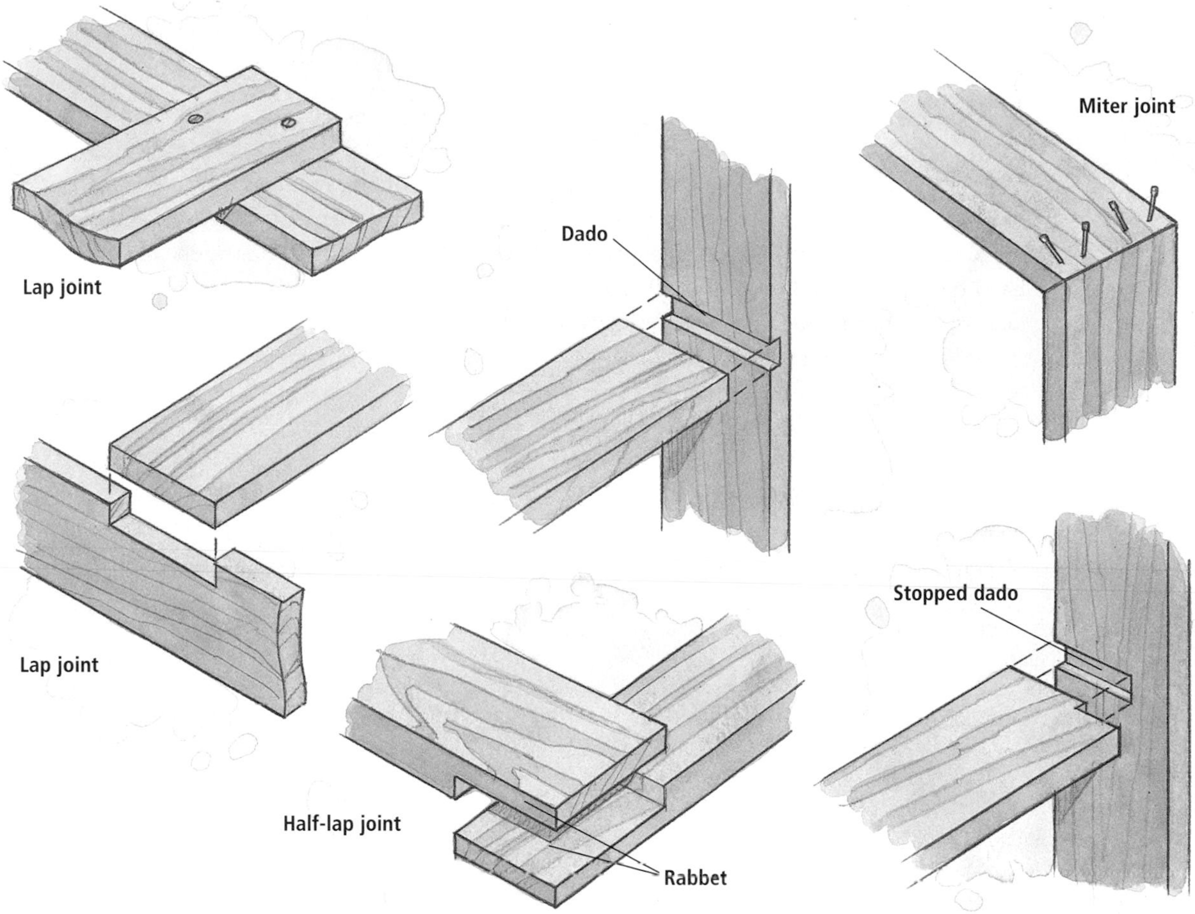

Lap joints

Lap joints are stronger than butt joints and often look better as well. To make a lap joint, lay one of the members on top of the other and nail or screw it in place.

For a lap joint on an edge, cut a notch into one member that is as deep as the second piece is thick. Glue and clamp the two pieces together, adding fasteners if you prefer.

To make a half-lap joint, rabbet each member to half its thickness, then glue, clamp, and add fasteners. The half lap is the strongest lap joint.

Dado joints

Dado joints are attractive and strong, but they're difficult to make because you must cut a dado across one member to hold the other. A stopped dado has the same strength and hides the joint.

Miter joints

For a finished-looking corner, make a miter joint. Cut the pieces at the same angle (45 degrees for a 90-degree corner), then glue the joint and drive in finishing nails at opposing angles. A miter joint is weak, so reinforce it with metal angles, gussets, or mending plates. If you think these add-ons will mar the appearance of the project, use splines–thin strips of wood glued into grooves cut into the mating faces–or dowels to strengthen the joint more discreetly.

Laying Out Posts

Some of the projects in this book call for posts to be set in straight lines and rectangular layouts with square corners. You can do that with a few 1×2s, some mason's twine, and simple arithmetic.

The illustrations on these pages show the essential steps in locating and lining up your posts. Before you start, check with the city or county zoning office to make sure your project will comply with building codes and ordinances regarding setback from your property line. Most locations have a single phone number you can call to have the buried pipes and wires on your property located and marked before you dig. Your local electric utility can probably provide the number. If you can't find the number, call the North American One Call Referral System at 888/258-0808.

Locating and Installing posts: Step-by-Step

1 Attach a crosspiece to stakes with screws as shown to make batterboards. Use a framing square to help you set a corner's two batterboards at right angles to each other. When you have installed all your batterboards, wrap a length of mason's twine several times around a crosspiece, pull it tight to the facing batterboard at an adjacent corner, and wrap it there.

2 Measure from one corner of your planned structure to a point 3 feet away on one string and mark the spot on a piece of masking tape folded over the string. Then measure the perpendicular string 4 feet out from the corner and mark that point. Measure between your two marks. If that distance equals 5 feet, the corner is square (90 degrees).

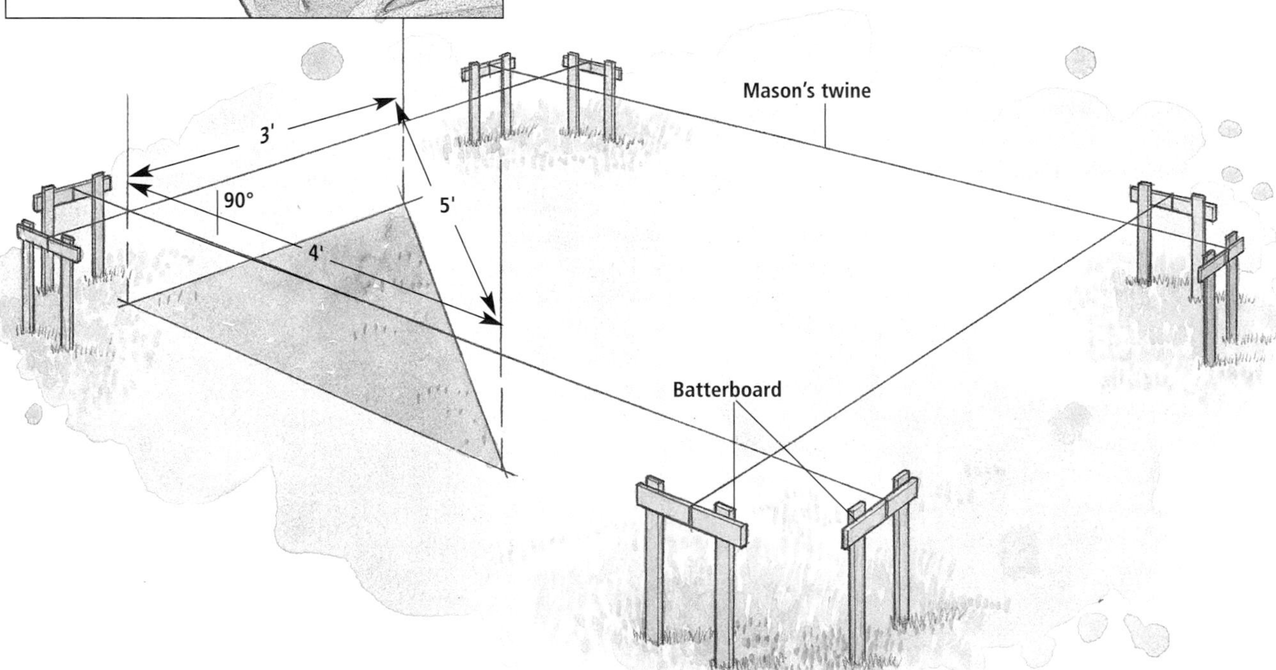

Get organized

You need little equipment to lay out posts for an outdoor structure. For an easy way to visualize its size and shape, use a tape measure and a garden hose to outline your project's dimensions on the ground. Then gather some 1×2 lumber; cut it into 3-foot lengths for batterboards. You also will need a heavy hammer to drive the upright stakes into the ground, a cordless drill/driver, a plumb bob, a spool of mason's twine, and 1½-inch deck screws for quick assembly.

You'll need a posthole digger, shovel, level, hammer, circular saw for trimming posts to length, tamping rod or board, and, if you're mixing your own concrete, a wheelbarrow or mixing box and a concrete hoe.

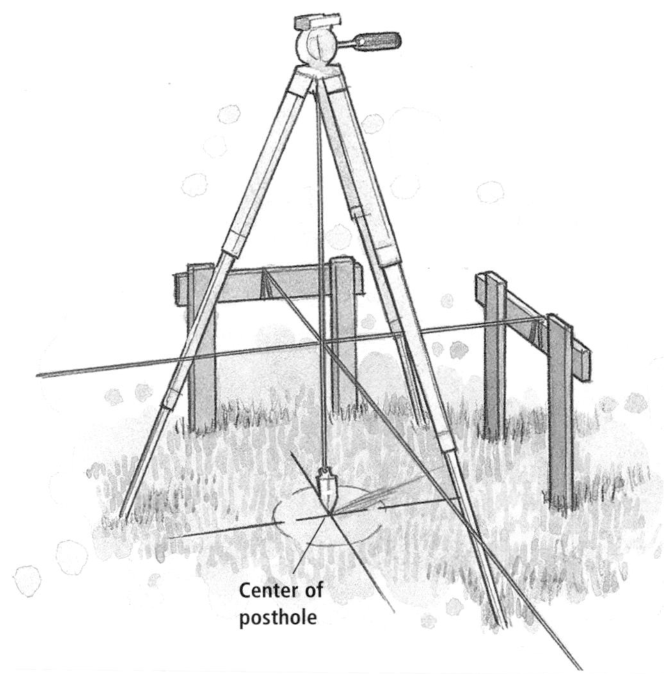

3 At each corner, transfer the strings' intersections to the ground with mason's line and a plumb bob. A camera or telescope tripod makes a handy holder. Keep the line about ⅛ inch away from the strings so that you don't push them out of position. The plumb bob points to the spot where the center of the posthole will be.

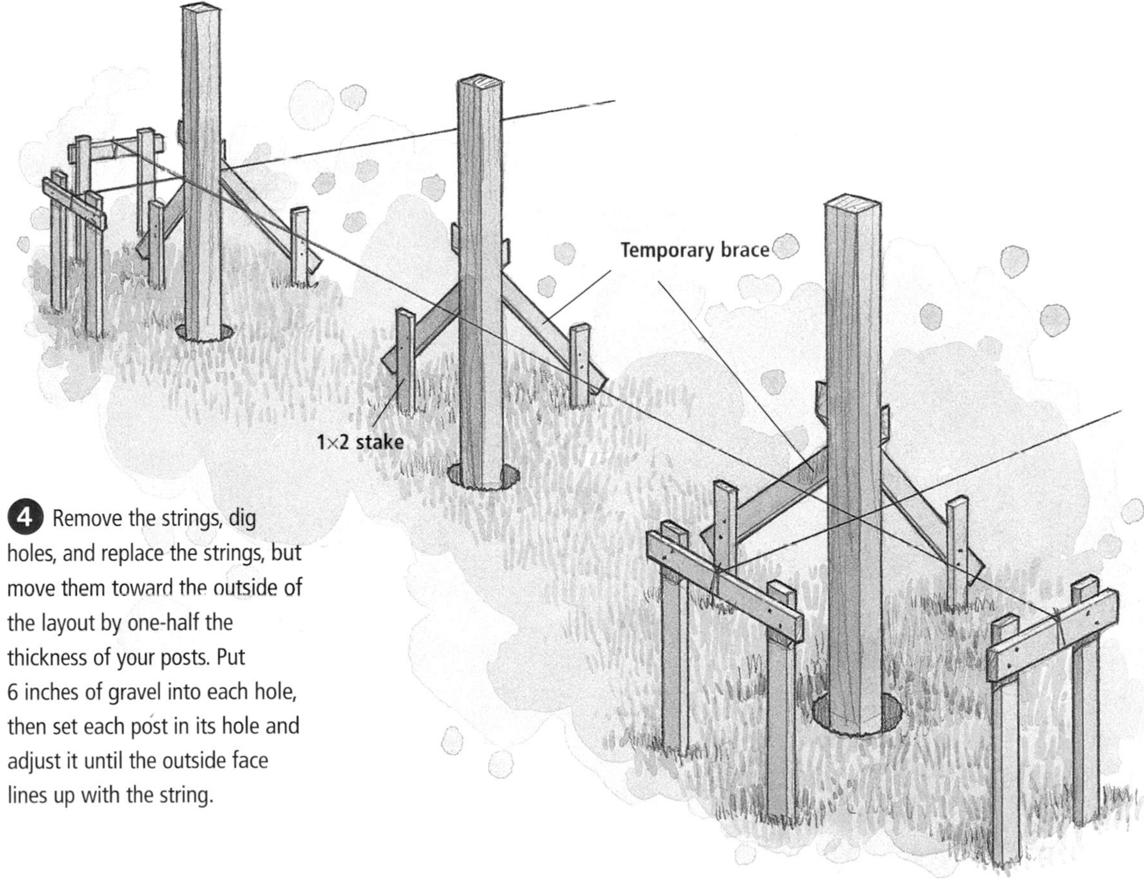

4 Remove the strings, dig holes, and replace the strings, but move them toward the outside of the layout by one-half the thickness of your posts. Put 6 inches of gravel into each hole, then set each post in its hole and adjust it until the outside face lines up with the string.

Setting posts in concrete

Posts set in the ground and anchored with concrete are the best way to support the playsets shown in this book. Some commercial playsets sit on the surface and are secured with anchors. Always follow the manufacturer's instructions for installing such a playset.

Mark each corner with a pair of batterboards. For each batterboard, make a pair of stakes by cutting a point on one end of two 1×2s. Attach a crossbar (see Step 1), and drive the batterboards into the ground. Set them 2 feet away from the planned corner. Locate them so that a line connecting the posthole centerlines will intersect the crossbar at about the center.

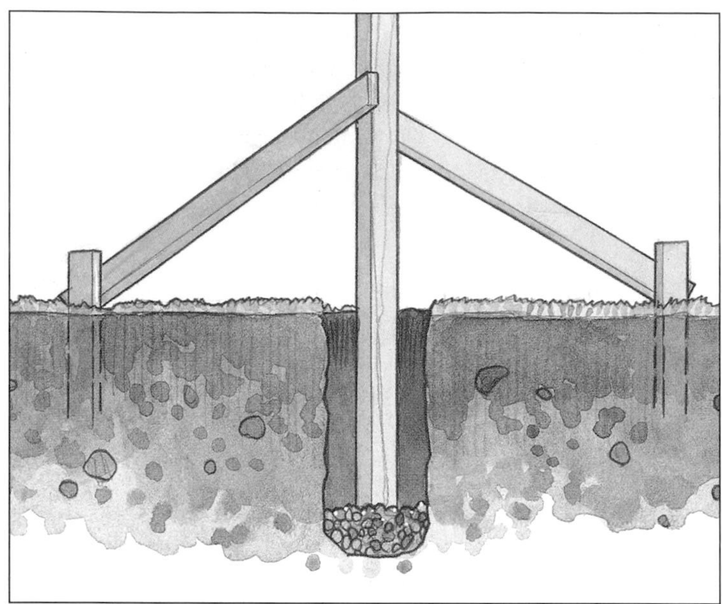

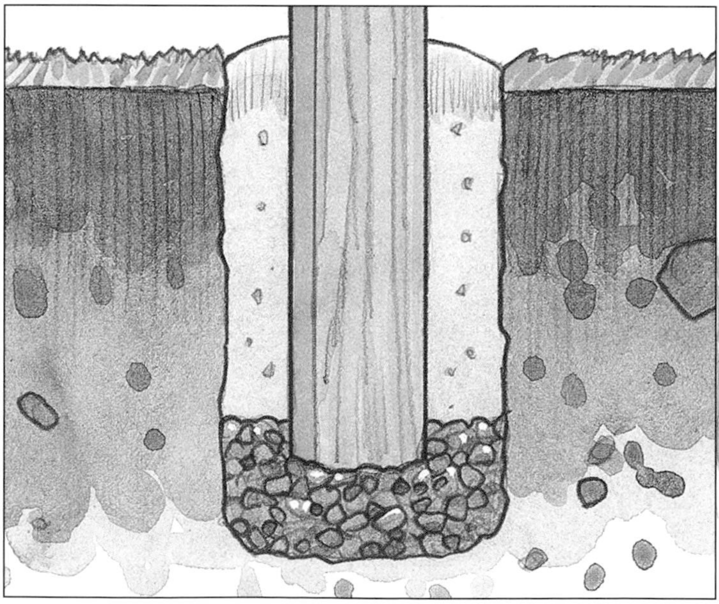

5 The 6-inch layer of gravel in the hole drains water away from the post base to help prevent rot. Set the post in place, plumb it on two sides, and brace it with outriggers in opposite directions. If you've dug the posthole too deep, add more gravel. If a hole is too shallow, dig deeper or saw off the post top.

6 Add more gravel around the post. Mix and pour in concrete, tamping as you fill to remove air bubbles from the mix. Mound concrete around the top of the hole as shown. This drains away water that might otherwise pool and cause rot. After the concrete sets, remove the outriggers.

7 For a watertight seal around posts in concrete, apply butyl caulk around the post base after the concrete cures. This ensures that even if a post shrinks a bit over time, it will be protected against rot. Use only cedar or redwood heartwood posts or lumber that has been pressure treated for ground contact.

Dig the postholes 6 inches deeper than the frost line in your area to counter the effects of frost heaving. Dig an 8-inch-diameter hole for each 4×4 post, using a power auger, hand auger, or posthole digger. A 6×6 post requires a 10-inch-diameter hole. For a neater job and added protection against heaving, line the postholes with cardboard form tubes (available at home centers) before you pour in the concrete.

Concrete choices

To save time and effort, consider buying premix concrete in bags. Premixed material has the correct amount of sand and gravel added to the cement; all you do is add water and mix.

Or buy the cement in bags, order sand and gravel, and mix the concrete yourself. Mixing it yourself is less expensive, but the convenience of premix concrete is usually worth the extra money. In either case, you will need gravel for the bottom of the postholes.

Mixing concrete

For most post-setting projects, use the standard mix of three parts gravel mix, two parts sand, and one part cement. When mixed with water, this mixture contains enough cement to coat each particle of sand and gravel, creating the bond that gives concrete its strength.

If you mix your own concrete, move the mixing container as close to your posts as possible. This will allow you easy access to keep the mixture thick and strong yet workable.

Mixing concrete is a lot like mixing cake batter. You have to follow the recipe (or adapt it slightly) to obtain the best results. Just as you can ruin a cake by adding too much liquid, you can weaken concrete if you add too much water in proportion to the other materials. On the other hand, too little water makes the concrete difficult to pour.

The amount of water needed depends on the sand. You'll need less water with wet sand than with dry sand. Test the wetness of the sand by balling some sand in your hand. If water runs out, the sand is too wet. If the ball compacts like moist clay, the sand is too dry. As you mix the concrete, add very small amounts of water at a time. The concrete may crumble at first, but as you add more water, it will begin to flow together like mud. When it becomes one color–medium gray–and has a plasticlike sheen, it's ready.

CONCRETE ESTIMATING

To estimate how much concrete you'll need, figure the volume of the postholes. Here's how to do that, using a hole 10 inches in diameter and 54 inches deep as an example:

- Multiply one-half the hole diameter times itself.
(5 inches × 5 inches = 25 square inches.)
- Multiply that result times Pi, about 3.14.
(25 square inches × 3.14 = 78.5 square inches.)
- Multiply that result times the depth of the hole. Subtract the depth of gravel in the bottom. The example hole has 6 inches of gravel in the bottom, so the depth is 48 inches.
(78.5 square inches × 48 inches = 3768 cubic inches.)
- Divide the volume in cubic inches by 1728 to find the volume in cubic feet.
(3768 cubic inches ÷ 1728 cubic inches/cubic foot = 2.18 cubic feet.)
- Multiply the volume of one hole times the number of holes.
(2.18 cubic feet × 4 holes = 8.72 cubic feet.)

To estimate how many 60-pound bags of premix you'll need, multiply volume times 2. Multiply by 3 for 40-pound bags or 1½ for 80-pound bags. (8.72 cubic feet × 2 bags/cubic foot = 17.44 60-pound bags.) Round this up to 18 bags; you should always mix full bags.

Applying Finish

Outdoor projects have to withstand more abuse than their indoor counterparts. Here's how to select a durable finish that's right for your structure.

Redwood, cedar, or pressure-treated wood left unfinished will soon take on the weathered look, complete with natural checks and slight surface imperfections. The wood will eventually turn gray–a color unappealing to many that signals the first stage in wood deterioration. If you prefer the rich, natural hue of brand-new lumber, apply a product that forms a film on the surface of the wood. The film must stand up to harsh outdoor conditions.

Wood left outdoors has two formidable foes: moisture and the ultraviolet (UV) rays in sunlight. Different exterior finishes provide different degrees of protection against them. Here's a survey of your choices:

Clear finishes for natural colors

Spar varnish, polyurethane varnish, water repellents, and penetrating oils shield wood from water while allowing all the color to show through. But clear finishes let UV rays penetrate into the grain. The wood cells react with these rays and begin to deteriorate under the film. The wood darkens, and the finish cracks, blisters, and peels.

Adding a UV filtering agent to the finish retards this reaction but doesn't eliminate it. If you use a clear finish, select one that has UV absorbers (the label will tell you). Even with UV protection, you'll have to reapply the finish at least every two years. If you wait until it peels, you'll face a tedious stripping job.

Semitransparent stains

With light pigmentation, semitransparent stains let the wood's natural grain and texture show through. These stains are available in tones that closely match various woods. Brighter stains can either contrast with or complement your house, deck, or patio. Semitransparent stains usually have an oil base and only fair resistance to UV rays, so you'll have to recoat the project every year or two.

Semisolid stains have more pigment than semitransparent stains and offer more UV resistance as well. But they're not completely opaque. You can expect a semisolid stain to last about two years.

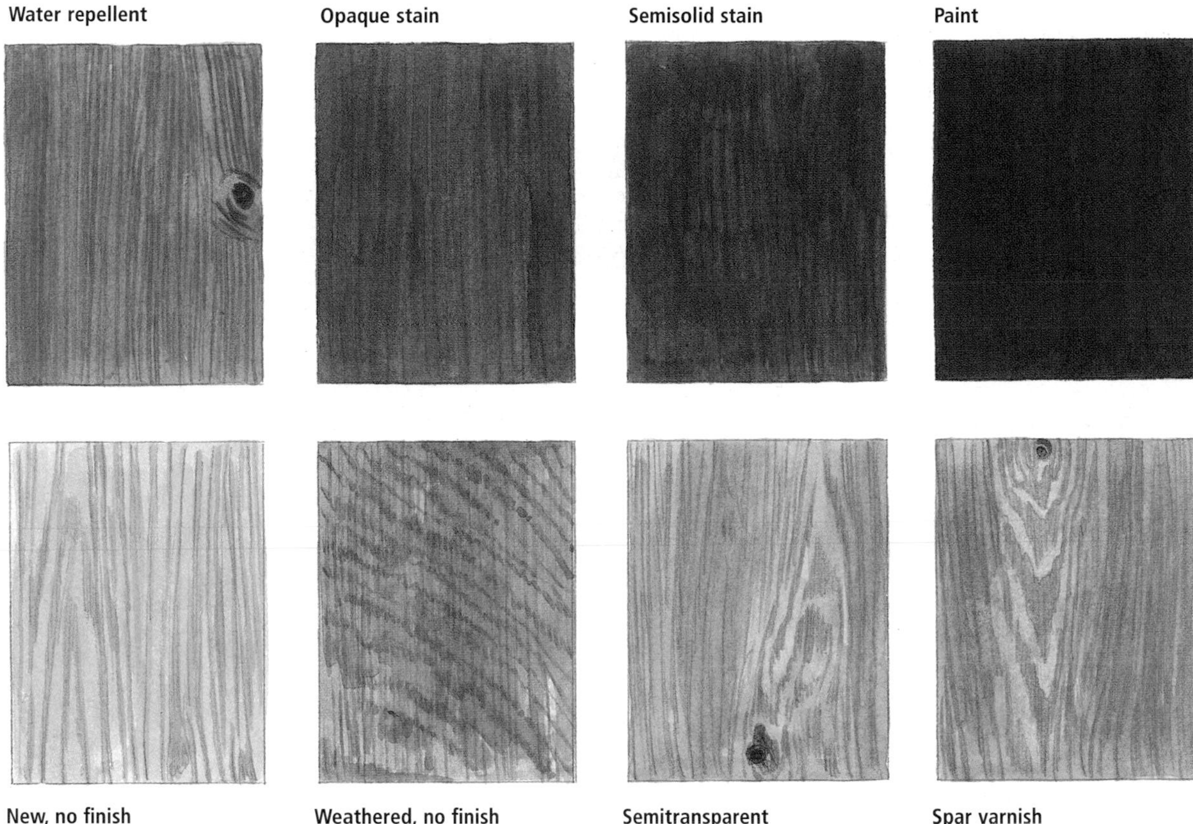

Opaque stains

Opaque stains, like paint, conceal the wood's natural color, yet they allow the texture to show. They're available in a variety of natural-looking colors and brighter hues and with either an oil or latex base. You also can choose either a flat opaque stain or a low-luster finish that's easier to wash.

Because the pigment in this type of stain is suspended in an oil or latex carrier, it's possible that it won't penetrate all wood surfaces equally. On horizontal surfaces especially, pigment that doesn't completely penetrate may collect, causing blotchy areas that wear off or blister. The California Redwood Association doesn't recommend using stains with a latex base on redwood products. Opaque stains usually need to be recoated every two years.

You need to select a compatible stain color for treated lumber because the chemical used to treat the wood imparts a color of its own that tends to alter the final appearance. You might want to experiment with several different stain colors on treated wood (use scraps left from the project) until you achieve the effect you want. (Some manufacturers offer special 4-ounce samples that you can experiment with before selecting a particular product.)

Paint

Paint is rarely used on the top grades of redwood or cedar because it hides grain, texture, and color. But it can be your solution to hiding the hue of treated wood, and it's the only way to protect metal parts.

GLOSSARY

A-B

Actual dimension: True size of a piece of lumber.

Batten: A narrow strip of wood used to cover joints between boards or panels.

Batterboard: A board frame supported by stakes set back from the corners of a structure.

Beam: A horizontal support member.

Bevel cut: A cut through the thickness of a piece of wood at an angle other than 90 degrees.

Blind-nail: To nail so that the head of the nail is not visible on the surface of the wood.

Board: Any piece of lumber that is less than 2 inches thick and more than 3 inches wide.

Board foot: The standard unit of measurement for wood; 1 square foot of wood 1 inch thick. One board foot is equal to a piece 1×12×12 inches (nominal size).

Butt joint: The joint formed by two pieces of material when fastened end to end, end to face, or end to edge.

C-F

Cantilever: A structural member that projects beyond a support member.

Casing: Trim around a door, window, or other opening.

Chalk line: A reel of string coated with colored chalk, used to mark straight lines.

Chamfer: A partial bevel cut made along the length of a board edge.

Concrete nails: Hardened steel nails that can be driven into concrete.

Cripple: A short stud above or below a door or window opening.

Dimension lumber: A piece of lumber at least 2 inches thick and at least 2 inches wide.

Eaves: The lower edge of a roof that projects beyond the wall.

Fascia: Horizontal trim attached to the outside ends of rafters or to the top of an exterior wall.

Footing: A thick concrete support for walls and other heavy structures built on firm soil and extending below the frost line.

Framing: The skeletal or structural support of a building. Sometimes called framework.

Frost line: The maximum depth frost normally penetrates the soil during the winter.

G-L

Gable: The triangular area on the end of a building's external wall located beneath the sloping parts of a roof and above the line that runs between the roof's eaves.

Galvanize: To coat steel or iron hardware with zinc to protect against corrosion.

Grain: The direction of fibers in a piece of wood; also refers to the pattern of the fibers.

Hardwood: Lumber derived from deciduous trees (those that have leaves), such as oaks, maples, and walnuts.

Header: The framing component spanning a door or window opening in a wall and supporting the weight above it.

Hip: The outside angle of a roof formed by the intersection of two sloped sides of the roof.

Jack studs: Studs on both sides of a door, window, or other opening that help support the header. Sometimes called trimmers.

Jamb: Pieces that form the top and sides of a door or window opening.

Joist: Horizontal framing member that supports a floor or ceiling.

King studs: Studs on both ends of a header that help support the header and run from the wall's soleplate to its top plate.

Lag bolt, lag screw: A heavy screw with a hexagonal head.

Lap joint: The joint formed when one member overlaps another.

M-R

Miter: To crosscut wood at an angle less than 90 degrees. A *miter joint* is formed when two pieces so cut meet.

Molding: Wood used to cover exposed edges or as decoration, often shaped with a decorative profile.

On center (OC): The distance from the center of one regularly spaced framing member or hole to the center of the next.

Plumb: The condition that exists when a surface is at true vertical.

Premix: Dry mixture of concrete ingredients in a bag.

Press under: Make a crease along the edge of a fabric, wrong sides together, and press with an iron.

Rafters: Parallel framing members that support a roof.

Rake: The inclined edge of the roof of a building.

Raw edge: The edge of the fabric with loose threads.

Ready-mix: Concrete mixed in a truck and delivered.

Ridge board: Topmost beam at a roof's peak.

Right side: The right side of a fabric is the front with the pattern (or brighter color), and the wrong side is the back.

Rip: To saw lumber or sheet goods parallel to the grain.

S-Z

Sash: The part of a window that can be opened, consisting of a frame and glass.

Seam allowance: The distance between the seam line (the line made by sewing) and the raw edge of the fabric.

Selvage: The edge on a length of fabric that prevents fraying, meant to be trimmed or removed when sewing.

Set: The process during which mortar or concrete hardens.

Setback: The distance a structure must be built from property lines, dictated by local zoning ordinances.

Setting nails: Driving the heads of nails slightly below the surface of the wood.

Sheathing: The first covering on a roof or exterior wall, usually fastened directly to the rafters or studs.

Shim: A thin piece of wood or other material used to fill a gap between two adjoining components or to help establish level or plumb.

Siding: Planks, boards, shingles, or sheet goods used as an external covering of the walls of a building.

Sill: The lowest horizontal piece of a window, door, or wall framework.

Soffit: Covering attached to the underside of eaves.

Softwood: Lumber derived from coniferous trees, such as pines, firs, cedars, or redwoods.

Soleplate: The bottommost horizontal part of a stud-framed partition. When a plate rests on a foundation, it's called a sill plate.

Span: The distance between supports.

Square: The condition that exists when two surfaces or parts meet at 90 degrees to each other. Also a tool used to determine square.

Straightedge: A tool, often a 1×4 or 2×4 with a straight edge, used to mark a line on material or to determine if a surface is even.

Studs: Vertical 2×4 or 2×6 framing members spaced at regular intervals within a wall.

Template: A pattern to follow when re-creating a precise shape.

Timber: A structural or framing member that is 5 inches or larger in the smallest dimension.

Toenail: To drive a nail at an angle to hold together two pieces of material.

Top plate: The topmost horizontal element of a stud-frame wall.

Valley: An intersection of roof slopes.

Warp: Any of several lumber defects caused by uneven shrinkage of wood cells.

Wrong side: See *Right Side.*

INDEX

INDEX (CONTINUED)

RESOURCES

Play Structures are available as plans, kits, and fully assembled from a variety of suppliers throughout North America. Those that follow are a good place to start. Those that are listed as carrying accessories sell rubberized mulch, swings, climbing walls, trapezes, etc. For more sources, both local and nationwide, search directories under "Play Structures."

PLANS:

JACK BOWSER

4419 Wee Laddie

Houston, TX 77084

281/345-1997

www.jacksbackyard.com

BETTER HOMES AND GARDENS

Reader Shopping Service

Dept 004, Box 9128

Des Moines, IA 50306-9128

www.bhg.com

ACCESSORIES ONLY:

PLAYSETPARTS.COM

PO Box 1363

Kingston, WA 98346

Phone: 866/297-PLAY

Fax: 360/626-0173

www.playsetparts.com/

PLANS, ACCESSORIES, KITS:

DETAILED PLAY SYSTEMS

PO Box 633

Springfield, NJ 07081

Phone: 800/398-7565

Fax: 973/376-8881

www.detailedplay.com

SWING-N-SLIDE

1212 Barberry Drive

Janesville, WI 53545

Phone: 800/888-1232

Fax: 800/755-7567

www.swing-n-slide.com

BACKYARDCITY.COM

1160 Vickcry Lanc

Suite 6

Cordova, TN 38018

Phone: 888/483-9159

Fax: 901/531-8145

www.backyardcity.com

PLAN-IT PLAY

1925 Shiloh Road Building 1

Kennesaw, GA 30144

Phone: 866/346-7529

Fax: 770/528-6677

www.planitplay.com